June 20, 2013
Seattle, Washington, USA

Association for
Computing Machinery

Advancing Computing as a Science & Profession

PLAS'13

Proceedings of the 2013 ACM SIGPLAN Workshop on
Programming Languages and Analysis for Security

Sponsored by:

ACM SIGPLAN

Co-located with:

PLDI 2013

Association for
Computing Machinery

Advancing Computing as a Science & Profession

The Association for Computing Machinery
2 Penn Plaza, Suite 701
New York, New York 10121-0701

ISBN: 978-1-4503-2144-0 (Digital)

ISBN: 978-1-4503-2440-3 (Print)

Additional copies may be ordered prepaid from:

ACM Order Department
PO Box 30777
New York, NY 10087-0777, USA

Phone: 1-800-342-6626 (USA and Canada)
+1-212-626-0500 (Global)
Fax: +1-212-944-1318
E-mail: acmhelp@acm.org
Hours of Operation: 8:30 am – 4:30 pm ET

Printed in the USA

Chairs' Welcome

It is our great pleasure to welcome you to the *ACM SIGPLAN Eighth Workshop on Programming Languages and Analysis for Security – PLAS'13*. As in previous years, our workshop continues to provide a unique forum for exploring and evaluating ideas on the use of programming language and program analysis techniques to improve the security of software systems.

The call for papers attracted 14 submissions from Asia, Europe, and North America. The program committee accepted 8 papers that cover a variety of topics, including 6 full papers and 2 position papers. We are also very happy to have two invited speakers: Philippa Gardner and David Sands. We hope that these proceedings will make for a vibrant workshop.

Putting together *PLAS'13* was a team effort. We thank the authors for providing the content of the program. We are grateful to the program committee, who worked very hard in reviewing papers and providing feedback for authors. We must also thank the organizing committee of PLDI'13, the ACM and Sheridan Communications for helping with organization of the workshop and its proceedings.

We hope that you will find this program interesting and thought-provoking and that the workshop will provide you with a valuable opportunity to share ideas with other researchers and practitioners from institutions around the world.

Prasad Naldurg
PLAS'13 Program Chair
IBM Research India

Nikhil Swamy
PLAS'13 Program Chair
Microsoft Research, USA

Table of Contents

ACM SIGPLAN 2013 Eighth Workshop on Programming Language and Analysis for Security

Program Chairs: Prasad Naldurg *(IBM Research India)*
Nikhil Swamy *(Microsoft Research Redmond)*

Program Committee: Aslan Askarov *(Harvard University)*
Karthikeyan Bhargavan *(INRIA)*
Nataliia Bielova *(INRIA-Rennes)*
Vinod Ganapathy *(Rutgers)*
Ana Almeida Matos *(Instituto Superior Técnico and Instituto de Telecomunicações)*
Prasad Naldurg (co-chair) *(IBM Research India)*
Grigore Rosu *(University of Illinois at Urbana-Champaign)*
Nikhil Swamy (co-chair) *(MSR Redmond)*
Ankur Taly *(Google)*

Additional reviewers: Jan Cederquist
Jorge Coelho
Manuel E Correia
Antoine Delignat-Lavaud
Michael May
Scott Moore
Alfredo Pironti
Jérémy Planul
José Fragoso Santos
Andrei Stefanescu
Danfeng Zhang

Sponsor: SIGPLAN

Co-located with: PLDI 2013 Seattle, USA

Fault-Tolerant Non-interference

[Invited Talk Abstract]

David Sands *

Chalmers University of Technology
Gothenburg
Sweden
dave@chalmers.se

Abstract

This work is about specifying and ensuring security in unreliable systems. We study systems which are subject to transient faults – soft errors that cause stored values to be corrupted. Transient faults occur in hardware when a high-energy particle strikes a transistor, resulting in a spontaneous bit-flip. Such events have been acknowledged as the source of major crashes in server systems. The trend towards lower threshold voltages and tighter noise margins means that susceptibility to transient faults is increasing.

From a security perspective, transient faults are a known attack vector. For instance, it has been shown that a single bit flip, regardless of how is triggered, can compromise the value of a secret key in some public key and authentication systems.

Fault tolerance techniques aim to preserve properties of systems despite such transient faults. Preservation of functional correctness, however, comes at a high cost, and seems to inevitably require some special form of hardware-level replication. For the predominantly-software-based techniques, with one or two notable exceptions, most works do not give precise, formal guarantees.

In this work, rather than attempting to preserve full functional behaviour in the presence of faults, we consider the novel problem of guaranteeing security: faults may cause a program to go wrong, but even if it goes wrong it should not leak sensitive data, no matter if the code is crafted with malicious intent. The particular security characterization we study is *non-interference*, an information-flow security property which says that public outputs of a program (the *low* security channel) do not reveal anything about its secrets (the *high* security inputs).

Our approach has two distinguishing features. Firstly, it does not rely on special purpose fault tolerant hardware, and secondly, it makes its assumptions precise and provides formal guarantees.

We study this problem for a RISC-style machine for which the only fault-tolerant component is the ROM containing the code, but otherwise contains no special fault-tolerant components. We devise a transformation technique for programs which generates fault-tolerant noninterfering code, up to a fixed number of faults. The method is based on a strong separation of resources between different security levels, inspired by the recent technique of Secure Multi-Execution, together with a carefully chosen code and data layout, and a robust protocol for data access and control flow modifications. We prove that the transformation method yields noninterfering programs in the presence of faults, and that it preserves the meaning of a class of reasonable programs – those which use a bounded amount of storage and which are not sensitive to exactly where in memory code and data are located.

Categories and Subject Descriptors D.1 [*Software*]: Programming Techniques

; F.3.1 [*Theory of Computation*]: Logics and Meanings of Programs—Specifying and Verifying and Reasoning about Programs

General Terms Security, Reliability, Theory, Verification

Keywords Non-interference, Transient faults

* This talk describes joint work with **Filippo Del Tedesco** and **Alejandro Russo**.

PLAS'13, June 20, 2013, Seattle, WA, USA.
ACM 978-1-4503-2144-0/13/06.

Knowledge Inference for Optimizing Secure Multi-party Computation

Aseem Rastogi Piotr Mardziel Michael Hicks Matthew A. Hammer
University of Maryland, College Park
{aseem, piotrm, mwh, hammer}@cs.umd.edu

Abstract

In secure multi-party computation, mutually distrusting parties cooperatively compute functions of their private data; in the process, they only learn certain results as per the protocol (e.g., the final output). The realization of these protocols uses cryptographic techniques to avoid leaking information between the parties. A protocol for a secure computation can sometimes be optimized without changing its security guarantee: when the parties can use their private data and the revealed output to infer the values of other data, then this other data need not be concealed from them via cryptography.

In the context of automatically optimizing secure multi-party computation, we define two related problems, *knowledge inference* and *constructive knowledge inference*. In both problems, we attempt to automatically discover when and if intermediate variables in a protocol will (eventually) be known to the parties involved in the computation. We formally state the two problems and describe our solutions. We show that our approach is sound, and further, we characterize its completeness properties. We present a preliminary experimental evaluation of our approach.

Categories and Subject Descriptors F.3.1 [*Logics and Meanings of Programs*]: Specifying and Verifying and Reasoning about Programs

General Terms Algorithms, Security, Verification

Keywords Secure Multi-party Computation;Program Verification;Information Flow

1. Introduction

Secure multi-party computation (SMC) protocols [5, 11, 23] enable a number of parties $p_1, ..., p_n$ to cooperatively compute a function f over their private inputs $x_1, ..., x_n$ in a way that every party directly sees only the output $f(x_1, ..., x_n)$ while keeping the variables x_i private. Initial implementations of SMC protocols [6, 18] compute f using a single, monolithic protocol, which can be very expensive. More recently, researchers have been exploring how program analysis can be used to optimize SMC protocols.

A key observation underlying many optimizations is that while SMC protocols typically only reveal the final output to each party, a party may be able to *infer* the results of intermediate computations given the final output, their inputs, and the function being computed. When such inference is possible, the inferable intermediate results need not be cryptographically concealed. Revealing inferable results does not change the *knowledge profile* of the protocol: If the party will eventually know the intermediate result (e.g., given the final output), then revealing it earlier does not change what is known to whom.[1] Beyond preserving a protocol's knowledge profile, decomposing monolithic protocols into smaller protocols that explicitly reveal intermediate results can significantly improve their performance.

As an example, consider the joint median computation between two parties Alice and Bob in Figure 1. Let `a1` and `a2` be Alice's inputs and `b1` and `b2` be Bob's. We also assume that these numbers are distinct, with `a1` < `a2` and `b1` < `b2`. At the end of the computation, both parties share the joint median output `m`.

In the unoptimized version of secure computation for this example, the whole program is computed as a single secure computation. However, one can show that, with the knowledge of `a1`, `a2`, and `m`, Alice can always infer the values of `x1` and `x2`, no matter what Bob's input values are [3]. Similarly, Bob can also infer the values of `x1` and `x2` from the knowledge of `b1`, `b2`, and `m`. Therefore, declassifying values of `x1` and `x2` *explicitly* to Alice and Bob during the computation would not compromise privacy, since they can infer them anyway, and it turns out that doing so it enables the following, more efficient SMC protocol:

[1] Throughout this paper, we assume the *honest-but-curious* threat model (also called *semi-honest*), where parties always follow a prearranged protocol to its completion. When parties are acting honestly they do not, for instance, unexpectedly stop participating halfway through the protocol.

PLAS'13, June 20, 2013, Seattle, WA, USA.

```
1  ## assume a1 < a2, b1 < b2, distinct(a1, a2, b1, b2)
2  int median(int a1, int a2, int b1, int b2)
3    bool x1, x2; int a3, b3, m;
4
5    x1 = a1 ≤ b1;
6    if x1 then { a3 = a2; } else { a3 = a1; }
7    if x1 then { b3 = b1; } else { b3 = b2; }
8    x2 = a3 ≤ b3;
9    if x2 then { m = a3; } else { m = b3; }
10   return m;
```

Figure 1. Joint median computation example [15]. `a1` and `a2` are Alice's inputs and `b1` and `b2` are Bob's. Both Alice and Bob can infer `x1` and `x2` given the final output.

Alice and Bob compute `a1` $\leq$ `b1` using secure computation and share the output `x1` (line 5). Alice *locally* computes `a3` (line 6). Bob *locally* computes `b3` (line 7). Alice and Bob compute `a3` $\leq$ `b3` using secure computation and share the output `x2` (line 8). If `x2` is `true`, Alice sends `a3` to Bob as the final median, else if `x2` is `false`, Bob sends Alice `b3` as the final median (line 9 and 10).

Thus, in the optimized version, only the two comparisons (line 5 and 8), need to be done securely. Moreover, Alice and Bob do not learn anything more than they did in the unoptimized version. For median computation on a joint set with 64 elements, Kerschbaum [15] shows 30x performance improvement using this optimization.

Building on and expanding work begun by Kerschbaum, this paper explores methods for inferring when and if variables like `x1` and `x2` in this example can be inferred by SMC participants, and thus may enable protocol optimizations like the one above. Specifically, we consider two related problems: *knowledge inference* and *constructive knowledge inference*. Both problems are specified by giving an SMC as a program that uses multiple parties' variables (as in Figure 1). From this program, a solution to the knowledge inference problem states which parties can learn which additional variables, if any, from a cooperative run of the unoptimized protocol. We call a knowledge inference solution *constructive* if, in addition to correctly asserting that a party p knows a variable y, the solution also gives an evidence of party p's knowledge of y in the form of a program that computes y from p's private data and the final output.

Contributions. We make the following contributions:

- Within the context of secure multi-party computation, we formally define notions of *knowledge* (of a program variable y to a party p), and the problems of *knowledge inference* and *constructive knowledge inference*.
- We give a solution to the knowledge inference problem (Section 3.2). We prove that our solution is sound (Theorem 5). Additionally, for the language that we consider, we also show that our solution is complete (Theorem 6).
- We give a solution to the constructive knowledge inference problem (Section 3.3). We prove that our solution is sound (Theorem 7), and we characterize conditions under which it is also complete (Theorems 8 and 9).
- We implement our solutions and evaluate them experimentally (Section 5).

2. Overview

In this section, we present an overview of our knowledge inference approaches with the help of some examples.

In our setting, party p knows the (deterministic) program (call it S), his own input set I, and his output O.[2] We say party p can *infer* the value of local variable $y \in S$ if there exists a function F such that $y = F(I, O)$ in all runs of S. Another way of putting it is that no matter the values of p's inputs or those of other participants of the SMC, p can always compute y given knowledge of only his inputs and the final result. Our goal to find all those variables in S that p can infer. We can do this by either showing merely that the required function F exists, without saying what it is, or we can produce F directly, thus constituting a constructive proof. In this paper we present approaches to both tasks.

2.1 Knowledge inference

To show that an intermediate variable can be expressed as a function of one party's inputs and outputs, we can attempt to prove that given any pair of runs of S that agree on the valuations of variables in I and O (but may not agree on the input and output variables of other parties), the valuations of y on those two runs must also agree. In other words, y can be determined uniquely from I and O, and thus a function F exists such that $F(I, O) = y$. We can construct such a proof in two steps.

First we use a program analysis to produce a formula ϕ_{post} that soundly approximates the final state of the program S (that is, the final values of all program variables) for all possible program runs. So that the meaning of a variable y mentioned in ϕ_{post} is unambiguous, we assume that a variable is assigned at most once during a program run.

One program analysis we might use to produce ϕ_{post} is symbolic execution [16]. Each feasible program path is characterized by a *path condition* φ_i, which is a set of predicates relating the program variables. The path conditions can be combined to provide a complete description of the program's behavior: $\phi_{post} \stackrel{\text{def}}{=} \bigvee_i \varphi_i$. For the median program of Figure 1, there are four possible paths, having the path conditions given in FIgure 2.

Consider the first path condition φ_1. Conceptually, it describes the program path in which `then` branch of both conditionals (lines 6 and 9) is taken. The remaining three paths constitute the other three possible branching combinations.

[2] Some SMCs may have different outputs for different parties; in the median example, there is a single output O = `m` known to both parties.

$$\varphi_1 \stackrel{\text{def}}{=} \texttt{a1} < \texttt{b1} \wedge \texttt{x1} = \textsf{true} \wedge \texttt{a3} = \texttt{a2} \wedge \texttt{b3} = \texttt{b1} \wedge$$
$$\texttt{a3} < \texttt{b3} \wedge \texttt{x2} = \textsf{true} \wedge \texttt{m} = \texttt{a3} \wedge \phi_{pre}$$
$$\varphi_2 \stackrel{\text{def}}{=} \texttt{a1} < \texttt{b1} \wedge \texttt{x1} = \textsf{true} \wedge \texttt{a3} = \texttt{a2} \wedge \texttt{b3} = \texttt{b1} \wedge$$
$$\texttt{a3} \geq \texttt{b3} \wedge \texttt{x2} = \textsf{false} \wedge \texttt{m} = \texttt{b3} \wedge \phi_{pre}$$
$$\varphi_3 \stackrel{\text{def}}{=} \texttt{a1} \geq \texttt{b1} \wedge \texttt{x1} = \textsf{false} \wedge \texttt{a3} = \texttt{a1} \wedge \texttt{b3} = \texttt{b2} \wedge$$
$$\texttt{a3} < \texttt{b3} \wedge \texttt{x2} = \textsf{true} \wedge \texttt{m} = \texttt{a3} \wedge \phi_{pre}$$
$$\varphi_4 \stackrel{\text{def}}{=} \texttt{a1} \geq \texttt{b1} \wedge \texttt{x1} = \textsf{false} \wedge \texttt{a3} = \texttt{a1} \wedge \texttt{b3} = \texttt{b2} \wedge$$
$$\texttt{a3} \geq \texttt{b3} \wedge \texttt{x2} = \textsf{false} \wedge \texttt{m} = \texttt{b3} \wedge \phi_{pre}$$

Figure 2. Path conditions for secure median

Note that each path also requires ϕ_{pre}. This formula defines the publicly-known constraints on all inputs; in the case of the median program we have $\phi_{pre} \stackrel{\text{def}}{=} \texttt{a1} < \texttt{a2} \wedge \texttt{b1} < \texttt{b2} \wedge \texttt{a1} \neq \texttt{b1} \wedge \texttt{a1} \neq \texttt{b2} \wedge \texttt{a2} \neq \texttt{b1} \wedge \texttt{a2} \neq \texttt{b2}$.

The next step is to prove that any two runs of the program S that agree on variables known to p will also agree on the value of y. This statement is a 2-safety property [8], and we can prove it using a technique called self-composition [4]. The idea is to reduce this two-run condition on program S to a condition on a single run of a *self-composed program* S_c, which is the sequential composition of S with itself, with the second copy of S's variables renamed, e.g., so that x is renamed to x'. Given the formula ϕ_{post}^{sc} for this self-composed program, we can ask whether, under the assumption that the normal and primed versions of p-visible variables are equal, that the normal and primed version of y is also equal.

As an example, Figure 3 shows self composition of the median function of Figure 1. We write $\texttt{median}'$ for the function `median` but with the local variables renamed to $\texttt{x1}', \texttt{x2}', \ldots$. The self-composed program effectively runs median twice, on two separate spaces of variables. We can express the question of knowledge inference as a question on the relationship between the two copies of the variables. Namely, Alice can infer `x1` if and only if for every feasible final state of the composed program, when the two copies of $\texttt{a1}, \texttt{a2}, \texttt{m}$ agree on their values then the copies of `x1` agree on their value. More formally we need to check the validity of the following formula for any feasible final state.

$$\phi_{post}^{sc} \wedge (\texttt{a1} = \texttt{a1'} \wedge \texttt{a2} = \texttt{a2'} \wedge \texttt{m} = \texttt{m'}) \Rightarrow (\texttt{x1} = \texttt{x1'})$$

Here, the formula ϕ_{post}^{sc} will involve sixteen path conditions (self-composition squares the number of paths). For example, among them will be:

$$\varphi_1^{sc} \stackrel{\text{def}}{=} \texttt{a1} < \texttt{b1} \wedge \texttt{x1} = \textsf{true} \wedge \texttt{a3} = \texttt{a2} \wedge \texttt{b3} = \texttt{b1} \wedge$$
$$\texttt{a3} < \texttt{b3} \wedge \texttt{x2} = \textsf{true} \wedge \texttt{m} = \texttt{a3} \wedge \phi_{pre} \wedge$$
$$\texttt{a1'} < \texttt{b1'} \wedge \texttt{x1'} = \textsf{true} \wedge \texttt{a3'} = \texttt{a2'} \wedge \texttt{b3'} = \texttt{b1'} \wedge$$
$$\texttt{a3'} < \texttt{b3'} \wedge \texttt{x2'} = \textsf{true} \wedge \texttt{m'} = \texttt{a3'} \wedge \phi'_{pre}$$

```
## a1 < a2, b1 < b2, distinct(a1, a2, b1, b2)
int m = median(a1, a2, b1, b2);

## a1'<a2', b1'<b2', distinct(a1', a2', b1', b2')
int m' = median'(a1', a2', b1', b2');
```

Figure 3. Median computation composed with itself.

The formula φ_1^{sc} is actually the conjunction of φ_1 with a version of φ_1 that has all its variables renamed to the primed versions. We can think of the entire post condition $\phi_{post}^{sc} = \varphi_1^{sc} \vee \ldots \vee \varphi_{16}^{sc}$ as the conjunction of the post condition ϕ_{post} with its primed version.

Being a quantifier-free formula in the theory of integer linear arithmetic, the final formula poses no problem for an SMT solver such as Z3 [2], which can indeed verify its validity. Additionally, the same can be said for Alice's knowledge of `x2` and `a3`, and Bob's knowledge of `x1`, `x2` and `b3`.

The knowledge inference question bears a close resemblance to deciding the property of *delimited release* [21]. We explore this connection in more detail in Section 4.

2.2 Constructive Knowledge Inference

The technique just described can establish that there exists some function F such that $y = F(I, O)$, where y is an intermediate variable in S, and I and O are variables known to party p. However, this technique cannot say what F actually is. To construct F we can leverage ideas from template-based program verification.

Program verification generally aims at inferring invariants in a program that are strong enough to verify some assertions of interest. Template-based program verification [12, 22] requires programmers to specify the structure of these invariants in the form of a template. The algorithm then generates verification constraints for the assertions, to be solved by an SMT solver (e.g. Z3 [2]). A solution to the constraints yields a valid proof of the correctness of the assertions as well as a solution to the template unknowns. Gulwani et. al. [12] present constraint-based verification techniques over the abstraction of linear arithmetic and Srivastava et. al. [22] present these techniques over the abstraction of predicates.

To infer p's knowledge of a variable y, our algorithm tries to infer a formula ϕ s.t. (a) at the end of the program $y = \phi$, and (b) ϕ only mentions the input and output variables known to p. If we add an assertion $y = \phi$ at the end of the program, and provide a template structure for ϕ (limited to formulae over variables known to p) this becomes a template-driven verification problem where the assertion and the invariant are the same. A successful verification of the assertion $y = \phi$ establishes p's knowledge of y, and also the solution for ϕ yields a formula for y in terms of input and output variables of p.

The template structure for this problem is defined as follows. Suppose y is a boolean variable. Then the template for ϕ requires it to be in *disjunctive normal form* (DNF) such that there are exactly d disjuncts each consisting of c conjuncts, with each conjunct drawn from a set of predicates Q. This set contains predicates over linear expressions involving I and O. In the median example, for Alice, one choice of Q is $\{v_1 \odot v_2 \mid v_1, v_2 \in \{\mathtt{a1}, \mathtt{a2}, \mathtt{m}\}, \odot \in \{>, \geq, <, \leq, =, \neq\}\}$. For Bob, similar Q would be $\{v_1 \odot v_2 \mid v_1, v_2 \in \{\mathtt{b1}, \mathtt{b2}, \mathtt{m}\}, \odot \in \{>, \geq, <, \leq, =, \neq\}\}$.

Our algorithm searches for a ϕ conforming to the prescribed template. For example, if $(c = 2, d = 2)$, then the search space for ϕ is all the boolean formulae $(q_1 \wedge q_2) \vee (q_3 \wedge q_4), q_1, q_2, q_3, q_4 \in Q$. We denote this search space for formulae as $\mathsf{DNF}(c, d, Q)$. A naive search algorithm would make $O(|Q|^{cd})$ queries to the SMT solver, one for every possible formula in $\mathsf{DNF}(c, d, Q)$. This algorithm is complete in the sense that if there exists a solution for ϕ in $\mathsf{DNF}(c, d, Q)$ then the naive search algorithm finds it. Our algorithm, on the other hand, makes $O(|Q|^c + |Q|^d)$ queries to the SMT solver, and still guarantees completeness, provided the existence of solution in $\mathsf{DNF}(c, d, Q)$.

Consider variable x1 from the median example. With Q_{Alice} and Q_{Bob} as above, and $(c = 1, d = 1)$, we are able to establish knowledge of x1 for both Alice and Bob as: $\mathtt{x1} = \mathtt{m} > \mathtt{a1}$ for Alice, and $\mathtt{x1} = \mathtt{m} \leq \mathtt{b1}$ for Bob. Interestingly, $(c = 1, d = 1)$ is insufficient to discover invariants describing Alice's and Bob's knowledge of x2. With $(c = 1, d = 2)$, we are able to establish Alice's knowledge of x2 as $\mathtt{x2} = (\mathtt{m} = \mathtt{a1} \vee \mathtt{m} = \mathtt{a2})$. And with $(c = 2, d = 1)$, we are able to establish Bob's knowledge of x2 as $\mathtt{x2} = (\mathtt{m} \neq \mathtt{b1} \wedge \mathtt{m} \neq \mathtt{b2})$. In general, starting with $(c = 1, d = 1)$, we can increment (c, d) in steps until either we find a solution or we leave x as being unknown to p.

We can also infer formulae for integer variables. In this case we use a different template structure, and leverage ideas from Gulwani et. al. [12]. We discuss the algorithm further in the next section.

Constructive knowledge inference problem is closely related to the problem of inferring output function in *required release* [7], a connection we explore more in Section 4.

3. Formal Development

In this section, we formally describe our knowledge inference algorithm. We first give the language syntax, operational semantics, and formal definition of *knowledge* in Section 3.1. We then present inference in Section 3.2, and constructive inference in Section 3.3.

3.1 Language Syntax

Let parties $p_1, \ldots, p_n$ want to compute a secure computation S whose syntax is given in Figure 4. The language is standard aside from the omission of a looping construct; this makes sense in our setting since most SMC methods forbid dynamic looping (rather, they require a static loop unrolling). Our methods support loops as well, but we elide them nevertheless to keep the formalization simpler. We also assume, for simplicity, that each program path is in single assignment form, i.e. in an execution of a program, every variable is assigned at most once.

$$
\begin{array}{rccl}
\text{Value} & v & ::= & n \mid \mathsf{true} \mid \mathsf{false} \\
\text{Exprn./Formula} & e, \phi & ::= & v \mid x \mid e_1 \odot e_2 \\
\text{Binary operator} & \odot & \in & \{\leq, \geq, >, <, =, \neq\} \\
 & & \cup & \{\wedge, \vee, \neg, \Rightarrow\} \cup \{+, -\} \\
\text{Statement} & S & ::= & x := e \mid S_1; S_2 \mid \mathsf{skip} \\
 & & \mid & \mathsf{if}\ e\ \mathsf{then}\ S_1\ \mathsf{else}\ S_2
\end{array}
$$

Figure 4. Syntax.

$$
\text{(E-VAR)}\ \frac{}{\langle \sigma, x \rangle \Downarrow \sigma[x]}
\qquad
\text{(E-VAL)}\ \frac{}{\langle \sigma, v \rangle \Downarrow v}
\qquad
\text{(E-BINOP)}\ \frac{\langle \sigma, e_1 \rangle \Downarrow v_1 \quad \langle \sigma, e_2 \rangle \Downarrow v_2}{\langle \sigma, e_1 \odot e_2 \rangle \Downarrow v_1 \odot v_2}
$$

$$
\text{(E-ASSIGN)}\ \frac{x \notin \mathsf{dom}(\sigma) \quad \langle \sigma, e \rangle \Downarrow v}{\langle \sigma, x := e \rangle \Downarrow \sigma[x \mapsto v]}
\qquad
\text{(E-SEQ)}\ \frac{\langle \sigma, S_1 \rangle \Downarrow \sigma' \quad \langle \sigma', S_2 \rangle \Downarrow \sigma''}{\langle \sigma, S_1; S_2 \rangle \Downarrow \sigma''}
$$

$$
\text{(E-IFTRUE)}\ \frac{\langle \sigma, e \rangle \Downarrow \mathsf{true} \quad \langle \sigma, S_1 \rangle \Downarrow \sigma'}{\langle \sigma, \mathsf{if}\ e\ \mathsf{then}\ S_1\ \mathsf{else}\ S_2 \rangle \Downarrow \sigma'}
\qquad
\text{(E-IFFALSE)}\ \frac{\langle \sigma, e \rangle \Downarrow \mathsf{false} \quad \langle \sigma, S_2 \rangle \Downarrow \sigma'}{\langle \sigma, \mathsf{if}\ e\ \mathsf{then}\ S_1\ \mathsf{else}\ S_2 \rangle \Downarrow \sigma'}
$$

$$
\text{(E-SKIP)}\ \frac{}{\langle \sigma, \mathsf{skip} \rangle \Downarrow \sigma}
\qquad
(\phi\text{-VALID})\ \frac{\langle \sigma, \phi \rangle \Downarrow \mathsf{true}}{\sigma \models \phi}
$$

Figure 5. Semantics.

The semantics of computations is given in Figure 5. The judgments have the form $\langle \sigma, S \rangle \Downarrow \sigma'$, meaning, statement S executed in state σ results in new state σ'. States σ are maps from variables x to values v; we write $\sigma[x]$ to look up x in σ, and we write $\sigma[x \mapsto v]$ to define a map identical to σ except that x maps to v. The figure also defines an auxiliary judgment for expressions having the form $\langle \sigma, e \rangle \Downarrow v$, meaning, expression e evaluated in state σ results in value v. The rules are standard, with one exception. The rule (E-ASSIGN) checks that $x \notin \mathsf{dom}(\sigma)$ to enforce single assignment form for the current program path. When an expression is viewed as a formula ϕ, we write $\sigma \models \phi$ to mean that in σ the formula ϕ evaluates to true. We also write predicate to mean a boolean valued formula.

Let V be a set of variables. We define two states as being *equivalent* on a set of variables as follows:

Definition 1 (Equivalence of States)**.** Two states, σ_1 and σ_2, are equivalent on a set of variables V, written as $\sigma_1 \stackrel{V}{\equiv} \sigma_2$, iff $\forall x \in V, \sigma_1[x] = \sigma_2[x]$.

$$\begin{array}{lcl} \varsigma(\mathsf{skip}, \phi) & = & \phi \\ \varsigma(\mathsf{x := e}, \phi) & = & \phi \wedge (x = e) \\ \varsigma(\mathsf{S_1; S_2}, \phi) & = & \varsigma(S_2, \varsigma(S_1, \phi)) \\ \varsigma(\mathsf{if}\ e\ \mathsf{then}\ S_1\ \mathsf{else}\ S_2, \phi) & = & (e \wedge \varsigma(S_1, \phi)) \vee \\ & & (\neg e \wedge \varsigma(S_2, \phi)) \end{array}$$

Figure 6. Postcondition of a predicate ϕ w.r.t. statement S.

Let ϕ_{pre} denote the precondition for a secure computation program S. It represents the assumptions that S makes about parties' inputs. In the median example from Figure 1, $\phi_{pre} = \mathtt{a1} < \mathtt{a2} \wedge \mathtt{b1} < \mathtt{b2} \wedge \mathtt{a1} \neq \mathtt{b1} \wedge \mathtt{a1} \neq \mathtt{b2} \wedge \mathtt{a2} \neq \mathtt{b1} \wedge \mathtt{a2} \neq \mathtt{b2}$. We are interested in executions $\langle \sigma, S \rangle \Downarrow \sigma'$ when $\sigma \models \phi_{pre}$.

We now define *knowledge* of a variable y to a party p in S, written as $\mathfrak{K}(S, p, y)$. Informally, y is known to p, if, whenever two final states of S are equivalent on the set of input and output variables of p, they are also equivalent on $\{y\}$.

Definition 2. [Knowledge of a Variable] Let S be a secure computation program with precondition ϕ_{pre}. For a party p in the computation, let I be the set of input variables of p, and O be the set of output variables of p. Then, a variable y in S is *known* to p, written as $\mathfrak{K}(S, p, y)$, if for all initial states σ_1, σ_2 s.t. $\sigma_1 \models \phi_{pre}$, $\sigma_2 \models \phi_{pre}$, and $\sigma_1 \overset{I}{\equiv} \sigma_2$, whenever $\langle \sigma_1, S \rangle \Downarrow \sigma_1'$ and $\langle \sigma_2, S \rangle \Downarrow \sigma_2'$ s.t. $\sigma_1' \overset{O}{\equiv} \sigma_2'$, we have $\sigma_1' \overset{\{y\}}{\equiv} \sigma_2'$.

The definition models the 2-safety property discussed in the Section 2. It says that the value of y can be uniquely determined from the knowledge of input and output variables of p, independent of the inputs of other parties in the computation. We now give the formal description of knowledge inference algorithm.

3.2 Knowledge Inference

The problem of knowledge inference is as follows. For a secure computation program S, we want to know whether a party p *knows* a program variable y according to Definition 2. We present our knowledge inference algorithm in Figure 8, but before that we give some auxiliary definitions.

Definition 3 (Validity of a Predicate)**.** A predicate ϕ is valid at the end of a program S with precondition ϕ_{pre}, if $\forall \sigma$ s.t. $\sigma \models \phi_{pre}$, $\langle \sigma, S \rangle \Downarrow \sigma'$, we have $\sigma' \models \phi$.

We define the postcondition of a predicate ϕ w.r.t. statement S, written as $\varsigma(S, \phi)$, in Figure 6. The following theorem states the properties of $\varsigma(S, \phi)$.

Theorem 4. *[Soundness and Completeness of Postcondition] For a program S with precondition ϕ_{pre}, $\varsigma(S, \phi_{pre})$ is valid at the end of program S (Soundness). Moreover, for any other predicate ϕ s.t. ϕ is valid at the end of S, $\varsigma(S, \phi_{pre}) \Rightarrow \phi$ (Completeness).*

Proof. Soundness – Structural induction on S. Completeness – Structural induction on S and using following lemma for each case. Let $\sigma \models \varsigma(S, \phi_{pre})$. Then, $\exists \sigma'$ s.t. $\sigma' \models \phi_{pre}$, $\langle \sigma', S \rangle \Downarrow \sigma$, and $\mathsf{dom}(\sigma') = \mathsf{dom}(\sigma) - \mathsf{Def}(S)$, where $\mathsf{Def}(S)$ is the set of variables defined by S. □

The theorem depends on the program paths being in single assignment form. Specifically, the postcondition rule for assignment statement assumes that x does not occur in ϕ.

We now define a variable renaming translation on predicates. The idea is to replace every variable in the predicate with a *copy* of the variable. Let θ be a mapping from variables to variables. The translation judgment is shown in Figure 7. We define similar translation judgments for statements and states and refer to them in the theorem proofs later on, however we do not show them here for lack of space.

Our algorithm is parameterized by an SMT solver (e.g. Z3 [2], STP [10]), that we denote as $\mathtt{alg}$. We use $\mathtt{alg}$ to determine whether a given predicate is a tautology (always true). We write $\vdash_{\mathtt{alg}} \phi$ as the query to $\mathtt{alg}$ for predicate ϕ.

(T-VAR1)
$$\frac{x \in \theta}{\langle \theta, x \rangle \rightsquigarrow \langle \theta, \theta[x] \rangle}$$

(T-VAR2)
$$\frac{x \notin \mathsf{dom}(\theta) \quad x' \text{ is fresh}}{\langle \theta, x \rangle \rightsquigarrow \langle \theta[x \mapsto x'], x' \rangle}$$

(T-BINOP)
$$\frac{\langle \theta, \phi_1 \rangle \rightsquigarrow \langle \theta', \phi_1' \rangle \quad \langle \theta', \phi_2 \rangle \rightsquigarrow \langle \theta'', \phi_2' \rangle}{\langle \theta, \phi_1 \odot \phi_2 \rangle \rightsquigarrow \langle \theta'', \phi_1' \odot \phi_2' \rangle}$$

(T-VAL)
$$\frac{}{\langle \theta, v \rangle \rightsquigarrow \langle \theta, v \rangle}$$

Figure 7. Variable renaming translation for a predicate.

```
InferKnowledge(S, φ_pre)
  for each party p
    let I be the set of p's input variables.
    let O be the set of p's output variables.
    φ_post := ς(S, φ_pre);
    ⟨ε, φ_post⟩ ⇝ ⟨θ, φ'_post⟩.
    φ_k := ⋀_{x∈I∪O} (x = θ[x]);
    for each program variable y
      φ := (φ_post ∧ φ'_post ∧ φ_k) ⇒ (y = θ[y]);
      if(⊢_alg φ)
        output y is known to p.
      else
        output y is not known to p.
```

Figure 8. Knowledge inference algorithm. ϕ_{pre} is the precondition of S. The algorithm first generates postconditions for two *different* runs of S (ϕ_{post} and ϕ'_{post}). To establish p's knowledge of a program variable y, it then tries to prove, using $\mathtt{alg}$, that whenever these two runs are equivalent on p's input and output variables, they are also equivalent on y.

The knowledge inference algorithm is shown in Figure 8. It takes as input the secure computation program S and its precondition ϕ_{pre}. For each party p and program variable y, it outputs whether p knows y or not.

The algorithm first computes the postcondition of ϕ_{pre} w.r.t. S (ϕ_{post}). It then performs variable translation on ϕ_{post} to generate ϕ'_{post}. Essentially ϕ_{post} and ϕ'_{post} model two *different* runs of the program. ϕ_k then asserts that $\forall x \in I \cup O$, x has same value across these two runs. Under these assumptions, if a program variable y also has same value across these two runs, the variable y is known to p.

The soundness theorem of our algorithm is as follows:

Theorem 5 (Soundness of Knowledge Inference). *Let S be a secure computation program with the precondition ϕ_{pre}. If* `InferKnowledge`(S, ϕ_{pre}) *outputs variable y is known to party p, then $\mathfrak{K}(S, p, y)$.*

Proof. We want to prove that for two states σ and σ' s.t. $\sigma \overset{I \cup O}{\equiv} \sigma'$, $\sigma[y] = \sigma[y']$ (see Definition 2). If we translate σ according to θ to yield σ' ($\mathsf{dom}(\sigma) \cap \mathsf{dom}(\sigma') = \epsilon$), then we can see that $\sigma \cup \sigma' \models \phi_{post}$, $\sigma \cup \sigma' \models \phi'_{post}$ (soundness of postcondition), and $\sigma \cup \sigma' \models \phi_k$ (using above equivalence). Thus, it follows from line 9 in Figure 8 that $\sigma \cup \sigma' \models (y = \theta[y])$. □

Moreover, we can also state a completeness theorem.

Theorem 6 (Completeness of Knowledge Inference). *Let S be a secure computation program with precondition ϕ_{pre}. For a program variable y and party p, if $\mathfrak{K}(S, p, y)$, then* `InferKnowledge`(S, ϕ_{pre}) *outputs variable y is known to party p.*

Proof. For a program S, let S' be the translation of S. Then, we can see that $\phi_{post} \wedge \phi'_{post} \wedge \phi_k = \varsigma(S; S', \phi_{pre} \wedge \phi'_{pre} \wedge \phi_k)$. By completeness of postcondition, if $y = \theta[y]$ is valid at the end of $S; S'$, line 9 in Figure 8 must be true. □

3.3 Constructive Knowledge Inference

The knowledge inference algorithm from Figure 8 establishes whether p knows y or not, however it does not give a formula for y in terms of p's input and output variables. In this section, we present constructive knowledge inference algorithms, that output such a formula.

Constructive knowledge inference for boolean variables. Define the verification condition of a predicate ϕ w.r.t. a statement S with precondition ϕ_{pre}, $\mathsf{VC}(S, \phi_{pre}, \phi)$, as $\varsigma(S, \phi_{pre}) \Rightarrow \phi$. Then, if $\vdash_{\mathtt{alg}} \mathsf{VC}(S, \phi_{pre}, \phi)$, the predicate ϕ is valid at the end of S.

Recall that to construct knowledge of variable y for a party p, we want to infer a formula ϕ, s.t. at the end of the program $y = \phi$ holds. For boolean variables, the search space for ϕ is $\mathsf{DNF}(c, d, Q)$, where Q is a set of predicates constructed from input and output variables of p.

```
ConstructKnowledgeB(S, φ_pre)
  for each party p
    construct the predicate set Q.
    for each boolean program variable y
      c = 1; d = 1;
      do
        φ := CFormula(y, c, d, Q);
        increment (c, d) in lockstep.
      while (φ is failure and c < c_max, d < d_max);
      if(φ = failure)
        output y is not known to p.
      else
        output y is known to p by φ.
```

Figure 9. Constructive knowledge inference for boolean variables. For each party p and each boolean program variable y, starting with $(c = 1, d = 1)$, it calls `CFormula` (Figure 10) to construct a formula for y in $\mathsf{DNF}(c, d, Q)$ template.

The algorithm for boolean variables is shown in Figure 9. For each party p, it first constructs a predicate set Q. As mentioned earlier, this can either be provided as input by the programmer, or it can be mined from the expressions appearing in the program. For each boolean program variable y, starting with $(c = 1, d = 1)$ and incrementing (c, d) in lockstep until (c_{max}, d_{max}), it tries to find ϕ. It uses an auxiliary routine `CFormula`, defined in Figure 10.

Figure 10 consists of the subroutine `CFormula` and two other subroutines, that it invokes, `CFormulaL` and `CFormulaR`. We divide the problem of constructing ϕ into subproblems of constructing ϕ_L and ϕ_R s.t. (a) ϕ_L and ϕ_R consist only of predicates from Q, and (b) at the end of the program, $\phi_L \Rightarrow y$, $y \Rightarrow \phi_R$, and $\phi_R \Rightarrow \phi_L$ hold. Then, we have $\phi = \phi_R$. `CFormulaL` constructs ϕ_L and `CFormulaR` constructs ϕ_R.

Construction of ϕ_L. To construct ϕ_L (`CFormulaL` in Figure 10), we perform breadth first search on the lattice of subsets of Q ordered by implication (i.e. $M \sqsubseteq N, M, N \in 2^Q$, iff $\vdash_{\mathtt{alg}} (\bigwedge_{q \in M} p) \Rightarrow (\bigwedge_{q' \in N} q')$) with $\top = \{\}$ and $\bot = Q$, and collect all nodes of the lattice that form a *solution* to $\phi_L \Rightarrow y$. A node N in the lattice is a solution to $\phi_L \Rightarrow y$ if $\vdash_{\mathtt{alg}} \mathsf{VC}(S, \phi_{pre}, (\bigwedge_{q \in N} q) \Rightarrow y)$. When we find a node N that is a solution, we delete the subtree rooted at N from the lattice, since any node in the subtree is a "weaker" solution than N (i.e. for any node M in the subtree under N, we have $\vdash_{\mathtt{alg}} (\bigwedge_{q \in M} q) \Rightarrow (\bigwedge_{q' \in N} q')$, and since $\vdash_{\mathtt{alg}} (\bigwedge_{q' \in N} q') \Rightarrow y$, we already have $\vdash_{\mathtt{alg}} (\bigwedge_{q \in M} q) \Rightarrow y$). Moreover, we also prune any subtree rooted at a node (including the node itself) whose size is greater than c (since the current search space is $\mathsf{DNF}(c, d, Q)$, we need not consider lattice nodes

```
CFormula(y, c, d, Q) ## construct φ s.t. y ⇔ φ
  let ℒ be the lattice (2^Q, ⇒, ⊤ = {}, ⊥ = Q).
  φ_L := CFormulaL(y, c, ℒ); φ_R := CFormulaR(y, d, Q);
  if(φ_L = failure || φ_R = failure)
     return failure;
  φ := VC(S, φ_pre, φ_R ⇒ φ_L);
  if(⊢_alg φ)
    return φ_R;
  else
    return failure;

CFormulaR(y, d, Q) ## construct φ_R s.t. y ⇒ φ_R
  𝒩 := {}; ## set of tuples that satisfy y ⇒ φ_R
  for all (q_1, ..., q_d) ∈ (Q ×_1 Q ··· ×_{d-1} Q)
    φ := VC(S, φ_pre, y ⇒ ⋁_{i=1}^{d} q_i);
    if(⊢_alg φ)
      𝒩 := 𝒩 ∪ {(q_1, ..., q_d)};
  if(𝒩 = {})
    return failure;
  else
    return ⋀_{(q_1,...,q_d)∈𝒩} (⋁_{i=1}^{d} q_i);
```

```
CFormulaL(y, c, ℒ) ## construct φ_L s.t. φ_L ⇒ y
  𝒩 := {}; ## set of lattice nodes that satisfy φ_L ⇒ y
  visit lattice ℒ nodes in BFS order,
    when node N is visited, do
      if(N = {})
        φ_N := true;
      else
        let N be {q_1, ..., q_n}.
        φ_N := ⋀_{i=1}^{n} q_i;
      φ := VC(S, φ_pre, φ_N ⇒ y);
      if(⊢_alg φ)
        𝒩 := 𝒩 ∪ {N};
        truncate sublattice rooted at N from BFS.
      else
        for each child M of N in ℒ
          if(|M| ≤ c && M is unvisited)
            add M to BFS worklist.
  if(𝒩 = {})
    return failure;
  else
    return ⋁_{{q_1,...,q_n}∈𝒩} (⋀_{i=1}^{n} q_i);
```

Figure 10. The routine CFormula constructs a formula for y in DNF(c, d, Q) template. It calls the subroutine CFormulaL to construct ϕ_L s.t. $\phi_L \Rightarrow y$, and subroutine CFormulaR to construct ϕ_R s.t. $y \Rightarrow \phi_R$. Finally, it checks that $\phi_R \Rightarrow \phi_L$, and if so, returns ϕ_R as the solution for y.

with more than c elements). Let $\mathcal{N}$ be the set of lattice nodes that are found as solutions. We assign $\phi_L = \bigvee_{N \in \mathcal{N}} (\bigwedge_{q \in N} q)$. If $\mathcal{N} = \{\}$, the algorithm fails to infer p's knowledge of y (under input values of c and d). Construction of ϕ_L makes $O(|Q|^c)$ queries to the SMT solver.

Construction of ϕ_R**.** To construct ϕ_R (CFormulaR in Figure 10), we consider all possible $(q_1, \ldots, q_d) \in (Q \times_1 Q \cdots \times_{d-1} Q)$, and collect all such tuples that form a *solution* to $y \Rightarrow \phi_R$. $(q_1, \ldots, q_d)$ is a *solution* to $y \Rightarrow \phi_R$ if $\vdash_{\texttt{pre}} \texttt{VC}(S, \phi_{pre}, y \Rightarrow \bigvee_{i=1}^{d} q_i)$. Let $\mathcal{N}$ be the set of such solutions. Then, we assign $\phi_R = \bigwedge_{(q_1,\ldots,q_d)\in\mathcal{N}} (\bigvee_{i=1}^{d} q_i)$. If $\mathcal{N} = \{\}$, the algorithm fails to infer P's knowledge of y (under input values of c and d). Construction of ϕ_R makes $O(|Q|^d)$ queries to the SMT solver.

Construction of ϕ**.** We now check that $\phi_R \Rightarrow \phi_L$ is valid at the end of the program using the formulae for ϕ_L and ϕ_R constructed above (CFormula in Figure 10). If it is, y is known to p using the formula ϕ_R, otherwise our algorithm returns y is not known to p (under input values of c and d).

Constructive knowledge inference for integer variables. For integer variables in the program S, constructive knowledge inference algorithm is shown in Figure 11. To verify ϕ on line 6, we use the algorithm given by Gulwani et. al. [12]. Their algorithm uses Farka's lemma to convert ϕ into SAT solver constraints, the solution of which returns a solution for the template unknowns a_i s.t. ϕ holds true at the end of S, and thus, $y = \sum_{i=1}^{n} a_i x_i$.

```
1  ConstructKnowledgeI(S, φ_pre)
2    for each party p
3      let {x_i}^{i∈1...n} be input and output variables of p.
4      for each integer program variable y
5        let a_i, i ∈ 1...n be n integer unknowns.
6        φ := -y + Σ_{i=1}^{n} a_i x_i ≥ 0 ∧ y + Σ_{i=1}^{n} -a_i x_i ≥ 0;
7        verify φ at the end of S.
8        if verification fails
9          output y is not known to p.
10       else
11         output y is known to p by Σ_{i=1}^{n} a_i x_i.
```

Figure 11. Constructive knowledge inference for integer variables. For each integer variable y, it tries to find a linear arithmetic formula for y in terms of input and output variables of p. To verify ϕ on line 6, it uses the algorithm by Gulwani et. al. [12].

We state soundness theorems for constructive knowledge inference algorithms as follows:

Theorem 7 (Soundness of Constructive Knowledge Inference). *Let S be a secure computation program with precondition ϕ_{pre}. If* `ConstructKnowledgeB`(S, ϕ_{pre}) *(Figure 9) and* `ConstructKnowledgeI`(S, ϕ_{pre}) *(Figure 11) output variable y is known to party p, then $\mathfrak{K}(S, p, y)$.*

Proof. If the algorithms infer $y = \phi$ for a party p, then $y = \phi$ is valid at the end of S. Moreover, since only variables in ϕ are variables from $I \cup O$ (input and output variables of p), p knows y by Definition 2. □

Moreover, constructive knowledge inference algorithms are also complete, provided a solution exists in the template form they consider.

Theorem 8 (Completeness of Constructive Knowledge Inference for Boolean Variables). *Let S be a secure computation program. For a party p, let Q be a set of predicates, where the only variables appearing in each predicate in Q are input and output variables of p. Let y be a boolean program variable in S. If $\exists \phi$ s.t. $x = \phi$ at the end of S, and ϕ is in $\mathsf{DNF}(c, d, Q)$ form, for some values of (c, d), then* `CFormula`(y, c, d, Q) *returns a solution (and not* `failure`*).*

Proof. We give an outline for $(c = 2, d = 2)$, the proof for general case follows similarly. Let $y = \phi$ at the end of S s.t. ϕ is in $\mathsf{DNF}(c, d, Q)$ form. Then, for some $q_1, q_2, q_3, q_4 \in Q$, $y = (q_1 \wedge q_2) \vee (q_3 \wedge q_4)$, equivalently, $y = (q_1 \vee q_3) \wedge (q_1 \vee q_4) \wedge (q_2 \vee q_3) \wedge (q_2 \vee q_4)$. Since `CFormulaR` considers all elements in $Q \times Q$, it would construct $\phi_R = (q_1 \vee q_3) \wedge (q_1 \vee q_4) \wedge (q_2 \vee q_3) \wedge (q_2 \vee q_4) \wedge \phi'$, for some ϕ' (possibly just true). On the other hand, since `CFormulaL` considers all lattice nodes up to size c, it would construct $\phi_L = (q_1 \wedge q_2) \vee (q_3 \wedge q_4) \vee \phi''$ for some ϕ'' (possibly just false). We can see that $\phi_R \Rightarrow \phi_L$, and hence `CFormula` returns ϕ_R. □

The following theorem of completeness for integer variables follows from the completeness of the algorithm by Gulwani et. al. [12][3].

Theorem 9 (Completeness of Constructive Knowledge Inference for Integer Variables). *Let S be a secure computation program. Let y be an integer variable in S. For a party p, let $\{x_i\}^{i \in 1 \ldots n}$ be the set of input and output variables of p. If $\exists a_i, i \in 1 \ldots n$ s.t. $y = \sum_{i=1}^{n} a_i x_i$ at the end of S, then* `ConstructKnowledgeI`(S, ϕ_{pre}) *(Figure 11) outputs y is known to p.*

Proof. Follows from the completeness of [12]. □

[3] Similar to the restriction in [12], the theorem holds if checking the invariant $y = \phi$ does not require integral reasoning.

4. Discussion

This section considers some aspects of our approach, including the relationship of knowledge inference to the property of *delimited release* [21], the relationship of constructive knowledge inference to *required release* [7], the effect of using a different program analysis to determine a program's final states, the possible use of type-based information flow analysis for knowledge inference, and finally the application of knowledge inference to allowing SMC computations with loops.

Relating knowledge inference to noninterference. As mentioned in Section 2.1, the knowledge inference problem bears some resemblance to the problem of proving noninterference, as evidenced by the similarity of our use of self-composition with its previous use in proving noninterference [4]. More precisely, knowledge inference is closely related Sabelfeld and Myers' *delimited release* [21] property. Next we define delimited release, and then show how a method for proving a program satisfies delimited release can be applied to knowledge inference.

In the setting of normal delimited release, we suppose there exists a *security labeling* Γ, which maps each program variable in S to one of two security labels, L (low) and H (high). We say that memories σ_1 and σ_2 are *low-equivalent*, written $\sigma_1 \sim_\Gamma \sigma_2$, if $\sigma_1(x) = \sigma_2(x)$ for all variables x such that $\Gamma(x) = L$. We also suppose that the program S may contain expressions `declassify(e)`, which signal that e's security label should be considered L, even if its contents may otherwise suggest its label should be H. (In an SMC, we can think of the output as being declassified; e.g., in Figure 1, we would change line 10 to be `return declassify(m)`.) We say that S enjoys *delimited release* with respect to Γ *iff* for all memories $\sigma_1, \sigma_2, \sigma'_1, \sigma'_2$ such that if $\sigma_1 \sim_\Gamma \sigma_2$, and $\langle S, \sigma_1 \rangle \Downarrow \sigma'_1$ and $\langle S, \sigma_2 \rangle \Downarrow \sigma'_2$ where $\langle \sigma'_1, e_i \rangle \Downarrow v \Leftrightarrow \langle \sigma'_2, e_i \rangle \Downarrow v$ for some v for all declassification expressions $e_i \in S$, then $\sigma'_1 \sim_\Gamma \sigma'_2$. In short, all pairs of program evaluations that agree on the results of declassified expressions e_i should also agree on other low-visible outputs. Satisfying this condition means that nothing is leaked via low outputs beyond what the declassification expressions already reveal.

We can describe knowledge inference for p in terms of delimited release. Let Γ_p map p-visible variables to L and all remaining variables to H. The set of declassification expressions is the set of output variables (e.g., `m` in the median example). Now, to see whether local variable y can be inferred by p, we simply label y with L and see whether S still satisfies delimited release. If so, revealing y to p provides no additional information.

The self-composition algorithm described in Section 2.1 is basically checking delimited release. For example, consider the condition presented for the median example:

$$\phi^{sc}_{post} \wedge (\texttt{a1} = \texttt{a1'} \wedge \texttt{a2} = \texttt{a2'} \wedge \texttt{m} = \texttt{m'}) \Rightarrow (\texttt{x1} = \texttt{x1'})$$

The ϕ^{sc}_{post} part captures the semantics of the two executions. The next two equalities are establishing $\sigma_1 \sim_\Gamma \sigma_2$, since they require Alice's two input variables to be equal. The third equality establishes the equality of the declassified output variable `m`. The final equality `x1` $=$ `x1'` establishes that $\sigma'_1 \sim_\Gamma \sigma'_2$ (where the other low-security variables are known to be equal by virtue of them appearing to the left of the implication, and the program respecting single-assignment semantics).

Constructive knowledge inference is related to *required release* [7]. In this setting, a program S satisfies required release of an input expression e to user p using output expression F if p can evaluate F (i.e. F only uses variables visible to p) and F evaluates to the same value as e, i.e. for all final states σ of S, $\langle \sigma, e \rangle \Downarrow v \Leftrightarrow \langle |\sigma|_p, F \rangle \Downarrow v$ where $|\sigma|_p$ denotes the state visible to p. The problem of constructive knowledge inference then is to infer the function F for a party p and program variable y such that the program S satisfies required release of y to party p using F.

Alternatives to $\varsigma(S, \phi)$. The role of $\varsigma(S, \phi)$ (Figure 6) is to provide a sound approximation of final states of executing the program S starting from an initial state that satisfies ϕ. We can use other program analyses to get such an approximation. In Section 2.1 we used symbolic execution for this purpose; for our language (Figure 4), which lacks loops, symbolic execution generates equivalent formula as ς.

While $\varsigma(S, \phi)$ as defined in Figure 6 provides a complete approximation of final program states (Theorem 4), for large programs the formula can become prohibitively large. In such cases, we can always trade completeness of the approximation, and use abstract interpretation [9] to provide a sound approximation. With such analyses, our knowledge inference algorithms are still sound, in that if they output y is known to p then $\mathfrak{K}(S, p, y)$, but they lose completeness.

Applying information flow analysis. In the limit, we can use a grossly over-approximating language-based information flow analysis [20] for knowledge inference. Following the formulation relating knowledge inference to delimited release given above, we can label each of party p's input variables as L and all other input variables as H, restricting valid flows in the program as $L \sqsubseteq H$ as usual, while explicitly declassifying the final output when it is returned. Then we can do type inference [19, 24] to determine whether any unlabeled, local variables can safely be given label L, and if so then we know these can be determined solely from knowledge of p's inputs.

Such a type-based analysis is less precise than the semantic analysis we have given to this point. It cannot, for example, infer the knowledge of `x1` and `x2` in the median example. As soon as it sees `x1` = `a1` $\leq$ `b1` (Figure 1, line 5) it assumes that there is information flow from both `a1` and `b1` to `x1`, and hence, neither Alice nor Bob can determine `x1` alone.

However, it is far less expensive than a semantic analysis, and there are some useful examples where such an analysis is enough to establish knowledge facts. Consider the joint economic lot size computation example from Kerschbaum [15], shown in Figure 12. The program computes an order quantity (or lot size) between a buyer (Bob) and vendor (Alice). The buyer's private inputs include the holding cost per item (`hbB`) and the fixed ordering costs per order (`fbB`). The vendor's private inputs include the holding cost per item (`hvA`), the fixed setup costs per order (`fvA`), and the capacity (`cA`). Both parties know the yearly demand of the buyer (`yd`). For vendor Alice, if we label `yd, fvA, cA, hvA` as L, `fbB, hbB` as H, and do type inference in an information flow type system, it can infer that `a, b, c, d` can have label L and are thus known to Alice. Similarly, it can infer that `e, f` are known to Bob. Using these knowledge facts, the SMC protocol can be optimized to compute lines 7-10 locally on Alice's host, and lines 12-13 locally on Bob's host, leaving only lines 15-17, and 19 to be computed securely.

```
1  ## variables with suffix A are Alice's inputs,
2  ## with suffix B are Bob's. yd is known to both.
3  int lot_size(int fvA, int cA, int hvA,
4               int fbB, int hbB, int yd)
5    int a, b, c, d, e, f, g, h, i;
6
7    a = 2 * yd;
8    b = a * fvA;
9    c = yd / cA;
10   d = c * hvA;
11
12   e = 2 * yd;
13   f = e * fbB;
14
15   g = f + b;
16   h = hbB + d;
17   i = g / h;
18
19   return sqrt(i); ## integer square root
```

Figure 12. Joint economic lot size example from [15]

Adding loops to the programs. SMC programs do not admit loop constructs because in many cases the execution of a loop, specifically the number of times it iterates, can potentially reveal information about parties' input values beyond what is revealed by the output. However, if we can prove that using their own input and output variables, all parties in the secure computation can infer the number of loop iterations, we can allow SMC programs to have loops in them, without compromising security. For example, for a loop `.. i = 0; while(i < n) { ... ++i;} ..` , if `n` is already known to all the parties in the computation, they can infer the number of loop iterations, and hence running this loop in SMC does not compromise security.

Constructive knowledge inference can be useful in this situation. In particular, we can use it to infer loop invariants in terms of known variables for a party, and if we can do so for all the parties, we can admit the loop in SMC.

5. Experiments

In this section, we present an experimental evaluation of our approach. We provide performance measurements for our algorithms on several example programs.

5.1 Implementation

We present evaluation of three implementations of our algorithms – two for the knowledge inference algorithm from Figure 8 that handle linear and non-linear arithmetic respectively, and one for the constructive knowledge inference algorithm from Figures 9 and 10.

Convex polyhedra based implementation. We have implemented the knowledge inference algorithm from Figure 8 using the polyhedra powerset domain as implemented in Parma Polyhedra Library (PPL, v0.11.2) [1]. This approach represents the program postcondition, ϕ_{post}, as a set of convex polyhedra (each of which is a conjunction of linear inequalities), interpreted over real-valued variables. We use polyhedra in the implementation to avoid reasoning about integers as much as possible. To verify the validity of ϕ (line 9 in Figure 8), we check if the negation of ϕ has an integer solution. This corresponds to checking, for every polyhedron/disjunct φ in $\phi_{post} \wedge \phi'_{post} \wedge \phi_k$, that the formulae $\varphi \wedge (y > y')$ and $\varphi \wedge (y < y')$ define convex regions with no real points (quick check) and no integer points (slower check). If so, ϕ is valid. This implementation only handles programs that use linear arithmetic.

Bitvectors based implementation. Our second implementation of the algorithm from Figure 8 uses a bitvector representation of program variables via the Simple Theorem Prover [10] (STP, revision 1671). This implementation handles non-linear arithmetic. It represents formulae (postcondition, ϕ) using logical and arithmetic expressions over fixed-width bit vectors. The validity of ϕ is checked using STP. In addition, STP allows us to construct formulas that relate individual bits of the integer variables, which means we can construct for every $1 \leq i \leq \mathbf{x}$ (for bit width **x**) the formula $\phi_{post} \wedge \phi'_{post} \wedge \phi_k \Rightarrow (y_i = y'_i)$ where y_i designates bit i of variable y. Checking validity of such formulas lets us conclude that parties can potentially infer individual bits, even if they cannot infer whole variables.

Constructive algorithm for boolean variables. We have implemented the constructive knowledge inference algorithm for boolean variables (Figure 9 and Figure 10) using the LLVM compiler infrastructure [17]. We use the Z3 SMT solver [2] for the validity queries.

5.2 Results

We have conducted the experiments on a Mac Pro with two 2.26 GHz quad-core Xeon processors, 16 GB RAM, and running OS X v10.8. The results are in Figure 13.

The top chart shows time taken (in log-scale) by our three implementations, **POLY** (convex polyhedra based), **BVx** (bit-vector based, for **x** as 8, 16, and 32), and **CONS** (constructive algorithm), on several example programs (discussed later). We evaluated **BVx** on all programs, whereas other implementations only on the (linear) median examples. In all programs, we try to infer all variables for both the parties. Additionally, in the case of **BVx**, we also try to infer every intermediate bit.

The bottom chart provides some characteristics of the test cases that contribute to the running times above: the total number of variables in the test cases, and for the linear programs, the number of convex disjuncts in program postcondition (see **POLY** implementation description).

Median example. We consider the joint median computation (Figure 1) for 2, 3, 4, and 5 inputs per party (these versions do not store intermediate integer values `a3`, `b3`, etc. as in Figure 1). Unsurprisingly, the time taken by non-constructive implementations increases with the number of inputs. **POLY** is especially susceptible to the large number of disjuncts in the program postcondition (due to the large number of paths), taking around 24 seconds for analyzing `median5`, up from as little as 0.044 seconds for analyzing `median2`.

For **CONS**, we consider the set Q for Alice as $\{\mathtt{m} \odot a_i\}$ and for Bob as $\{\mathtt{m} \odot b_i\}$, where $\odot \in \{<, \leq, >, \geq, =, \neq\}$, and a_i and b_i range over inputs of Alice and Bob respectively. We used $(c = 2, d = 2)$ for all input sizes. It is able to infer knowledge of all comparisons for all the median programs. However, as the number of candidate predicates ($|Q|$) increases, the algorithm takes more time. For median with 4 inputs, for example, $|Q_{\text{Alice}}| = |Q_{\text{Bob}}| = 24$, and it takes ~41 seconds to infer all the variables for both parties, as compared to ~2 seconds in the case of 2 inputs per party and $|Q_{\text{Alice}}| = |Q_{\text{Bob}}| = 12$.

We note that at present, our implementation does not aggressively optimize the use of the SMT solver (like caching query responses etc.) that can potentially bring down the inference time since there are lots of redundant validity queries. Moreover, the **CONS** implementation computes ς for every to-be-inferred variable, something that can be optimized as well.

Lot size example. The joint computation of economic lot size in Figure 12 is a non-linear arithmetic example. As described in Section 4, information flow analysis infers that Alice knows `a, b, c, d` and Bob knows `e, f`. Using **BVx**, for **x** as 8, 16, and 32, we infer the same conclusions. In addition, various bits of some other variables are inferred. For example, Alice knows bit 1 of `f` and g, while Bob knows bit

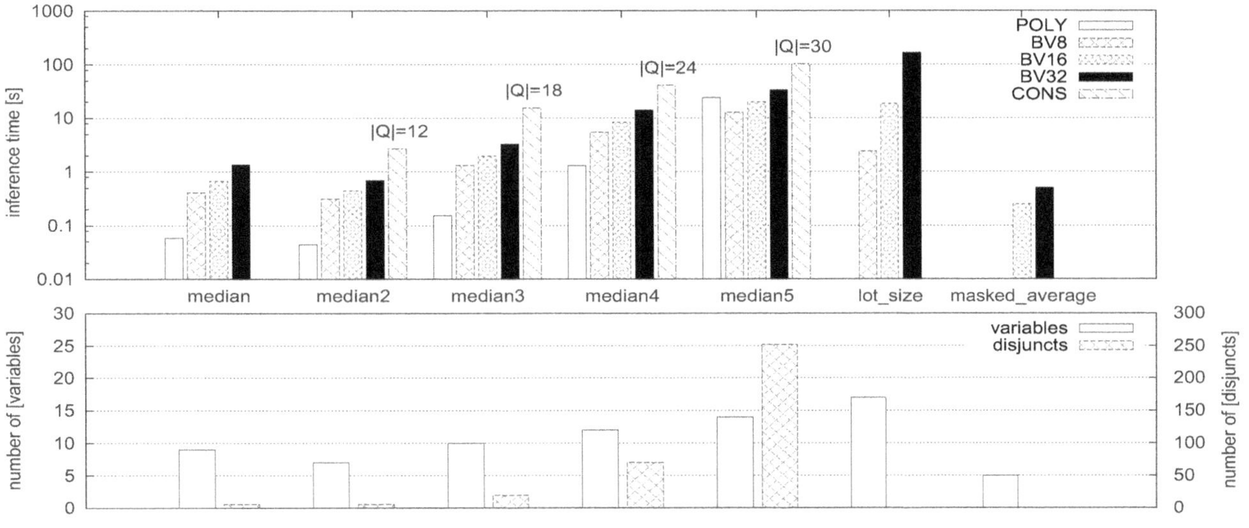

Figure 13. Results (Section 5.2).

1 of b and g. These are due to the multiplications by 2 on lines 9 and 15, resulting in null bits of lowest order. The performance of **BVx** for this test case naturally decreases as **x** is increased. For **x** as 8, the analysis takes around 2.4 seconds, while for **x** as 32, it takes 165 seconds. Note that a significant portion of this additional time is spent checking a much larger number of bits for partial inference (when complete variables cannot be inferred).

```
## assume 0 <= a,b < 0x0fff
int masked_average (int a, int b)
  int sum = a + b;
  int avg = sum / 2;
  return (avg & 0xfff0);
```

Figure 14. Masked average

Masked average example. Our final example serves to better demonstrate the inference of bits of variables that cannot be inferred completely. Inference on the scale of bits lets us determine bit-width requirements of a circuit implementing some computation, as well as determine which bits can be revealed ahead of time due to the output of the computation. Consider a `masked_average` function in Figure 14. The function outputs the high-order bits of the average of two 16 (or 32) bit inputs, which are assumed to be 12 bits big. **BVx** implementations for **x** as 16 and 32, analyzes this function in 0.25 and 0.50 seconds respectively.

If we only consider the input assumptions (view the program as outputting nothing), then both parties can infer the null values of `sum` at bits 14-16 and of `avg` at bits 13-16 . Additionally, since the function returns all but the lower 4 bits of the average, knowledge inference lets us conclude that bits 6-13 of `sum` and bits 5-12 of `avg` can be inferred given the output. An optimized circuit for this function would (a) reduce the size of sum and avg to 13 and 12 bits respectively, and (b) reveal bits 6-13 of `sum` after computing it, so that the final division circuit can be performed with just 5 bits.

6. Related Work

Knowledge inference in SMC. In contrast to SMC compilers that compute a function as a monolithic secure computation [6, 18], recent research has focused on knowledge inference driven optimized SMC protocols. Huang et. al. [14] identify this limitation of previous compilers, and present a framework for implementing optimized, modular SMC protocols. However, they leave the automatic generation of optimized SMC protocols to future work [13].

Kerschbaum [15] solves the knowledge inference problem using a custom program analysis based on epistemic modal logic inference rules. He shows that his approach works on the median example (Figure 1), and the lot size computation example (Figure 12). Our work can be viewed as a generalization and improvement of his approach, making several advances. First, we formally define the notion of *knowledge* in SMC, and the problem of knowledge inference. Second, we prove our algorithms are sound and (relatively) complete. Moreover, our algorithms are built on top of SMT solvers, thus leveraging recent advances in SMT solving techniques. Indeed, we present experimental measurements to characterize the performance of our algorithms while he does not.

Self-composition and noninterference. Our approach to (non-constructive) knowledge inference takes advantage of the connection between the problem and methods for deciding noninterference-like properties using *self-composition* [4]. As far as we are aware, we are the first to observe that knowledge inference can be reduced to the question of deciding delimited release [21], and we are the first to show how to decide this property using self-composition [4]. Moreover, in the form of constructive knowledge inference, we are the first to propose inference algorithms for inferring the output function to decide the problem of required release [7]. Inferring local variables known to p via information flow analysis, as described earlier, is similar to the splitting algorithm employed by Jif/Split [24], which partitions a program to run on multiple hosts. Jif/Split does not employ SMCs, but rather relies on trusted third parties, and employs a simple syntactic algorithm incapable of inferring deeper relationships, e.g., it would not be able to deduce that Alice can infer `x1` and `x2` in the median example.

Template based program verification. Our constructive knowledge inference algorithms (Figure 11, Figure 10, and Figure 9) are inspired by template driven program verification techniques [12, 22]. However, our algorithms take advantage of features specific to our problem. Our templates, instead of having arbitrary structure, have restricted form of $\phi_L \Rightarrow y \wedge y \Rightarrow \phi_R$. For *negative* variables (i.e., variables on the left side of an implication), independent of c and d, we never have to consider more than one lattice, since we always have only one template variable on the left of implication. Second, as mentioned in the inference of ϕ_L earlier, in addition to pruning the subtree of a solution node, we also prune subtrees whose root node has size greater than c. Finally, we infer ϕ_L independent of ϕ_R, i.e. solve $\phi_L \Rightarrow y$ separately from $y \Rightarrow \phi_R$, which is different from [22], where *negative* variables are inferred for every permutation of *positive* variables (variables on the right side of an implication). Again, the simple structure of our templates enables us to do so.

7. Conclusion

In this paper, we considered the problem of knowledge inference in the context of optimizing secure multi-party computation. We formally defined the notion of knowledge in SMC, and the problems of knowledge inference and constructive knowledge inference. We gave solutions to the knowledge inference problems and proved that our solutions are sound, and characterized conditions under which they are complete. Finally, we presented an experimental evaluation of our solutions.

Acknowledgments. We thank anonymous reviewers for their helpful feedback. This research was sponsored by NSF grant CNS-1111599, and the US Army Research laboratory and the UK Ministry of Defence under Agreement Number W911NF-06-3-0001. The views and conclusions contained in this document are those of the authors and should not be interpreted as representing the official policies, either expressed or implied, of the US Army Research Laboratory, the US Government, the UK Ministry of Defense, or the UK Government. The US and UK Governments are authorized to reproduce and distribute reprints for Government purposes notwithstanding any copyright notation hereon.

References

[1] PPL: Parma polyhedral library. `www.cs.unipr.it/ppl`.

[2] Z3 theorem prover. `research.microsoft.com/en-us/um/redmond/projects/z3`.

[3] G. Aggarwal, N. Mishra, and B. Pinkas. Secure computation of the k th-ranked element. In *EUROCRYPT*. Springer, 2004.

[4] G. Barthe, P. R. D'Argenio, and T. Rezk. Secure information flow by self-composition. In *CSFW*, 2004.

[5] D. Beaver, S. Micali, and P. Rogaway. The round complexity of secure protocols. In *STOC*, 1990.

[6] A. Ben-David, N. Nisan, and B. Pinkas. FairplayMP: a system for secure multi-party computation. In *CCS*, 2008.

[7] S. Chong. Required information release. In *CSF*, 2010.

[8] M. R. Clarkson and F. B. Schneider. Hyperproperties. In *CSF*, 2008.

[9] P. Cousot and R. Cousot. Static determination of dynamic properties of programs. In *Proceedings of the Second International Symposium on Programming*, 1976.

[10] V. Ganesh and D. L. Dill. A decision procedure for bit-vectors and arrays. In *CAV*, 2007.

[11] O. Goldreich, S. Micali, and A. Wigderson. How to play ANY mental game. In *STOC*, 1987.

[12] S. Gulwani, S. Srivastava, and R. Venkatesan. Program analysis as constraint solving. In *PLDI*, 2008.

[13] Y. Huang, P. Chapman, and D. Evans. Privacy-preserving applications on smartphones. In *HOTSEC*, 2011.

[14] Y. Huang, D. Evans, J. Katz, and L. Malka. Faster secure two-party computation using garbled circuits. In *USENIX Security*, 2011.

[15] F. Kerschbaum. Automatically optimizing secure computation. In *CCS*, 2011.

[16] J. C. King. Symbolic execution and program testing. *Commun. ACM*, 19(7):385–394, 1976.

[17] LLVM. `http://llvm.org`.

[18] D. Malkhi, N. Nisan, B. Pinkas, and Y. Sella. Fairplay: a secure two-party computation system. In *USENIX Security*, 2004.

[19] F. Pottier and V. Simonet. Information flow inference for ML. *ACM TOPLAS*, 25(1):117–158, Jan. 2003.

[20] A. Sabelfeld and A. C. Myers. Language-based information-flow security. *IEEE JSAC*, 2003.

[21] A. Sabelfeld and A. C. Myers. A model for delimited information release. In *International Symp. on Software Security*, 2004.

[22] S. Srivastava and S. Gulwani. Program verification using templates over predicate abstraction. In *PLDI*, 2009.

[23] A. C.-C. Yao. How to generate and exchange secrets. In *FOCS*, 1986.

[24] S. Zdancewic, L. Zheng, N. Nystrom, and A. C. Myers. Untrusted hosts and confidentiality: secure program partitioning. In *SOSP*, 2001.

Faceted Execution of Policy-Agnostic Programs

Thomas H. Austin
UC Santa Cruz
taustin@ucsc.edu

Jean Yang
MIT CSAIL
jeanyang@csail.mit.edu

Cormac Flanagan
UC Santa Cruz
cormac@ucsc.edu

Armando Solar-Lezama
MIT CSAIL
asolar@csail.mit.edu

Abstract

It is important for applications to protect sensitive data. Even for simple confidentiality and integrity policies, it is often difficult for programmers to reason about how the policies should interact and how to enforce policies across the program. A promising approach is *policy-agnostic programming*, a model that allows the programmer to implement policies separately from core functionality. Yang et al. describe Jeeves [48], a programming language that supports information flow policies describing how to reveal sensitive values in different output channels. Jeeves uses symbolic evaluation and constraint-solving to produce outputs adhering to the policies. This strategy provides strong confidentiality guarantees but limits expressiveness and implementation feasibility.

We extend Jeeves with *faceted values* [6], which exploit the structure of sensitive values to yield both greater expressiveness and to facilitate reasoning about runtime behavior. We present a faceted semantics for Jeeves and describe a model for propagating multiple views of sensitive information through a program. We provide a proof of termination-insensitive non-interference and describe how the semantics facilitate reasoning about program behavior.

Categories and Subject Descriptors D.3.3 [*PROGRAMMING LANGUAGES*]: Language Constructs and Features

General Terms Languages, Security
Language design, run-time system, privacy, security

1. Introduction

It is increasingly important for applications to protect user privacy. Even for simple confidentiality and integrity policies, it is often difficult for programmers to reason about how the policies should interact and how to enforce policies across the program.

Policy-agnostic programming has the goal of allowing the programmer to implement core functionality separately from privacy policies. The programmer specifies policies as declarative rules and relies on the system to produce outputs adhering to the policies. Yang et al. describe Jeeves [48], a language that supports confidentiality policies describing how to reveal views of sensitive values based on the output channel. Sensitive values are pairs $\langle \ell \,?\, v_H : v_L \rangle$, where v_H is the high-confidentiality value, v_L is the low-confidentiality value, and guard ℓ is a *label*. The initial implementation of Jeeves relies on symbolic evaluation and constraint-solving to produce outputs adhering to the policies. This strategy provides strong confidentiality guarantees, but at the cost of expressiveness and implementation feasibility. For instance, this implementation restricts recursion under symbolic conditionals and requires the cumulative constraint environment to persist.

In this paper, we present a faceted semantics for Jeeves that exploits the structure of sensitive values in order to increase expressiveness, facilitate reasoning about runtime behavior, and automatically enforce confidentiality policies. We base the Jeeves evaluation strategy on Austin et al.'s *faceted execution* [6], which manipulates explicit representations of sensitive values. With this strategy, labels variables are the only symbolic variables, allowing Jeeves to lift restrictions on the flow of sensitive values. To further improve ease of reasoning, Jeeves allows policies to only constrain labels to **low**. This guarantees that the constraint environment is always consistent, a property that allows for policy garbage-collection.

In this paper we make the following contributions:

- We present a faceted evaluation semantics for Jeeves, a language for automatically enforcing confidentiality policies. The execution model exploits the structure of sensitive values in order to increase expressiveness and to facilitate reasoning about runtime behavior.
- We present a dynamic semantics for faceted execution of Jeeves in terms of the λ^{jeeves} core language. We prove termination-insensitive non-interference, and policy compliance. We show that it is possible to reason about termination, policy consistency, and policy independence: properties that were not possible to reason about with the original semantics of Jeeves [48].
- We describe our implementation of Jeeves as an embedded domain-specific language in Scala and our experience using Jeeves to implement a conference management system that interacts with a web-based frontend and a persistent database.

2. Jeeves and Faceted Evaluation

We introduce faceted values into Jeeves in order to provide confidentiality guarantees, and compare its design with systems that rely on a declassification primitive and with the symbolic execution strategy used in an earlier implementation of Jeeves.

In this section, we present Jeeves using an ML-like concrete syntax, shown in Figure 1. Jeeves extends the λ-calculus with refer-

PLAS'13, June 20, 2013, Seattle, WA, USA.

ences, facets ($\langle \ell ~?~ Exp_H : Exp_L \rangle$), a label construct for introducing labels that guard access to facets, and a **restrict** construct for introducing policies on labels. Jeeves statements include let-bound expressions and the effectful **print** statement.

2.1 Jeeves for Confidentiality

Jeeves allows the programmer to introduce a variable name that can be either "Alice" or "Anonymous" depending on the output channel:

```
let name: string = label a in
  <a ? "Alice" : "Anonymous" >
in ...
```

The above code introduces a label a that determines whether the private (high-confidentiality) value "Alice" or the public (low-confidentiality) "Anonymous" should be revealed. Labels take on the values { **low**, **high** }.

A simple policy on a sensitive value name is that the user must be the user alice to have high-confidentiality status:

```
let name: string = label a in
  restrict a: λ(c: User).(c == alice) in
    <a ? "Alice" : "Anonymous">
in ...
```

The **restrict** statement introduces a rule that strengthens the policy relating the output channel to the high-confidentiality value. To produce an assignment to label, the Jeeves system translates this rule to the declarative constraint !(c == alice) ⇒ (a == **low**). This rule is not used until evaluation of **print**, so other policies could further restrict the label to be **low**.

In Jeeves programs, sensitive values can be used as regular program values and effectful statements such as **print** require a context parameter:

```
let msg: string = "Sender is " + name in
print { alice } msg /* Output: "Sender is Alice" */
```

During program evaluation, the Jeeves runtime ensures that only the user alice can see her name appearing as the author in the string msg. User bob sees the string "Sender is Anonymous":

```
let msg = "Sender is " + name in
print { bob } msg     /* Output: "Sender is Anonymous" */
```

Unlike the previous implementation of Jeeves [48], which performs symbolic evaluation, Jeeves evaluation propagates *faceted values*, such as the following faceted value for msg:

```
<a ? "Sender is Alice" : "Sender is Anonymous">
```

Producing concrete outputs involves finding assignments to labels that satisfy the policies. The Jeeves system tries to assign labels to **high**, setting labels to **low** only if the policies require it. Assigning all labels to **low** always yields a consistent solution.

Jeeves allows the output channel to be sensitive:

```
let u: user = label b in
  restrict b: λ(c: User).(c == alice) in <b ? alice : nobody>
in print {u} u.name
```

There is a circular dependency: the context u is a sensitive value <b ? alice : nobody> guarded by a policy depending on the context. Such a policy allows two outcomes: b is **high** and we display alice.name to user alice and b is **low** and we display nobody.name to user nobody. The Jeeves runtime ensures maximal functionality: if the policies allow a labels to be **high** or **low**, the value will be **high**.

2.2 A Health Database in Jeeves

To show how to use Jeeves for real-world applications, let us build a simple health database with records of the following form:

```
type Patient { identity : User ref
             ; doctor: User ref
             ; meds: ( Medication list ) ref }
```

In these records, each of the fields identity, doctor, and meds could be sensitive values that show different values of the correct type to low-confidentiality output channels.

In this example, the output context has type HealthCtxt, which we define as follows:

```
type HealthCtxt { viewer: User, time: Date }
```

This context contains information not just for the viewer but also for the current date, allowing policies to define activation and expiration times for visibility.

The idiomatic way of attaching policies to a value is to create sensitive values for each field and then attach policies:

```
let mkPatient ( identity : User) (doctor: User)
      ( meds: Medication list ) : Patient =
  label np, dp, mp in
  let p = { identity  = <np ? identity : nobody>
          ; doctor    = <dp ? doctor : nobody>
          ; meds      = <mp ? meds : []> in
  addNamePolicy          p np;
  addDoctorPolicy        p dp;
  addMedicationsPolicy   p mp;
in p
```

This function introduces labels, creates sensitive values, attaches policies to the labels, and returns the resulting Patient record. The function makes use of the add... Policy functions for attaching policies to the labels. The add... Policy functions take a Patient record and a labels and uses the record fields to attach a policy to the label. We define addMedicationsPolicy as:

```
let addMedicationsPolicy (p: Patient) (mp: label): unit =
  restrict mp: λ(c: HealthCtxt).
      (c.viewer == p.identity || c.viewer == p.doctor)
in ...
```

This policy sets the label to **low** unless the viewer is the patient or the patient's doctor. Jeeves automatically handles dependencies between policies and sensitive values: to have access to the medication list, the viewer needs to be able to see that their identity is equal to either p. identity or p.doctor.

2.3 Comparison to Declassification

Declassification primitives are used in many systems that make information flow guarantees. For instance, in an auction system the last bid might be considered private information until the auction has been completed, at which point the final bid should be made public. In a system with a declassification primitive instead of support for policy-agnostic programming, the relevant code to allow the release of this data might look something like the following:

```
let finalBid : (int ref) = ref label a in <a ? 42 : 0>
in let ...
  if currentTime < closeOfBid
    then finalBid := declassify ( finalBid )
in print { bidder } { ! finalBid }
```

At each print statement involving the final bid, the above code would need to be repeated. These declassification statements refine the core policy. The original paper on faceted values [6] shows how a declassification primitive may be designed for faceted evaluation.

The downside with this approach is that the effective policy for the system is littered throughout the code, leading to obvious

x			variables
ℓ			labels
p, r			primitives, records
$Label$	::=	**low** | **high**	labels
τ	::=	**int** | **bool** | **string** | **record** $\overrightarrow{x : \tau}$	types
	|	$\tau_2 \to \tau_2$ | τ **ref** | $Label$	
Exp	::=	x | p | r	expressions
	|	$\lambda x : \tau.Exp$	
	|	Exp_1 (op) Exp_2	
	|	**if** Exp_1 **then** Exp_t **else** Exp_f	
	|	Exp_1 Exp_2	
	|	Exp_1 ; Exp_2	
	|	! Exp	
	|	$x := Exp$	
	|	$\langle \ell ? Exp_{high} : Exp_{low} \rangle$	
	|	**let** $x = Exp$ **in** Exp	
	|	label ℓ **in** Exp	
	|	**restrict** ℓ : Exp_p **in** Exp	
$Stmt$	::=	**let** $x : \tau = Exp$ **in** Exp_b	statements
	|	**print** $\{Exp_c\} Exp$	

Figure 1: Jeeves syntax.

Identity	Doctor
$\langle a$? alice : default$\rangle$	$\langle e$? erica : default$\rangle$
$\langle b$? bob : default$\rangle$	$\langle f$? fred : default$\rangle$
$\langle c$? claire : default$\rangle$	$\langle f'$? fred : default$\rangle$

Table 1. Sample patient records.

problems with the readability and maintainability of the policy-related code. In aspect-oriented [25] terminology, this approach suffers from a *tangling of aspects*.

While declassification can provide the flexibility needed in real-world systems, we argue that policy-agnostic programming is a more elegant solution. Since the policy code is kept separately, it is easier to get a holistic picture of the policy for data in the system, resulting in improved readability and maintainability. Also, since policy code can be kept separate, it might potentially be easier to protect policy mechanisms from abuse by malicious third parties than it would be to protect the use of a declassification primitive.

Continuing with the auction example, the policy code for the final bid is shown below. No matter how many channels we write to with the print statement, we do not need to repeat the policy code that determines if the value of finalBid can be released.

```
let finalBid : (int ref) = ref label a in
  restrict a: λ (x: bool). currentTime < closeOfBid in
    <a ? 42 : 0> /* The starting high bid is 42 */
in ...
```

As an additional benefit, we note that policy-agnostic programming offers a good solution for approaches such as secure multi-execution [17] that rely on separate processes. Since policy code is only applied when data is released, it eliminates the need for coordinating between processes (assuming that the policy is consistent).

2.4 Advantages of Faceted Execution over Symbolic Execution

Explicit representation of facets allows the runtime to prune branches of execution. Consider the following function, which takes a list of patients and a doctor and calls fold to count of the number of patients with a doctor field matching the doctor argument, on the records in Table 1 with doctor = erica.

```
let countPatients (patients: Patient list) (doctor: User): int
  = fold (λ (p: Patient) . λ (accum: int) .
        ( if (p.doctor == doctor)
              then (accum + 1)
              else accum)
        0 patients)
in ...
```

Consider the behavior of this function on the records in Table 1 with a call to countPatients with doctor = erica. Evaluation of <e ? erica : default> == erica yields the expression <e ? erica == erica : default == erica>, which can be simplified to <e ? **true** : **false**>. Evaluation of faceted function applications creates a new faceted value resulting from applying the function to each facet. If e is in the set of path condition assumptions, then only the high facet is used. Evaluation of the conditional produces the expression

<e ? **if** (**true**) **then** (accum + 1) **else** accum : **if** (**false**) ... >,

which simplifies to <e ? accum + 1 : accum>. Depending on whether the output user is allowed to see that p.doctor is equal to erica, the resulting sum is either accum or accum + 1.

Storing an explicit representation for facets allows the runtime to prune branches. For instance, if the doctor is not equal to erica on either facet, then the faceted evaluation only needs to store a single value. The system may also prune facets based on path assumptions: if evaluation is occurring under the assumption that guard k is true, then subsequent evaluation can assume guard k. This is particularly advantageous when there are a small number of labels corresponding to a fixed set of principals.

3. Core Semantics

We model the semantics of Jeeves with λ^{jeeves}, a simple core language that extends the faceted execution semantics of Austin and Flanagan [6] with a declarative policy language for confidentiality. The λ^{jeeves} semantics describes how to evaluate faceted values, store policies, and use the policy environment to provide assignments to labels for producing concrete outputs. We use these semantics to prove non-interference and policy compliance guarantees.

We show the source syntax in Figure 2. The language λ^{jeeves} extends the λ-calculus with expressions for allocating references (ref e), dereferencing ($!e$), assignment ($e_1 := e_2$), creating faceted

Syntax:

$e ::=$		*Term*
	x	variable
	c	constant
	$\lambda x.e$	abstraction
	$e_1\ e_2$	application
	ref e	reference allocation
	$!e$	dereference
	$e{:=}e$	assignment
	$\langle k\ ?\ e_1 : e_2\rangle$	faceted expression
	label k in e	label declaration
	restrict(k, e)	policy specification
$S ::=$		*Statement*
	let $x = e$ in S	let statement
	print $\{e\}$ e	print statement
$c ::=$		*Constant*
	f	file handle
	b	boolean
	i	integer
x, y, z		*Variable*
k, l		*Label*

Standard encodings:

$$\begin{aligned}
true &\stackrel{\text{def}}{=} \lambda x.\lambda y.x \\
false &\stackrel{\text{def}}{=} \lambda x.\lambda y.y \\
\text{if } e_1 \text{ then } e_2 \text{ else } e_3 &\stackrel{\text{def}}{=} (e_1\ (\lambda d.e_2)\ (\lambda d.e_3))\ (\lambda x.x) \\
\text{if } e_1 \text{ then } e_2 &\stackrel{\text{def}}{=} \text{if } e_1 \text{ then } e_2 \text{ else } 0 \\
\text{let } x = e_1 \text{ in } e_2 &\stackrel{\text{def}}{=} (\lambda x.e_2)\ e_1 \\
e_1 \wedge_f e_2 &\stackrel{\text{def}}{=} \lambda x.e_1\ x \wedge e_2\ x \\
e_1 \wedge e_2 &\stackrel{\text{def}}{=} \text{if } e_1 \text{ then } e_2 \text{ else } false
\end{aligned}$$

Figure 2: The source language λ^{jeeves}

expressions ($\langle k\ ?\ e_1 : e_2\rangle$), specifying policy (restrict(k, e)), and declaring labels (label k in e). Additional statements exist for let-statements (let $x = e$ in S) and printing output (print $\{e_1\}$ e_2). Conditionals are encoded in terms of function application.

In λ^{jeeves}, values V contain *faceted values* of the form

$$\langle k\ ?\ V_H : V_L\rangle$$

A viewer authorized to see k-sensitive data will observe the private facet V_H. Other viewers will instead see V_L. For example, the value $\langle k\ ?\ 42 : 0\rangle$ specifies a value of 42 that should only be viewed when k is **high** according to the policy associated with k. When the policy specifies **low**, the observed value should instead be 0.

A *program counter label* pc records when execution is influenced by public or private facets. For instance, in the conditional test

$$\text{if } (\langle k\ ?\ true : false\rangle) \text{ then } e_1 \text{ else } e_2$$

our semantics needs to evaluate both e_1 and e_2. The label k is added to pc during the evaluation of e_1. By doing so, our semantics records the influence of k on this computation. Similarly, $\overline{k}$ is added to pc during the evaluation of e_2 to record that the execution should have no effects observable to k. A *branch* h is either a label k or its negation $\overline{k}$. Therefore pc is a set of branches that never contains both k and $\overline{k}$, since that would reflect influences from both the private and public facet of a value.

The operation $\langle\!\langle\ pc\ ?\ V_1 : V_2\ \rangle\!\rangle$ creates a faceted value. The value V_1 is visible when the specified policies correspond with *all* branches in pc. Otherwise, V_2 is visible instead.

$$\begin{aligned}
\langle\!\langle\ \emptyset\ ?\ V_n : V_o\ \rangle\!\rangle &\stackrel{\text{def}}{=} V_n \\
\langle\!\langle\ \{k\} \cup rest\ ?\ V_n : V_o\ \rangle\!\rangle &\stackrel{\text{def}}{=} \langle k\ ?\ \langle\!\langle\ rest\ ?\ V_n : V_o\ \rangle\!\rangle : V_o\rangle \\
\langle\!\langle\ \{\overline{k}\} \cup rest\ ?\ V_n : V_o\ \rangle\!\rangle &\stackrel{\text{def}}{=} \langle k\ ?\ V_o : \langle\!\langle\ rest\ ?\ V_n : V_o\ \rangle\!\rangle\rangle
\end{aligned}$$

For example, $\langle\!\langle\ \{k, l\}\ ?\ V_H : V_L\ \rangle\!\rangle$ returns $\langle k\ ?\ \langle l\ ?\ V_H : V_L\rangle : V_L\rangle$. We occasionally abbreviate $\langle\!\langle\ \{k\}\ ?\ V_H : V_L\ \rangle\!\rangle$ as $\langle\!\langle\ k\ ?\ V_H : V_L\ \rangle\!\rangle$.

The semantics are defined via the big-step evaluation relation:

$$\Sigma, e \Downarrow_{pc} \Sigma', V$$

This relation evaluates an expression e in the context of a store Σ and program counter label pc. It returns a modified store Σ' reflecting updates and a value V. In Figure 3 we show the evaluation rules, which uses additional runtime syntax (also shown in Figure 3).

Our language includes support for reference cells, which introduce additional complexities in handling implicit flows. The rule [F-REF] handles reference allocation (ref e). It evaluates an expression e, encoding any influences from the program counter pc to the value V, and adds it to the store Σ' at a fresh address a. Facets in V inconsistent with pc are set to 0. (Critically, to maintain non-interference, $\Sigma(a) = 0$ for all a not in the domain of Σ.)

The rule [F-DEREF] for dereferencing ($!e$) evaluates the expression e to a value V, which should either be an address or a faceted values where all of the "leaves" are addresses. The rule uses a helper function $deref(\Sigma', V, pc)$ (defined in Figure 3), which takes the addresses from V, retrieves the appropriate values from the store Σ', and combines them in the return value V'. As an optimization, addresses that are not compatible with pc are ignored.

The rule [F-ASSIGN] for assignment ($e_1{:=}e_2$) is similar to [F-DEREF]. It evaluates e_1 to a possibly faceted value V_1 corresponding to an address and e_2 to a value V'. The helper function $assignOp(\Sigma_2, pc, V_1, V')$ defined in Figure 3 decomposes V_1 into separate addresses, storing the appropriate facets of V' into the returned store Σ'. The changes to the store may come from both V_1 and pc.

The rule [F-LABEL] dynamically allocates a label (label k in e), adding a fresh label to the store with the default policy of $\lambda x.true$. Any occurrences of k in e are α-renamed to k' and the expression is evaluated with the updated store. Policies may be further refined (restrict(k, e)) by the rule [F-RESTRICT], which evaluates e to a policy V that should be either a lambda or a faceted value comprised of lambdas. The additional policy check is restricted by pc, so that policy checks cannot themselves leak data. It is then joined with the existing policy for k, ensuring that policies can only become more restrictive.

When a faceted expression $\langle k\ ?\ e_1 : e_2\rangle$ is evaluated, both sub-expressions must be evaluated in sequence, as per the rule [F-SPLIT]. The influence of k is added to the program counter for the evaluation of e_1 to V_1 and $\overline{k}$ for the evaluation of e_2 to V_2, tracking the branch of code being taken. The results of both evaluations are joined together in the operation $\langle\!\langle\ k\ ?\ V_1 : V_2\ \rangle\!\rangle$. As an optimization, only one expression is evaluated if the program counter already contains either k or $\overline{k}$, as indicated by the rules [F-LEFT] and [F-RIGHT].

Function application ($e_1\ e_2$) is somewhat complex in the presence of faceted values. The rule [F-APP] evaluates e_1 to V_1, which should either be a lambda or a faceted value containing lambdas, and evaluates e_2 to the function argument V_2. It then delegates the application $(V_1\ V_2)$ to an auxiliary relation defined in Figure 4:

$$\Sigma, (V_1\ V_2) \Downarrow_{pc}^{\mathsf{app}} \Sigma', V'$$

Runtime Syntax

$$
\begin{array}{lclcl}
e & \in & \mathit{Expr} & ::= & \ldots \mid a \\
\Sigma & \in & \mathit{Store} & = & (\mathit{Address} \to_p \mathit{Value}) \cup (\mathit{Label} \to \mathit{Value}) \\
R & \in & \mathit{RawValue} & ::= & c \mid a \mid (\lambda x.e) \\
a & \in & \mathit{Address} & & \\
V & \in & \mathit{Val} & ::= & R \mid \langle k \; ? \; V_1 : V_2 \rangle \\
h & \in & \mathit{Branch} & ::= & k \mid \overline{k} \\
pc & \in & \mathit{PC} & = & 2^{\mathit{Branch}}
\end{array}
$$

Expression Evaluation Rules $\boxed{\Sigma, e \Downarrow_{pc} \Sigma', V}$

$$\frac{}{\Sigma, R \Downarrow_{pc} \Sigma, R} \quad \text{[F-VAL]}$$

$$\frac{\Sigma, e \Downarrow_{pc} \Sigma', V' \quad a \notin dom(\Sigma') \quad V = \langle\!\langle \, pc \; ? \; V' : 0 \, \rangle\!\rangle}{\Sigma, (\text{ref } e) \Downarrow_{pc} \Sigma'[a := V], a} \quad \text{[F-REF]}$$

$$\frac{\Sigma, e \Downarrow_{pc} \Sigma', V \quad V' = \mathit{deref}(\Sigma', V, pc)}{\Sigma, !e \Downarrow_{pc} \Sigma', V'} \quad \text{[F-DEREF]}$$

$$\frac{\Sigma, e_1 \Downarrow_{pc} \Sigma_1, V_1 \quad \Sigma_1, e_2 \Downarrow_{pc} \Sigma_2, V' \quad \Sigma' = \mathit{assign}(\Sigma_2, pc, V_1, V')}{\Sigma, e_1 := e_2 \Downarrow_{pc} \Sigma', V'} \quad \text{[F-ASSIGN]}$$

$$\frac{\Sigma, e_1 \Downarrow_{pc} \Sigma_1, V_1 \quad \Sigma_1, e_2 \Downarrow_{pc} \Sigma_2, V_2 \quad \Sigma_2, (V_1 \; V_2) \Downarrow_{pc}^{\text{app}} \Sigma', V'}{\Sigma, (e_1 \; e_2) \Downarrow_{pc} \Sigma', V'} \quad \text{[F-APP]}$$

$$\frac{k \notin pc \text{ and } \overline{k} \notin pc \quad \Sigma, e_1 \Downarrow_{pc \cup \{k\}} \Sigma_1, V_1 \quad \Sigma_1, e_2 \Downarrow_{pc \cup \{\overline{k}\}} \Sigma', V_2 \quad V' = \langle\!\langle \, k \; ? \; V_1 : V_2 \, \rangle\!\rangle}{\Sigma, \langle k \; ? \; e_1 : e_2 \rangle \Downarrow_{pc} \Sigma', V'} \quad \text{[F-SPLIT]}$$

$$\frac{k \in pc \qquad \Sigma, e_1 \Downarrow_{pc} \Sigma', V}{\Sigma, \langle k \; ? \; e_1 : e_2 \rangle \Downarrow_{pc} \Sigma', V} \quad \text{[F-LEFT]}$$

$$\frac{\overline{k} \in pc \qquad \Sigma, e_2 \Downarrow_{pc} \Sigma', V}{\Sigma, \langle k \; ? \; e_1 : e_2 \rangle \Downarrow_{pc} \Sigma', V} \quad \text{[F-RIGHT]}$$

$$\frac{k' \mathit{fresh} \quad \Sigma[k' := \lambda x.\mathit{true}], e[k := k'] \Downarrow_{pc} \Sigma', V}{\Sigma, \text{label } k \text{ in } e \Downarrow_{pc} \Sigma', V'} \quad \text{[F-LABEL]}$$

$$\frac{\Sigma, e \Downarrow_{pc} \Sigma_1, V \quad \Sigma' = \Sigma_1[k := \Sigma_1(k) \wedge_f \langle\!\langle \, pc \cup \{k\} \; ? \; V : \lambda x.\mathit{true} \, \rangle\!\rangle]}{\Sigma, \text{restrict}(k, e) \Downarrow_{pc} \Sigma', V} \quad \text{[F-RESTRICT]}$$

Auxiliary Functions

$$
\begin{array}{lcl}
\mathit{deref} : \mathit{Store} \times \mathit{Val} \times \mathit{PC} & \to & \mathit{Val} \\
\mathit{deref}(\Sigma, a, pc) & = & \Sigma(a) \\
\mathit{deref}(\Sigma, \langle k \; ? \; V_H : V_L \rangle, pc) & = & \begin{cases} \mathit{deref}(\Sigma, V_H, pc) & \text{if } k \in pc \\ \mathit{deref}(\Sigma, V_L, pc) & \text{if } \overline{k} \in pc \\ \langle\!\langle \, k \; ? \; \mathit{deref}(\Sigma, V_H, pc) : \mathit{deref}(\Sigma, V_L, pc) \, \rangle\!\rangle & \text{otherwise} \end{cases}
\end{array}
$$

$$
\begin{array}{lcl}
\mathit{assign} : \mathit{Store} \times \mathit{PC} \times \mathit{Val} \times \mathit{Val} & \to & \mathit{Store} \\
\mathit{assign}(\Sigma, pc, a, V) & = & \Sigma[a := \langle\!\langle \, pc \; ? \; V : \Sigma(a) \, \rangle\!\rangle] \\
\mathit{assign}(\Sigma, pc, \langle k \; ? \; V_H : V_L \rangle, V) & = & \Sigma' \quad \text{where } \Sigma_1 = \mathit{assign}(\Sigma, \; pc \cup \{k\}, V_H, V) \\
 & & \qquad \text{and } \; \Sigma' = \mathit{assign}(\Sigma_1, pc \cup \{\overline{k}\}, V_L, V)
\end{array}
$$

Figure 3: Faceted Evaluation Semantics

Application Rules $\boxed{\Sigma, (V_1\ V_2) \Downarrow_{pc}^{\mathsf{app}} \Sigma', V'}$

[FA-FUN]

$$\frac{\Sigma, e[x := V] \Downarrow_{pc} \Sigma', V'}{\Sigma, ((\lambda x.e)\ V) \Downarrow_{pc}^{\mathsf{app}} \Sigma', V'}$$

[FA-LEFT]

$$\frac{k \in pc \qquad \Sigma, (V_{\mathrm{H}}\ V_2) \Downarrow_{pc}^{\mathsf{app}} \Sigma', V}{\Sigma, (\langle k\ ?\ V_{\mathrm{H}} : V_{\mathrm{L}} \rangle\ V_2) \Downarrow_{pc}^{\mathsf{app}} \Sigma', V}$$

[FA-SPLIT]

$$\frac{\begin{array}{c} k \notin pc \qquad \overline{k} \notin pc \\ \Sigma, (V_{\mathrm{H}}\ V_2) \Downarrow_{pc \cup \{k\}}^{\mathsf{app}} \Sigma_1, V_{\mathrm{H}}' \\ \Sigma_1, (V_{\mathrm{L}}\ V_2) \Downarrow_{pc \cup \{\overline{k}\}}^{\mathsf{app}} \Sigma', V_{\mathrm{L}}' \\ V' = \langle\!\langle\, k\ ?\ V_{\mathrm{H}}' : V_{\mathrm{L}}' \,\rangle\!\rangle \end{array}}{\Sigma, (\langle k\ ?\ V_{\mathrm{H}} : V_{\mathrm{L}} \rangle\ V_2) \Downarrow_{pc}^{\mathsf{app}} \Sigma', V'}$$

[FA-RIGHT]

$$\frac{\overline{k} \in pc \qquad \Sigma, (V_{\mathrm{L}}\ V_2) \Downarrow_{pc}^{\mathsf{app}} \Sigma', V}{\Sigma, (\langle k\ ?\ V_{\mathrm{H}} : V_{\mathrm{L}} \rangle\ V_2) \Downarrow_{pc}^{\mathsf{app}} \Sigma', V}$$

Statement Evaluation Rules $\boxed{\Sigma, S \Downarrow V_p, f : R}$

[F-LET]

$$\frac{\begin{array}{c} \Sigma, e \Downarrow_{\emptyset} \Sigma', V \\ \Sigma, S[x := V] \Downarrow V_p, f : R \end{array}}{\Sigma, \text{let } x = e \text{ in } S \Downarrow V_p, f : R}$$

[F-PRINT]

$$\frac{\begin{array}{c} \Sigma, e_1 \Downarrow_{\emptyset} \Sigma_1, V_f \\ \Sigma_1, e_2 \Downarrow_{\emptyset} \Sigma_2, V_c \\ e_p = \lambda x.\mathit{true} \wedge_f \Sigma_2(k_1) \wedge_f \ldots \wedge_f \Sigma_2(k_n) \\ \Sigma_2, e_p\ V_f \Downarrow_{\emptyset} \Sigma_3, V_p \\ \{\, k_1 \ldots k_n \,\} \text{ includes all labels in } V_f,\ V_c,\ V_p \\ \text{pick } pc \text{ such that } pc(V_f) = f,\ pc(V_c) = R,\ pc(V_p) = \mathit{true} \end{array}}{\Sigma, \text{print } \{e_1\}\ e_2 \Downarrow V_p, f : R}$$

Semantics for Derived Encodings

[F-IF-TRUE]

$$\frac{\begin{array}{c} \Sigma, e_1 \Downarrow_{pc} \Sigma_1, \mathit{true} \\ \Sigma_1, e_2 \Downarrow_{pc} \Sigma', V \end{array}}{\Sigma, \text{if } e_1 \text{ then } e_2 \text{ else } e_3 \Downarrow_{pc} \Sigma', V}$$

[F-IF-FALSE]

$$\frac{\begin{array}{c} \Sigma, e_1 \Downarrow_{pc} \Sigma_1, \mathit{false} \\ \Sigma_1, e_3 \Downarrow_{pc} \Sigma', V \end{array}}{\Sigma, \text{if } e_1 \text{ then } e_2 \text{ else } e_3 \Downarrow_{pc} \Sigma', V}$$

[F-IF-SPLIT]

$$\frac{\begin{array}{c} \Sigma, e_1 \Downarrow_{pc} \Sigma_1, \langle k\ ?\ V_H : V_L \rangle \\ e_H = \text{if } V_H \text{ then } e_2 \text{ else } e_3 \\ e_L = \text{if } V_L \text{ then } e_2 \text{ else } e_3 \\ \Sigma_1, \langle k\ ?\ e_H : e_L \rangle \Downarrow_{pc} \Sigma', V \end{array}}{\Sigma, \text{if } e_1 \text{ then } e_2 \text{ else } e_3 \Downarrow_{pc} \Sigma', V}$$

Figure 4: Faceted Evaluation Semantics for Application and Statements

This relation breaks apart faceted values and tracks the influences of the labels through the rules [FA-SPLIT], [FA-LEFT], and [FA-RIGHT] in a similar manner to the rules [F-SPLIT], [F-LEFT], and [F-RIGHT] discussed previously. The actual application is handled by the [FA-FUN] rule. The body of the lambda ($\lambda x.e$) is evaluated with the variable x replaced by the argument V.

Conditional branches (if e_1 then e_2 else e_3) are Church-encoded as function calls for the sake of simplicity. However, Figure 4 shows direct rules for evaluating conditionals in the presence of faceted values. Under the rule [F-IF-SPLIT], If the condition e_1 evaluates to a faceted value $\langle k\ ?\ V_H : V_L \rangle$, the if statement is evaluated twice with V_H and V_L as the conditional tests.

While expressions handle most of the complexity of faceted values, statements in λ^{jeeves} illustrate how faceted values may be concretized when exporting data to an external party. The semantics for statements are defined via the big-step evaluation relation:

$$\Sigma, S \Downarrow V_p, f : R$$

The rules for statements are specified in Figure 4. The rule [F-LET] handles let expressions (let $x = e$ in S), evaluating an expression e to a value V, performing the proper substitution in statement S. The rule [F-PRINT] handles print statements (print $\{e_1\}$ e_2), where the result of evaluating e_2 is printed to the channel resulting from the evaluation of e_1. Both the channel V_f and the value to print V_c may be faceted values, and furthermore, we must select the facets that correspond with our specified policies. The expression e_p contains all relevant policies included in the store Σ_2. It is evaluated and applied to V_f, returning the policy check V_p that is a faceted value containing booleans. A program counter pc is chosen such that the policies are satisfied, which determines the channel f and the value to print R. Note that there exists a $pc' \in PC$ where all branches are set to **low**, which may always be displayed, thereby ensuring that there is always at least one valid choice for pc.

This property allows garbage collection of policies and facets. Because the constraints are always consistent, the only set of policies relevant to an expression e to output are associated with the transitive closure of labels L_e appearing in e and the policies associated with L_e. Thus any policy associated with an out-of-scope variable may be garbaged-collected. In addition, once a policy has been set to the equivalent of $\lambda x.\mathit{false}$ for a label k, k-sensitive facets and policies cannot be used in a print statement. These properties are advantages over the previous symbolic-execution strategy used by an earlier implementation of Jeeves [48], since the earlier approach could introduce inconsistent policies.

4. Properties

We prove that a single execution with faceted values is equivalent to multiple different executions without faceted values. From this we know that if execution terminates on each facet of a sensitive value, then faceted execution terminates. Jeeves does not have this property because execution keeps sensitive values as symbolic; thus Jeeves restricts applications of recursive functions.

We also prove that the system cannot leak sensitive information either via the output or by the choice of output channel.

4.1 Projection Theorem

A key property of faceted evaluation is that it simulates multiple executions. In other words, a single execution with faceted values *projects* to multiple different executions without faceted values.

$$pc : \mathit{Expr} \text{ (with facets)} \to \mathit{Expr} \text{ (with fewer facets)}$$

$$pc(\langle k\ ?\ e_1 : e_2\rangle) = \begin{cases} pc(e_1) & \text{if } k \in pc \\ pc(e_2) & \text{if } \overline{k} \in pc \\ \langle k\ ?\ pc(e_1) : pc(e_2)\rangle & \text{otherwise} \end{cases}$$

$$pc(\langle k\ ?\ V_1 : V_2\rangle) = \begin{cases} pc(V_1) & \text{if } k \in pc \\ pc(V_2) & \text{if } \overline{k} \in pc \\ pc(V_1) & \text{if } pc(V_1) = pc(V_2) \\ \langle k\ ?\ pc(V_1) : pc(V_2)\rangle & \text{otherwise} \end{cases}$$

$$pc(\dots) = \text{compatible closure}$$

We extend pc to project faceted stores $\Sigma \in \mathit{Store}$ into stores with fewer facets.

$$\begin{array}{lcl} pc : \mathit{Value} & \to & \mathit{Value} \\ pc(\Sigma) & = & \lambda a.\ pc(\Sigma(a)) \cup \lambda k.\ pc(\Sigma(k)) \end{array}$$

Thus pc projection does not remove policies, it only removes some labels on expressions or values. We say that pc_1 and pc_2 are *consistent* if

$$\neg\exists k.\ (k \in pc_1 \wedge \overline{k} \in pc_2) \vee (\overline{k} \in pc_1 \wedge k \in pc_2)$$

We note some key lemmas regarding projection.

Lemma 1. *If* $V = \langle\!\langle\, pc\ ?\ V_1 : V_2 \,\rangle\!\rangle$ *then* $\forall q \in PC$

$$q(V) = \begin{cases} \langle\!\langle\, pc \setminus q\ ?\ q(V_1) : q(V_2) \,\rangle\!\rangle & \text{if } q \text{ is consistent with } pc \\ q(V_2) & \text{otherwise} \end{cases}$$

Lemma 2. *If* $V' = \mathit{deref}(\Sigma, V, pc)$ *then* $\forall q \in PC$ *where* q *is consistent with pc,* $q(V') = \mathit{deref}(q(\Sigma), q(V), pc \setminus q)$.

Lemma 3. *If* $\Sigma' = \mathit{assign}(\Sigma, pc, V_1, V_2)$ *then* $\forall q \in PC$

$$q(\Sigma') = \begin{cases} \mathit{assign}(q(\Sigma), pc \setminus q, q(V_1), q(V_2)) & \text{if } q \text{ consistent with } pc \\ q(\Sigma) & \text{otherwise} \end{cases}$$

Lemma 4. *Suppose pc and q are not consistent and that either*

$$\begin{array}{rl} & \Sigma, e \Downarrow_{pc} \Sigma', V \\ \text{or} & \Sigma, (V_1 V_2) \Downarrow_{pc}^{\text{app}} \Sigma', V \end{array}$$

Then $q(\Sigma) = q(\Sigma')$.

The following projection theorem shows how a single faceted evaluation simulates (or projects) to multiple executions, each with fewer facets, or possibly with no facets at all (if for each label k in the program, either k or $\overline{k}$ is in q).

Theorem 1 (Projection Theorem). *Suppose*

$$\Sigma, e \Downarrow_{pc} \Sigma', V$$

Then for any $q \in PC$ *where pc and q are consistent*

$$q(\Sigma), q(e) \Downarrow_{pc \setminus q} q(\Sigma'), q(V)$$

This theorem significantly extends the projection property of Austin and Flanagan [6], in that it supports dynamic label allocation and flexible, dynamically specified policies, and is also more general in that it can either remove none, some, or all top-level labels in a program, depending on the choice of the projection $PC\ q$. A full proof of the projection theorem is available in the appendix.

4.2 Termination-Insensitive Non-Interference

The projection property captures that data from one collection of executions, represented by the corresponding set of branches pc, does not leak into any incompatible views, thus enabling a straightforward proof of non-interference.

Two faceted values are *pc-equivalent* if they have identical values for the set of branches pc. This notion of pc-equivalence naturally extends to stores ($\Sigma_1 \sim_{pc} \Sigma_2$) and expressions ($e_1 \sim_{pc} e_2$):

$$\begin{array}{lcl} (V_1 \sim_{pc} V_2) & \text{iff} & pc(V_1) = pc(V_2) \\ (\Sigma_1 \sim_{pc} \Sigma_2) & \text{iff} & pc(\Sigma_1) = pc(\Sigma_2) \\ (e_1 \sim_{pc} e_2) & \text{iff} & pc(e_1) = pc(e_2) \end{array}$$

The notion of pc-equivalence and the projection theorem enable a concise statement and proof of termination-insensitive non-interference.

Theorem 2 (Termination-Insensitive Non-Interference). *Let pc be any set of branches. Suppose* $\Sigma_1 \sim_{pc} \Sigma_2$ *and* $e_1 \sim_{pc} e_2$*, and that:*

$$\Sigma_1, e_1 \Downarrow_\emptyset \Sigma_1', V_1 \qquad \Sigma_2, e_2 \Downarrow_\emptyset \Sigma_2', V_2$$

Then $\Sigma_1' \sim_{pc} \Sigma_2'$ *and* $V_1 \sim_{pc} V_2$.

Proof. By the Projection Theorem:

$$\begin{array}{c} pc(\Sigma_1), pc(e_1) \Downarrow_\emptyset pc(\Sigma_1'), pc(V_1) \\ pc(\Sigma_2), pc(e_2) \Downarrow_\emptyset pc(\Sigma_2'), pc(V_2) \end{array}$$

The pc-equivalence assumptions imply that $pc(\Sigma_1) = pc(\Sigma_2)$ and $pc(e_1) = pc(e_2)$. Hence $pc(\Sigma_1') = pc(\Sigma_2')$ and $pc(V_1) = pc(V_2)$ since the semantics is deterministic. □

4.3 Termination-Insensitive Policy Compliance

While we have shown non-interference for a set of labels, the labels do not directly correspond to the output revealed to a given observer. In this section we show how we can prove termination-insensitive *policy compliance*; data is revealed to an external observer only if it is allowed by the policy specified in the program. Thus if S_1 and S_2 are terminating programs that differ only in k-labeled components and the computed policy V_i for each program does not permit revealing k-sensitive data to the output channel, then the set of possible outputs from each program is identical. Here, an output $f : v$ combines both the output channel f and the value v, to ensure that sensitive information is not leaked either via the output value or by the choice of output channel.

Theorem 3. *Suppose for* $i \in 1, 2$*:*

$$\begin{array}{l} S_i = \mathit{print}\ \{e\}\ C[\langle k\ ?\ e_i : e_l\rangle] \\ \emptyset, S_1 \Downarrow V_{p1}, f_1 : R_1 \\ \emptyset, S_2 \Downarrow V_{p2}, f_2 : R_2 \\ \forall pc' \text{ with } k \in pc',\ pc'(V_{p1}) \neq \mathit{true} \text{ and } pc'(V_{p2}) \neq \mathit{true} \end{array}$$

Then $\{\, f : R \mid \emptyset, S_1 \Downarrow V_p, f : R \,\} = \{\, f : R \mid \emptyset, S_2 \Downarrow V_p, f : R \,\}$.

Proof. We show left-to-right containment as follows. (The converse containment holds by a similar argument.) Suppose

$$\begin{array}{l} \emptyset, S_1 \Downarrow V_{p1}, f_1 : R_1 \\ \emptyset, S_2 \Downarrow V_{p2}, f_2 : R_2 \end{array}$$

Then by the [F-PRINT] rule

$\emptyset, e \Downarrow_\emptyset \Sigma_{11}, V_{f1}$
$\Sigma_{11}, C[\langle k \ ?\ e_1 : e_l \rangle] \Downarrow_\emptyset \Sigma_{12}, V_{c1}$
$e_{p1} = \Sigma_{12}(k_1) \wedge_f \ldots \wedge_f \Sigma_{12}(k_n)$ where $\{ k_1 \ldots k_n \}$ includes all labels in V_{f1}, V_{c1}, V_{p1}
$\Sigma_{12}, e_{p1}\ V_{f1} \Downarrow_\emptyset \Sigma_{13}, V_{p1}$
$pc_1(V_{f1}) = f_1,\ pc_1(V_{c1}) = R_1,\ pc_1(V_{p1}) = true,$ so $\overline{k} \in pc_1$

Also by the [F-PRINT] rule for the second execution

$\emptyset, e \Downarrow_\emptyset \Sigma_{21}, V_{f2}$
$\Sigma_{21}, C[\langle k \ ?\ e_2 : e_l \rangle] \Downarrow_\emptyset \Sigma_{12}, V_{c2}$
$e_{p2} = \Sigma_{22}(k_1) \wedge_f \ldots \wedge_f \Sigma_{22}(k_n)$ where $\{ k_1 \ldots k_n \}$ includes all labels in V_{f2}, V_{c2}, V_{p2}
$\Sigma_{22}, e_{p2}\ V_{f2} \Downarrow_\emptyset \Sigma_{23}, V_{p2}$
$pc_2(V_{f2}) = f_2,\ pc_2(V_{c2}) = R_2,\ pc_2(V_{p2}) = true,$ so $\overline{k} \in pc_2$

By determinism, $\Sigma_{11} = \Sigma_{21}\ V_{f1} = V_{f2}$.
Also, $C[\langle k \ ?\ e_1 : e_l \rangle] \sim_{\{\overline{k}\}} C[\langle k \ ?\ e_2 : e_l \rangle]$.
Hence by the projection theorem

$$\begin{array}{lll} \Sigma_{12} \sim_{\{\overline{k}\}} \Sigma_{22} & V_{c1} \sim_{\{\overline{k}\}} V_{c2} & e_{p1} \sim_{\{\overline{k}\}} e_{p2} \\ \Sigma_{13} \sim_{\{\overline{k}\}} \Sigma_{23} & V_{p1} \sim_{\{\overline{k}\}} V_{p2} & \end{array}$$

Pick $pc_2 = pc_1$. Then $R_2 = R_1$ and $f_2 = f_1$ as required. □

5. Scala Implementation

We have implemented Jeeves as an embedded domain-specific language in the Scala programming language [37]. We use Scala's overloading capabilities to implement faceted execution, constraint collection, and interaction with the Z3 SMT solver [33].[1] The implementation defines Scala classes for integers, booleans, objects, and functions that support operations over expressions e or faceted expressions $\langle k\ ?\ e_H : e_L \rangle$. The implementation overloads operators on these types so that faceted values can be used interchangeably with concrete values. For instance, the Expr[Int] class represents the type of concrete and faceted integer expressions. We use Scala's implicit type conversions to lift concrete Scala values.

We have implemented a Scala trait that stores a runtime environment to support methods creating labels, declaring policies, and concretizing expressions. The trait maintains the logical and default constraint environments as lists of functions of type Expr[T] ⇒ Formula, where Formula is a boolean expression that may contain facets. We have a partial evaluation procedure that simplifies expressions based on the value of each facet and the current path assumptions.

To assign values to labels, the implementation evaluates policies according to the context and heap state and invokes Z3 for resolving constraints. Our implementation translates constraints to the QF_LIA logic of SMT-LIB2 [7]. There are only quantifier-free boolean constraints. Labels are the only free variables. We use incremental scripting to implement default values according to default logic [2]. The implementation relies on Scala's support for dynamic invocation to resolve field dereferences. We use zero values (null, 0, or false) to represent undefined fields in SMT.

Our Jeeves library interface supports the introduction of labels, declaration of policies, creation of sensitive variables, and concretization of sensitive expressions. It also has functions for assignment, conditionals, and function evaluation according to the Jeeves semantics.

The library has the following API methods for introducing sensitive values and policies:

```
def mkLabel: Label
def restrict (lvar: Label, f: Expr[T] ⇒ Formula)
def mkSensitive( lvar: Label , high: Expr[T], low: Expr[T]):
    Expr[T]
```

The programmer introduces labels, which are boolean logic variables mapped to HIGH and LOW, into scope by calling the mkLabel method. The restrict method for introducing policies takes a labels and a function that takes a context expression and returns a formula. The library stores policy functions and applies them with respect to the output context and output heap state to produce concrete outputs adhering to the policies. The programmer introduces sensitive values through the mkSensitive method, which takes a labels along with high-confidentiality and low-confidentiality views. To support evaluation with sensitive expressions, programs should accommodate values of type Expr[T] (*e.g.* IntExpr rather than BigInt). The library has methods for producing concrete state:

```
def concretize [T](ctxt: Expr[T], e: Expr[T]): T
def jprint [T](ctxt: Expr[T], e:Expr[T]): Unit
```

These functions take a context and an expression, both of which may be sensitive, and provides assignments to the labels to produce concrete views that adhere to the policies. The implementation treats the mutable state as part of the context in the concretize call to ScalaSMT. All classes that are used in constraint must extend the JeevesRecord class. The set of allocated JeevesRecords is supplied at concretization. This way, policies that refer to mutable parts of the heap will produce correct constraints for the snapshot of the system at concretization. The library provides support for evaluating conditionals and function applications:

```
def jif [T] (c: Formula, t : Unit ⇒ T, f: Unit ⇒ T): Unit
def jfun [A, B] (f : FunctionExpr[A, B], arg : A): B
```

The library stores the path condition as a set of labels and their negations. The jif method evaluates the condition and manages the path condition for each branch appropriately in order to produce a potentially faceted result. The jfun method behaves similarly. Both of these methods check against the path condition to avoid performing unnecessary computations.

6. Case Study: Conference Management

We have implemented JConf, a conference management system that uses Jeeves for confidentiality guarantees. The JConf backend interacts with a web-based frontend and a persistent database store. The original JConf implementation, written using an earlier implementation of Jeeves that used symbolic evaluation rather than faceted execution, was up for several hours at a time and a cumulative total of several days, processing submissions for the Student Research Competition for the Programming Language Design and Implementation Conference 2012. Our experience with this system motivated some of the design decisions in Jeeves, including the decision to use faceted execution.

The implementation of JConf has a backend written in Jeeves that defines Scala objects corresponding to data types (for instance, for representing users and papers) and associates policies with fields of these objects; object constructors add the policies. The backend contains functionality that supports the creation of, lookup of, updates to, and search over these objects. The frontend web code, written using the Scalatra web framework [1], makes calls to the backend functionality and to accessors of the objects. The JConf backend contains a layer that interacts with a MySQL database for persistent storage. The frontend web code and database-interaction code remain agnostic to the policies: the same code is used, for instance, to render a page (for instance, displaying appropriately anonymized information about a paper review) for an author, a reviewer, and a program committee member. Interaction with the Jeeves backend takes on the order of seconds; solving in the Z3

[1] The code is available at `http://code.google.com/p/jeeveslib/`.

File	Total LOC	Policy LOC
ConfUser.scala	212	21
PaperRecord.scala	304	75
PaperReview.scala	116	32
ConfContext.scala	6	0
Backend + Squeryl	800	0
Frontend (Scalatra)	629	0
Frontend (SSP)	798	0
Total	**2865**	**128**

Table 2. Lines of code vs. policy in JConf.

SMT solver takes well under one second. The bulk of execution is involved in propagating sensitive values.

The JConf conference management system provides support for creating new users and updating profiles, creating papers and updating information, submitting papers, assigning reviews, and reviewing papers. We show the breakdown of the system in Table 2: classes describing the data (users, papers, paper reviews, and the context), backend code for accessing the data (including the interface to the database), the Scalatra code for the frontend web request handlers, and the Scalatra Server Page (SSP) code defining the browser pages themselves.

Policy code (calls to `mkLabel`, `mkSensitive`, `restrict`, and `concretize`) is concentrated in the data classes, enabling modular updates to the policy and core functionality. For instance, we can change the review process from double-blind to single-blind simply by tweaking the policies associated with paper and review fields. The policy code makes up less than 5% of the total lines of code.

The programmer defines a *getter*, a *setter*, and a *show function* for each sensitive field. The getter returns the sensitive value, the setter creates a new sensitive value based on the views, and the show function calls `concretize` to return a concrete value of the appropriate type. The programmer creates the sensitive value with a label in scope to which policies can be attached. It may make sense to share labels between field for some applications. The frontend calls the show functions to access concrete versions of values. We use the database only for persistent storage; all queries use Jeeves to ensure policy compliance.

7. Related Work

Jeeves follows a line of research in language-based information flow that began with the work of Denning [15, 16]. Sabelfeld and Myers [41] survey much of the literature in the field in subsequent years. Volpano et al. [47] develop a type system that guarantees non-interference for the language that Denning outlines. Heintze and Riecke [22] design a type system guaranteeing non-interference for a functional language, extended with constructs for reference cells, concurrency, and integrity guarantees. Smith [43] discusses some of the core concepts in information flow analysis.

Languages for verifying information flow security include Jif [34], Fine [12], F* [45], and Ur/Web [13]. Nanevski et al. [36] verify information flow policies through the use of dependent types. Hunt and Sands [23] describe a flow-sensitive type system. Zhang et al. [51] describe a type-based approach to mitigating timing channels. These static approaches have no dynamic overhead. Myers [34] discusses JFlow, a variant of Java with security types to provide strong information flow guarantees. Le Guernic et al. [20] examine code from branches not taken, increasing precision at the expense of run-time performance overhead. Shroff et al. [42] use a purely-dynamic analysis to track variable dependencies and reject more insecure programs over time. Jeeves mitigates programmer burden by guaranteeing that programs adhere to the desired properties by construction, but with dynamic overhead. Systems like Fabric [28] combine static and dynamic techniques, but the focus of the dynamic analyses is on checking rather than on helping the programmer produce correct outputs. Russo and Sabelfeld [40] discuss trade-offs between static and dynamic analyses.

Jeeves is also related to systems that provide support for inserting information flow checks. Broberg and Sands [9] describe flow locks for dynamic information flow policies. Birgisson et al. [8] show how capabilities can guarantee information flow policies. The system-level data flow framework Resin [49] allows the programmer to insert checking code to be executed at output channels. Privacy Integrated Queries (PINQ) [30] is a capability-based system that enforces differential privacy policies in declarative database queries. SEAL [35] specifies policies for label-based access control systems.

There are parallels with dynamic approaches that run multiple executions for security guarantees. Capizzi et al.'s *shadow executions* [10] maintain confidentiality by running both a public and private copy of the application. The public copy can communicate with the outside world but cannot access private data; the private copy has access to private information but lacks network access. Devriese and Piessens' *secure multi-execution* strategy [17] applies this approach to JavaScript code. Kashyap et al. [24] discuss properties of timing and termination for secure multi-execution.

Austin and Flanagan [6] simulate secure multi-execution with a single execution through the use of faceted values, avoiding overhead when code does not depend on confidential data, noticeably improving performance. The same paper also show how declassification may be performed with facets, though with Jeeves's policies, declassification is largely unnecessary. Rozzle [27] uses symbolic execution to detect malware, treating environment-specific data as symbolic and exploring both paths whenever a value branches on a symbolic value in a manner similar to faceted evaluation. Jeeves allows more complex policies, for instance ones that may depend on sensitive values. Faceted values are related to the non-interference work by Pottier and Simonet for *Core ML* [38]. Their proof approach involves a Core ML^2 language that has expression pairs and value pairs, similar to faceted expressions and faceted values respectively. While their approach is not intended as a dynamic enforcement mechanism, their work does include evaluation rules for Core ML^2 that may supplement understanding of faceted values.

The automatic policy enforcement is related to work in constraint functional programming and executing specifications. Like constraint functional languages, Jeeves integrates declarative constraints into a non-declarative programming model. Jeeves differs from languages such as Mercury [44], Escher [29], Curry [21], and Kaplan [26], which support rich operations over logic variables at the cost of potentially expensive runtime search and undecidability. In Jeeves, the logical environment is always consistent and the runtime only performs decidable search routines. Jeeves differs from the Squander system [31] for unified execution of imperative and declarative code in that Jeeves propagates constraints alongside the core program rather than executing isolated constraint-based subprocedures. As with relaxed approximate programs [11], Jeeves nondeterministically provides an acceptable output for a specific class of acceptability properties.

Jeeves is related to declarative domain-specific languages. Frenetic [19] provides a query language programming distributed collections of network switches. Engage [18] uses constraints to mitigate programmer burden in configuring, installing, and managing applications. Jeeves differs in that its target domain of privacy is cross-cutting with respect to other functionality.

Declassification is an important area of research for information flow analysis and overlaps a great deal with the applications of computable policies. Zdancewic [50] uses integrity labels to provide *robust declassification.* permitting only high-integrity declassification decisions. Askarov and Myers [3] consider a similar approach for endorsement, *checked endorsements.* arguing that *checked endorsements* are needed to prevent an attacker from endorsing an unauthorized declassification. Chong and Myers [14] use a framework for application-specific declassification policies. Askarov and Sabelfeld [4] study a declassification framework specifying what and where data is released. Vaughan and Chong [46] infer declassification policies for Java programs.

The termination channel is another area of particular concern for information flow analysis. Askarov et al. [5] highlight complications of *intermediary output channels*, which allow an attacker to observe the output of a program during its execution, and discuss *progress-sensitive noninteference*. Moore et al. [32] include the concept of a budget for possible information loss through the termination channel, terminating the program when the budget has been exceeded. Rafnnson et al. [39] buffer output to reduce data lost from intermediary output channels and termination behavior.

8. Conclusions

Jeeves allows the programmer to implement core functionality separately from confidentiality policies. Our execution strategy exploits the structure of sensitive values to facilitate reasoning about runtime behavior. We present a semantics for faceted execution of Jeeves in terms of the λ^{jeeves} core language, and prove non-interference and policy compliance for confidentiality. We describe how Jeeves enables reasoning about termination, policy consistency, and policy independence. Finally, we describe our implementation of Jeeves in Scala and our experience using Jeeves to implement an end-to-end conference management system.

Acknowledgments

This work was supported by NSF grant CNS-0905650, by the U.S. Government under the DARPA UHPC, and by Facebook Fellowship programs. The views and conclusions contained herein are those of the authors and should not be interpreted as representing the official policies, either expressed or implied, of the U.S. Government or of Facebook Inc.

References

[1] Scalatra: A tiny Sinatra-like web framework for Scala. `http://www.scalatra.org/`.

[2] G. Antoniou. A tutorial on default logics. *ACM Computing Surveys (CSUR)*, 31(4), 1999.

[3] A. Askarov and A. Myers. A semantic framework for declassification and endorsement. In *European Symposium on Programming (ESOP)*, 2010.

[4] A. Askarov and A. Sabelfeld. Tight enforcement of information-release policies for dynamic languages. In *IEEE Computer Security Foundations Symposium*. IEEE Computer Society, 2009.

[5] A. Askarov, S. Hunt, A. Sabelfeld, and D. Sands. Termination-insensitive noninterference leaks more than just a bit. In *ESORICS '08*. Springer-Verlag, 2008.

[6] T. H. Austin and C. Flanagan. Multiple facets for dynamic information flow. In *Symposium on Principles of Programming Languages (POPL)*, 2012.

[7] C. Barrett, A. Stump, and C. Tinelli. The SMT-LIB standard: Version 2.0. In *SMT Workshop*, 2010.

[8] A. Birgisson, A. Russo, and A. Sabelfeld. Capabilities for information flow. In *Workshop on Programming Languages and Analysis for Security (PLAS)*, 2011.

[9] N. Broberg and D. Sands. Flow locks: Towards a core calculus for dynamic flow policies. In *European Symposium on Programming (ESOP)*, 2006.

[10] R. Capizzi, A. Longo, V. Venkatakrishnan, and A. Sistla. Preventing information leaks through shadow executions. In *Annual Computer Security Applications Conference (ACSAC)*, dec 2008.

[11] M. Carbin, D. Kim, S. Misailovic, and M. Rinard. Proving acceptability properties of relaxed nondeterministic approximate programs. In *Conference on Programming Language Design and Implementation (PLDI)*, 2012.

[12] J. Chen, R. Chugh, and N. Swamy. Type-preserving compilation of end-to-end verification of security enforcement. In *Conference on Programming Language Design and Implementation (PLDI)*, 2010.

[13] A. Chlipala. Static checking of dynamically-varying security policies in database-backed applications. In *USENIX Conference on Operating Systems Design and Implementation (OSDI)*, 2012.

[14] S. Chong and A. C. Myers. Security policies for downgrading. In *Conference on Computer and Communications Security (CCS)*, 2004.

[15] D. E. Denning. A lattice model of secure information flow. *Commun. ACM*, 19(5), 1976.

[16] D. E. Denning and P. J. Denning. Certification of programs for secure information flow. *Commun. ACM*, 20(7):504–513, 1977.

[17] D. Devriese and F. Piessens. Noninterference through secure multi-execution. *IEEE Symposium on Security and Privacy*, 2010.

[18] J. Fischer, R. Majumdar, and S. Esmaeilsabzali. Engage: a deployment management system. In *Conference on Programming Language Design and Implementation (PLDI)*, 2012.

[19] N. Foster, R. Harrison, M. J. Freedman, C. Monsanto, J. Rexford, A. Story, and D. Walker. Frenetic: a network programming language. In *International Conference on Functional Programming (ICFP)*, 2011.

[20] G. L. Guernic, A. Banerjee, T. P. Jensen, and D. A. Schmidt. Automata-based confidentiality monitoring. In *ASIAN*, 2006.

[21] M. Hanus, H. Kuchen, J. J. Moreno-Navarro, R. Aachen, and I. Ii. Curry: A truly functional logic language, 1995.

[22] N. Heintze and J. G. Riecke. The SLam calculus: Programming with secrecy and integrity. In *Symposium on Principles of Programming Languages (POPL)*, 1998.

[23] S. Hunt and D. Sands. On flow-sensitive security types. In *Symposium on Principles of Programming Languages (POPL)*, 2006.

[24] V. Kashyap, B. Wiedermann, and B. Hardekopf. Timing- and termination-sensitive secure information flow: Exploring a new approach. In *IEEE Symposium on Security and Privacy*, 2011.

[25] G. Kiczales, J. Lamping, A. Mendhekar, C. Maeda, C. V. Lopes, J.-M. Loingtier, and J. Irwin. Aspect-Oriented Programming. In *ECOOP*, 1997.

[26] A. Köksal, V. Kuncak, and P. Suter. Constraints as control. In *Symposium on Principles of Programming Languages (POPL)*, 2012.

[27] C. Kolbitsch, B. Livshits, B. Zorn, and C. Seifert. Rozzle: De-cloaking internet malware. Technical Report MSR-TR-2011-94, Microsoft Research Technical Report, 2011.

[28] J. Liu, M. D. George, K. Vikram, X. Qi, L. Waye, and A. C. Myers. Fabric: a platform for secure distributed computation and storage. In *Symposium on Operating System Principles (SOSP)*, 2009.

[29] J. W. Lloyd. Programming in an integrated functional and logic language. *Journal of Functional and Logic Programming*, 3, 1999.

[30] F. McSherry. Privacy integrated queries: an extensible platform for privacy-preserving data analysis. In *International Conference on Management of Data (SIGMOD)*, 2009.

[31] A. Milicevic, D. Rayside, K. Yessenov, and D. Jackson. Unifying execution of imperative and declarative code. In *International Conference on Software Engineering (ICSE)*, 2011.

[32] S. Moore, A. Askarov, and S. Chong. Precise enforcement of progress-sensitive security. In *ACM Conference on Computer and Communications Security*, pages 881–893, 2012.

[33] L. D. Moura and N. Björner. Z3: An efficient SMT solver. In *Tools and algorithms for the construction and analysis of systems (TACAS)*, 2008.

[34] A. C. Myers. JFlow: Practical mostly-static information flow control. 1999.

[35] P. Naldurg and R. K. R. Seal: a logic programming framework for specifying and verifying access control models. In *ACM Symposium on Access Control Models and Technologies*, pages 83–92, 2011.

[36] A. Nanevski, A. Banerjee, and D. Garg. Verification of information flow and access control policies with dependent types. In *IEEE Symposium on Security and Privacy*, 2011.

[37] M. Odersky, P. Altherr, V. Cremet, B. Emir, S. Maneth, S. Micheloud, N. Mihaylov, M. Schinz, E. Stenman, and M. Zenger. An overview of the scala programming language. Technical report, Citeseer, 2004.

[38] F. Pottier and V. Simonet. Information flow inference for ML. *ACM Transactions on Programming Languages and Systems (TOPLAS)*, 25 (1), 2003.

[39] W. Rafnsson and A. Sabelfeld. Limiting information leakage in event-based communication. In *Workshop on Programming Languages and Analysis for Security (PLAS)*. ACM, 2011.

[40] A. Russo and A. Sabelfeld. Dynamic vs. static flow-sensitive security analysis. In *IEEE Computer Security Foundations Symposium*. IEEE Computer Society, 2010.

[41] A. Sabelfeld and A. C. Myers. Language-based information-flow security. *IEEE Journal on Selected Areas in Communications*, 21(1), 2003.

[42] P. Shroff, S. F. Smith, and M. Thober. Dynamic dependency monitoring to secure information flow. In *CSF*, 2007.

[43] G. Smith. Principles of secure information flow analysis. In M. Christodorescu, S. Jha, D. Maughan, D. Song, and C. Wang, editors, *Malware Detection*, volume 27 of *Advances in Information Security*, pages 291–307. Springer, 2007. ISBN 978-0-387-32720-4.

[44] Z. Somogyi, F. J. Henderson, and T. C. Conway. Mercury, an efficient purely declarative logic programming language. In *Australian Computer Science Conference*, 1995.

[45] N. Swamy, J. Chen, C. Fournet, P.-Y. Strub, K. Bhargavan, and J. Yang. Secure distributed programming with value-dependent types. In *International Conference on Functional Programming (ICFP)*, 2011.

[46] J. Vaughan and S. Chong. Inference of expressive declassification policies. In *IEEE Security and Privacy*, 2011.

[47] D. Volpano, C. Irvine, and G. Smith. A sound type system for secure flow analysis. *Journal of Computer Security*, 4(2-3), 1996.

[48] J. Yang, K. Yessenov, and A. Solar-Lezama. A language for automatically enforcing privacy policies. In *Symposium on Principles of Programming Languages (POPL)*, 2012.

[49] A. Yip, X. Wang, N. Zeldovich, and M. F. Kaashoek. Improving application security with data flow assertions. In *Symposium on Operating System Principles (SOSP)*, 2009.

[50] S. Zdancewic. A type system for robust declassification. In *19th Mathematical Foundations of Programming Semantics Conference*, 2003.

[51] D. Zhang, A. Askarov, and A. C. Myers. Predictive mitigation of timing channels in interactive systems. In *Conference on Computer and Communications Security (CCS)*, 2011.

A. Proof of Projection

Theorem 1. *Suppose*

$$\Sigma, e \Downarrow_{pc} \Sigma', V$$

Then for any $q \in PC$ *where pc and q are consistent*

$$q(\Sigma), q(e) \Downarrow_{pc \setminus q} q(\Sigma'), q(V)$$

Proof. We prove a stronger inductive hypothesis, namely that for any $q \in PC$ where $\neg \exists k.(k \in pc \land \overline{k} \in q) \lor (\overline{k} \in pc \land k \in q)$

1. If $\Sigma, e \Downarrow_{pc} \Sigma', V$ then $q(\Sigma), q(e) \Downarrow_{pc \setminus q} q(\Sigma'), q(V)$.
2. If $\Sigma, (V_1\ V_2) \Downarrow^{\mathsf{app}}_{pc} \Sigma', V$ then $q(\Sigma), (q(V_1)\ q(V_2)) \Downarrow^{\mathsf{app}}_{pc \setminus q} q(\Sigma'), q(V)$.

The proof is by induction on the derivation of $\Sigma, e \Downarrow_{pc} \Sigma', V$ and the derivation of $\Sigma, (V_1\ V_2) \Downarrow^{\mathsf{app}}_{pc} \Sigma', V$, and by case analysis on the final rule used in that derivation.

- For case [F-LABEL], $e =$ label k in e'.
  By the antecedents of this rule:
  $$k' \text{ fresh}$$
  $$\Sigma[k' := \lambda x.\mathit{true}], e'[k := k'] \Downarrow_{pc} \Sigma', V$$
  By induction
  $$q(\Sigma[k' := \lambda x.\mathit{true}]), q(e'[k := k']) \Downarrow_{pc \setminus q} q(\Sigma'), q(V)$$
  Since $k' \notin \Sigma$, we know that $k' \notin q(\Sigma)$.
  Therefore, $q(\Sigma)[k' := \lambda x.\mathit{true}] = q(\Sigma[k' := \lambda x.\mathit{true}])$.
  By α-renaming, we assume $k \notin q$, $\overline{k} \notin q$, $k' \notin q$, and $\overline{k}' \notin q$.
  Therefore $q(e')[k := k'] = q(e'[k := k'])$.
- For case [F-RESTRICT], $e =$ restrict(k, e'). By the antecedents of this rule:
  $$\Sigma, e' \Downarrow_{pc} \Sigma_1, V$$
  $$\Sigma' = \Sigma_1[k := \Sigma_1(k)\ \land_f\ \langle\!\langle\, pc \cup \{k\} \,?\, V : \lambda x.\mathit{true} \,\rangle\!\rangle]$$
  By induction, $q(\Sigma), q(e') \Downarrow_{pc \setminus q} q(\Sigma_1), q(V)$.
  $$\begin{aligned} q(\Sigma') &= q(\Sigma_1[k := \Sigma_1(k) \land_f \langle\!\langle\, pc \cup \{k\} \,?\, V : \lambda x.\mathit{true} \,\rangle\!\rangle]) \\ &= q(\Sigma_1)[k := q(\Sigma_1(k)) \land_f \\ &\qquad q(\langle\!\langle\, pc \cup \{k\} \,?\, V : \lambda x.\mathit{true} \,\rangle\!\rangle)] \\ &= q(\Sigma_1)[k := q(\Sigma_1(k)) \land_f \\ &\qquad \langle\!\langle\, pc \cup \{k\} \setminus q \,?\, q(V) : \lambda x.\mathit{true} \,\rangle\!\rangle)] \\ &\quad \text{by Lemma 1} \end{aligned}$$
- For case [F-VAL], $e = V$.
  Since $\Sigma, V \Downarrow_{pc} \Sigma, V$ and $q(\Sigma), q(V) \Downarrow_{pc \setminus q} q(\Sigma), q(V)$, this case holds.
- For case [F-REF], $e =$ ref e'. Then by the antecedents of the [F-REF] rule:
  $$\Sigma, e' \Downarrow_{pc} \Sigma'', V'$$
  $$a \notin \mathit{dom}(\Sigma'')$$
  $$V'' = \langle\!\langle\, pc \,?\, V' : 0 \,\rangle\!\rangle$$
  $$\Sigma' = \Sigma''[a := V'']$$
  $$V = a$$
  By induction, $q(\Sigma), q(e') \Downarrow_{pc \setminus q} q(\Sigma''), q(V')$.
  Since $a \notin \mathit{dom}(\Sigma'')$, $a \notin \mathit{dom}(q(\Sigma''))$.
  By Lemma 1, $q(V'') = \langle\!\langle\, pc \setminus q \,?\, q(V') : q(0) \,\rangle\!\rangle$.
  Since $\Sigma' = \Sigma''[a := V'']$, $q(\Sigma') = q(\Sigma'')[a := q(V'')]$.
  Therefore $q(\Sigma)$, ref $q(e') \Downarrow_{pc \setminus q} q(\Sigma'), q(V)$.
- For case [F-DEREF], $e = \,!e'$. Then by the antecedents of the [F-DEREF] rule:
  $$\Sigma, e' \Downarrow_{pc} \Sigma', V'$$
  $$V = \mathit{deref}(\Sigma', V', pc)$$
  By induction, $q(\Sigma), q(e') \Downarrow_{pc \setminus q} q(\Sigma'), q(V')$.
  By Lemma 2, $q(V) = \mathit{deref}(q(\Sigma'), q(V'), pc \setminus q)$.
  Therefore $q(\Sigma), q(!e') \Downarrow_{pc \setminus q} q(\Sigma'), q(V)$.
- For case [F-ASSIGN], $e = (e_a := e_b)$.
  By the antecedents of the [F-ASSIGN] rule:
  $$\Sigma, e_a \Downarrow_{pc} \Sigma_1, V_1$$
  $$\Sigma_1, e_b \Downarrow_{pc} \Sigma_2, V$$
  $$\Sigma' = \mathit{assign}(\Sigma_2, pc, V_1, V)$$

By induction

$$q(\Sigma), q(e_a) \Downarrow_{pc \setminus q} q(\Sigma_1), q(V_1)$$
$$q(\Sigma_1), q(e_b) \Downarrow_{pc \setminus q} q(\Sigma_2), q(V)$$

By Lemma 3, $q(\Sigma') = assign(q(\Sigma_2), pc \setminus q, q(V_1), q(V))$. Therefore $q(\Sigma), q(e_a{:=}e_b) \Downarrow_{pc \setminus q} q(\Sigma'), q(V)$.

- For case [F-APP], $e = (e_a\ e_b)$. By the antecedents of the [F-APP] rule:

$$\Sigma, e_a \Downarrow_{pc} \Sigma_1, V_1$$
$$\Sigma_1, e_b \Downarrow_{pc} \Sigma_2, V_2$$
$$\Sigma_2, (V_1\ V_2) \Downarrow_{pc}^{\mathsf{app}} \Sigma', V$$

By induction

$$q(\Sigma), q(e_a) \Downarrow_{pc \setminus q} q(\Sigma_1), q(V_1)$$
$$q(\Sigma_1), q(e_b) \Downarrow_{pc \setminus q} q(\Sigma_2), q(V_2)$$
$$q(\Sigma_2), (q(V_1)\ q(V_2)) \Downarrow_{pc \setminus q}^{\mathsf{app}} q(\Sigma'), q(V)$$

Therefore $q(\Sigma), q(e_a\ e_b) \Downarrow_{pc \setminus q} q(\Sigma'), q(V)$.

- For case [F-LEFT], $e = \langle k\ ?\ e_a : e_b \rangle$. By the antecedents of this rule

$$k \in pc$$
$$\Sigma, e_a \Downarrow_{pc} \Sigma', V$$

  - If $k \in q$, then $q(\langle k\ ?\ e_a : e_b \rangle) = q(e_a)$. By induction $q(\Sigma), q(e_a) \Downarrow_{pc \setminus q} q(\Sigma'), q(V)$.
  - Otherwise $k \notin q$ and $\overline{k} \notin q$. Therefore $q(\langle k\ ?\ e_a : e_b \rangle) = \langle k\ ?\ q(e_a) : q(e_b) \rangle$. Since $k \in pc \setminus q$, it holds by induction that

$$q(\Sigma), \langle k\ ?\ q(e_a) : q(e_b) \rangle \Downarrow_{pc \setminus q} q(\Sigma'), q(V)$$

- Case [F-RIGHT] holds by a similar argument as [F-LEFT].
- For case [F-SPLIT], $e = \langle k\ ?\ e_a : e_b \rangle$. By the antecedents of the [F-SPLIT] rule:

$$\Sigma, e_a \Downarrow_{pc \cup \{k\}} \Sigma_1, V_1$$
$$\Sigma_1, e_b \Downarrow_{pc \cup \{\overline{k}\}} \Sigma', V_2$$
$$V = \langle k\ ?\ V_1 : V_2 \rangle$$

  - Suppose $k \in q$. Then $q(e) = q(e_a)$ and $q(V_1) = q(V)$. By induction, $q(\Sigma), q(e_a) \Downarrow_{pc \cup \{k\} \setminus q} q(\Sigma_1), q(V_1)$. Lemma 4 implies $q(\Sigma_1) = q(\Sigma')$, so this case holds.
  - If $\overline{k} \in q$, Then $q(e) = q(e_b)$ and $q(V_2) = q(V)$. By Lemma 4 we know that $q(\Sigma) = q(\Sigma_1)$. By induction, $q(\Sigma_1), q(e_b) \Downarrow_{pc \cup \{k\} \setminus q} q(\Sigma'), q(V_2)$.
  - If $k \notin q$ and $\overline{k} \notin q$, then by induction

$$q(\Sigma), q(e_a) \Downarrow_{pc \cup \{k\} \setminus q} q(\Sigma_1), q(V_1)$$
$$q(\Sigma_1), q(e_b) \Downarrow_{pc \cup \{\overline{k}\} \setminus q} q(\Sigma'), q(V_2)$$

  By Lemma 1, $q(V) = \langle\!\langle\, pc \setminus q\ ?\ q(V_1) : q(V_2) \,\rangle\!\rangle$.

- For case [FA-FUN], $V_1 = \lambda x.e'$. By the antecedent of this rule

$$\Sigma, e'[x := V_2] \Downarrow_{pc} \Sigma', V$$

We know that $q(\lambda x.e'\ V_2) = q(e'[x := V_2])$. By induction $q(\Sigma), q(e'[x := V_2]) \Downarrow_{pc \setminus q} q(\Sigma'), q(V)$.

- Both cases [FA-LEFT] and [FA-RIGHT] hold by a similar argument as [F-LEFT].
- Case [FA-SPLIT] holds by a similar argument as [F-SPLIT].

□

Security Completeness: Towards Noninterference in Composed Languages

Andreas Gampe
The University of Texas at San Antonio
agampe@cs.utsa.edu

Jeffery von Ronne
The University of Texas at San Antonio
vonronne@cs.utsa.edu

Abstract

Ensuring that software protects its users' privacy has become an increasingly pressing challenge. Requiring software to be certified with a secure type system is one enforcement mechanism. Protecting privacy with type systems, however, has only been studied for programs written entirely in a single language, whereas software is frequently implemented using multiple languages specialized for different tasks.

This paper presents an approach that facilitates reasoning over composed languages. It outlines sufficient requirements for the component languages to lift privacy guarantees of the component languages to well-typed composed programs, significantly lowering the burden necessary to certify that such composite programs safe. The approach relies on computability and security-level separability. This paper defines completeness with respect to secure computations and formally establishes conditions sufficient for a security-typed language to be complete. We demonstrate the applicability of the results with a case study of three seminal security-typed languages.

Categories and Subject Descriptors D.2.4 [*Software/Program Verification*]: Formal methods; Correctness proofs

General Terms Languages, Security, Verification

Keywords Security; noninterference; type systems; composition

1. Introduction

In contemporary software engineering practice, it is becoming more common to use several languages while implementing large systems. This ranges from using separate languages in different files (e.g., configuration files in XML or libraries coded in different languages) to using code in one language being directly embedded in the code of another language. As an example, one commonly embedded language is SQL, which is used to declaratively retrieve data. Such languages are common even in the mobile app space: both Android and iOS expose bindings for SQL systems (e.g., SQLite) to applications written primarily in Java and Objective C, respectively.

At the same time, privacy is becoming an increasingly important property of software. Mobile platforms like smartphones and tablets, for example, are built around "app stores", where users can download new applications. These applications can gain access to private information that is stored on the device, like contacts, phone logs, location information, etc. In the mobile space, major vendors have chosen two ways to help users: either, a simple form of static permissions, as used on the Android platform, or a review of every application, as in the case of iOS. Neither approach is very satisfying: several cases of apps that violate the privacy of the owner's device have become known recently for both platforms. A formal and sound mechanism that can be applied to formally verify such software against privacy policies would greatly improve this situation. Type systems enforcing noninterference can provide such a mechanism.

Noninterference [5] ensures that any compliant program cannot leak private information to public channels. Type systems are a common method to guarantee noninterference, e.g., [1, 6, 12, 16, 17], for an overview see [15], and the approach has been extended to cover entire distributed systems [9]. In all of this work, however, exactly one language is treated.

The question then is: How can we (statically) guarantee the safety of programs that are composed from elements in different languages such that a client can check a program for compliance with security policies? The solution we propose is to compose security-typed languages into *composed languages*, such that well-typed programs in a composed language can be guaranteed to comply with noninterference. Focusing on the more general end of the language composition spectrum, we will consider the case where a composed language is created by extending a *host language* so that

PLAS'13, June 20, 2013, Seattle, WA, USA.

code from an *embedded language* can replace certain constructs in otherwise valid host language programs.

This paper describes an approach (in Section 3) where, under certain assumptions, it is possible to leverage proofs of non-interference of well-typed host language and well-typed embedded language programs to prove noninterference of well-typed composed language programs. In order to generalize this composition over security-typed host and security-typed embedded languages that use different proofs that well-typed programs are noninterferent, our approach relies on host languages being complete with respect to being able to compute any noninterferent function over its data types. This allows us to establish that executing noninterferent code does not introduce any behaviors that could not be observed in the host language. Our initial conjecture is that all non-trivial security type systems will satisfy this requirement.

Suppose one has a noninterferent function $f(x, y)$ that produces a public output from public input x and secret input y. To obtain a typeable version f' of f, one can first define a function g to be the same function as f, but type both of g's inputs as public, and its output also as public. Intuitively, assuming that the underlying language is Turing complete, and that any function that involves only a single security level is typeable, g can be expressed and typed. Now, one can define $f'(x, y) = g(x, c)$, for some suitable constant c, which is well-typed since, usually, constants are public. A typical noninterference theorem guarantees that $f(x, y_1) = f(x, y_2)$, for all y_1, y_2, which ensures that $f = f'$.

This basic argument may seem trivial; actually showing that it holds for classes of languages providing operations over certain classes of data types (rather than a specific language with integer data) brings up several issues. Our basic approach for establishing this property is first described in Section 4 and formalized in Section 5. We then, in Sections 6 and 7, show how more complex data types and references can be supported, which adds additional requirements on the host language that would generally be expected to be satisfied by languages that support such entities. Note that the current work does not support extending the types of inputs and outputs to functions. Finally, in Section 8, we show that the requirements placed on host languages are reasonable by showing how three languages, the system of [16], FlowML [13], and work in [1] satisfy the requirements.

The contributions of this paper include

- identifying a general framework for leveraging the proofs of the noninterference of security-typed languages to establish the noninterference of their composition,
- showing how arbitrary noninterferent functions can be computed in certain classes of security-typed languages, and
- showing that the classes of languages are reasonable

2. Background

2.1 Language Definition

We assume languages provide values, programs and states, and are associated with a semantics such that a program and a state get reduced to a value and a state. We only consider deterministic languages here, that is, the semantics can be considered a (partial) function. We use p to range over programs, and f, g over functions represented by such programs.

Type systems assign types to values, programs and states in a judgment. If a type system makes a judgment, a certain property is guaranteed. For example, traditionally type systems enforce that programs cannot go wrong, that is, get stuck or end with an error.

Most security-typed languages can be seen as annotated versions of a ground typed language. These annotations may be on programs, values and states, as well as on types. The annotations are used to maintain local security invariants that allow judgments to guarantee security properties for the whole program.

2.2 Security

Our work is in the realm of lattice-based security [2], with security information taken from a lattice of security "levels". The simplest non-trivial lattice is $\{L, H\}$ with the obvious ordering, but many more complicated lattices have been proposed. Flows can be formulated by the partial order of levels in the lattice. Informally, (1) computations that involve private=high information need to be classified private, (2) we cannot allow direct assignments of private information to public storage and (3) we cannot allow indirect leaks, that is, assignments to public storage in a private context. Examples for violations of these cases are

```
(1) d{H} * 3{L} => 15{L}
(2) var tmp{L} = salary{H}
(3) if age{H}>65 then
      tmp{L}=1 else tmp{L}=0 end
```

In the first case, one can deduce that the private input d must have been 5. In the second case, we *declassified* formerly private information and store it in a public field. In the third case, we gain one bit of information about the private age information by case analysis of the value of `tmp`.

Noninterference can be generalized with the help of an indistinguishability relation that defines which parts of values may be distinguishable (and thus should not be influenced).

3. Approach to Composition

Our ultimate goal is to *prove* safe the composition of practical languages. For example, we are interested in the embedding of SQL into JIF [12], which would allow us to write code like the following, executing a SQL statement and retrieving the result in the host language.

```
int{high} age = SELECT age FROM employees
```

```
WHERE name=$name;
```

In this fragment, the (confidential) age of the employee with the name given in the Java variable `name`, embedded into the SQL statement by `$name`, is retrieved from the database table employees.

We now assume that SQL is secure by use of a security-type system. For example, we could assign security types to each column in each table of the database to trace flows through queries. In the example, this might derive that the result of the query should better be confidential.

Embedding can be formalized by extending the host language with an evaluation construct, maybe named `eval`. We would add evaluation and typing rules that connect the host and embedded language. For example, `eval` could be resolved by computing its parameters, translating them to the embedded language, running the embedded program, and translating the result back to the host. For typing purposes, we need a translation of types between the languages the preserve security properties. This translation needs to be monotonic and round-trip non-decreasing to not leak information. Furthermore, indistinguishable input must be translated to indistinguishable output. With such rules in place, and assuming that the type systems for both JIF and SQL are secure, we would like to prove that the composed language is also secure.

3.1 Limitations of Proof Manipulation

A strawman approach to proving noninterference for well-typed composed programs is by defining a mechanical procedure for directly manipulating the proofs of noninterference of programs in the host and embedded languages. However, this seems to be tied closely to the format and details of the noninterference proof of the host language. For example, if that proof was done syntactically via a subject reduction theorem, as for example in [13], that theorem would need to be extended. Subject reduction is usually shown by some inductive argument, for example over the input typing. As such, we could extend the case analysis of the induction with a specific argument for `eval` that is derived from the typing constraints, and hope to get a well-formed proof for the composed language.

However, the picture is not that simple. While adding a case to subject reduction is simple and (mostly) independent from the other constructs, other cases may use their own nested inductive arguments, auxillary lemmas, or inversions. [13], for example, uses auxillary lemmas for weakening, projection, and substitution, with all lemmas ranging over *all* constructs in the language. Without a detailed knowledge of the proof and the statements necessary, it seems impossible to generically prove correctness by manipulating an (in details) unknown proof.

3.2 Computability

We instead try to reuse the existing proofs completely and without modifications, by focussing on computability in a three-step process:

1. Embedded-language programs can be simulated in the host
2. The simulation is noninterferent and can be typed
3. Replace embeddings with the simulation; the now pure-host program is typable, implying noninterference of the composed program

Assume that the embedded language is Turing-computable, that is, every program computes a Turing-computable function. Furthermore assume that the host language is Turing-complete, that is, there is a program for every Turing-computable function. Then the host language is able to *functionally* simulate any embedded language program (fragment). Since the original program was noninterferent - the `eval` forces a typing, which guarantees noninterference - the simulation is also noninterferent. Note that this argument requires compatible notions of noninterference. For example, if the embedded-language fragment was termination-sensitive noninterferent, then it will be termination-sensitive or termination-insensitive noninterferent in the host language.

However, not all termination-insensitive noninterferent programs are termination-sensitive noninterferent. In that case a totally faithful representation is impossible. We sketch the following solution. We can change the semantics of the embedded program to be total by selecting an arbitrary indistinguishable result in the nonterminating cases, which allows representation in the host. The resulting program is an overapproximation, but ensures that the original semantics with nontermination is now termination-*insensitive* noninterferent.

It remains to show that there is a legal program, that is, a *typable* host language program that computes the simulation. If such a program exists *and* the host language allows us to substitute the `eval` with our typed simulation, we end up with a pure host-language program that is typed and computes the same function as the composed-language program. The host language security-type system now guarantees this program to be noninterferent, which means that the functionally equivalent composed-language version is noninterferent, too.

Note that step 3 is specific to each host language, but can be reused for all compositions of that language. In general, a proof of this step is similar to a standard substitution lemma. One has to show that the program remains typed, and retains its meaning.

In this paper, we focus on step 2. We try to answer this key question: if a function is computable (there is a, not necessarily typable, program) and noninterferent, is there a security-typable program that computes the (exact) same function? This is formulated in the following definition.

Definition 1 (Security Completeness). *A security-typed language $\mathcal{L}$ is security-complete if and only if for every (not necessarily typable) program p that computes a function f, where f is noninterfering with respect to security signature S, there exists a program p' that also computes f and is typable corresponding to S.*

Our working conjecture here is the following.

Conjecture 2. *All non-trivial security-typed languages are security-complete.*

Note that, while the conjecture might seem obviously valid, "the devil is in the details." This statement is rather strong. While it is easy to show that it holds for simple formalizations of noninterference with primitive input and output types (e.g., `int`), it actually does *not* hold for all computations in all non-trivial languages when we consider more complex datastructures - noninterference and indistinguishability do not always provide enough context for a typable program. It remains to be seen what requirements on $\mathcal{L}$, $\mathcal{T}$ and f are sufficient to prove a corresponding theorem.

3.3 Applicability

One might ask if embedding a less powerful language is useful at all, and thus if our approach is realistic in practice. For one, in practice many embedded languages are only powerful in certain domains (i.e., domain specific languages). Most embedded languages show their advantages in the conciseness and expressivity in just this limited domain. For example, SQL is a query language for databases and is (in its basic incarnation) not Turing-complete, but can describe a complex set of relational queries with a relatively small amount of code. The SQL semantics could be simulated precisely in a general-purpose language, albeit with simulation overhead. Thus, SQL can clarify the meaning and intention of some part of a program, improving that and only that part over a general-purpose implementation. Also, most host languages are general-purpose languages that are Turing-complete and thus as powerful as realistically possible.

Second, we would like to stress that any simulation overhead is not relevant in practice. The simulation is a tool for guaranteeing noninterference of the extended semantics of the composed language. Thus, the size of the simulation would not matter, since it would *not* be used in practice.

Another relevant question is whether our requirements are too strong. While we require noninterferent input programs, type systems are still important once one already knows that a function is noninterferent. For example, a typing can act as a certificate for a program, such that remote clients can check for actual noninterference. Also, our overarching goal is to formally establish the safety of a composed language from its components. Typing for a known noninterferent embedded program still needs to be liftable to the overall language, which our approach provides.

4. Approach

The section details our approach in the simplified case of output indistinguishability being output equivalence, as used in the previous section. This is for example the case if the output is just a single integer value that is assumed to be public, which is a common form to formalize noninterference (e.g., [13]). We will formalize this setting in the next section, and the following sections will detail generalizations to more complicated values. A subsection treats the differences between termination-sensitive and termination-insensitive noninterference.

4.1 Basic Approach

If a function f is computable, then there exists a program p that computes f, that is, the output of p agrees with f under the same inputs for the right meaning of inputs and output. Noninterference is a dependency problem, If a program is noninterferent, then the (low) result does not depend on high inputs. This means that, for any high inputs, the low output value will be the same. We are thus able to substitute arbitrary constants for those inputs when computing only low outputs. However, we need to prove the existence or wellformed-ness of said program. We approach this from a computability direction, where constant functions and function composition are guaranteed by primitive recursion.

We prefer a composition requirement over more direct manipulations because it abstracts the exact syntax and semantics of the language involved. Note that we do not need to inspect programs at all, as required by, for example, a slicing approach. Instead, we show the existence of some separate program that is typable and computes an equivalent function. This allows us a generalization that can accept, for example, both imperative and functional languages. Note that it is important to find an *equivalent* function: for our simulation argument, it is not enough to compute correctly up to indistinguishability.

The final step is showing typability of this intuitive construction. We observe that, trivially, every function is noninterferent if all inputs are considered public - noninterference resolves to determinism (or some similar notion in the case of nondeterministic languages). This generalizes to any single security level. It seems reasonable to require that a non-trivial security-type system should be able to type a program with a security typing assigning a single level to everything. This is our first requirement for a security-typed language.

Next, projection and constant functions should be typable at the respective levels. Under projection we understand here functions of multiple inputs that return one of those inputs. For example, projection $\pi_1(x, y) = x$ should be typable as $\ell_x \times \ell_y \mapsto \ell_x$ for any ℓ_x and ℓ_y. The constant function is noninterferent no matter the security typing, since the output is always the same and does not depend on the inputs. Our

a := (x + y) − (y − x);	$[\mathrm{x} : L,\ \mathrm{y} : H,\ \mathrm{a} : L]$
$\mathrm{t}^{\mathrm{x}}_1$:= x; $\mathrm{t}^{\mathrm{y}}_1$:= y; $\mathrm{t}^{\mathrm{o}}_1$:= $\mathrm{t}^{\mathrm{x}}_1$;	$[\mathrm{t}^{\mathrm{x}}_1 : L,\ \mathrm{t}^{\mathrm{y}}_1 : H,\ \mathrm{t}^{\mathrm{o}}_1 : L]$ $\mathrm{t}^{\mathrm{o}}_1 = \pi_1(x, y)$
$\mathrm{t}^{\mathrm{x}}_2$:= x; $\mathrm{t}^{\mathrm{y}}_2$:= y; $\mathrm{t}^{\mathrm{o}}_2$:= 0;	$[\mathrm{t}^{\mathrm{x}}_2 : L,\ \mathrm{t}^{\mathrm{y}}_2 : H,\ \mathrm{t}^{\mathrm{o}}_2 : L]$ $\mathrm{t}^{\mathrm{o}}_2 = c_0(x, y)$
$\mathrm{t}^{\mathrm{x}}_3$:= $\mathrm{t}^{\mathrm{o}}_1$; $\mathrm{t}^{\mathrm{y}}_3$:= $\mathrm{t}^{\mathrm{o}}_2$; $\mathrm{t}^{\mathrm{o}}_3$:= $(\mathrm{t}^{\mathrm{x}}_3 + \mathrm{t}^{\mathrm{y}}_3) - (\mathrm{t}^{\mathrm{y}}_3 - \mathrm{t}^{\mathrm{x}}_3)$;	$[\mathrm{t}^{\mathrm{x}}_3 : L,\ \mathrm{t}^{\mathrm{y}}_3 : L,\ \mathrm{t}^{\mathrm{o}}_3 : L]$ $\mathrm{t}^{\mathrm{o}}_3 = p^L(\mathrm{t}^{\mathrm{o}}_1, \mathrm{t}^{\mathrm{o}}_2)$
a := $\mathrm{t}^{\mathrm{o}}_3$;	

Figure 1. Simple Program with Security Context

requirement is that it can be typed with any result level, including public.

Last, we require that composition is typable if the components are typable and agree on input and output types. By construction, the input types of the composition agree with the security typing for the original program, and the output type with the output type of said program. Then a typing states the same (or extended) noninterference property that we intended for the original program, and the construction guarantees functional equivalence.

A demonstration is shown in Figure 1 for program p = a := (x + y) − (y − x) computing $f(x, y) = 2x$. The result is shown below the double lines. The first block projects x, the second block is the constant 0 function, the third block represents the original program in a low-typable version, and the fourth block is the final result. The overhead comes from the necessity to rename variables when composing in imperative languages to prevent side effects. The original program is not typable under the signature that assumes x low and y high, because the assignment cannot be typed. The new construction, however can be typed and computes essentially the same function.

4.2 Termination Sensitivity

The development in the previous subsection only holds if we consider termination-sensitive noninterference. In that case, two runs on indistinguishable inputs have to agree on their termination behaviour, that is, the first run terminates if and only if the second run terminates. Termination-insensitive noninterference, on the other hand, only makes a statement over two terminating runs, considering that an attacker might not be able to observe (non-)termination, or at most gain one bit of knowledge from it. In that case, the approach outlined in the previous subsection cannot be guaranteed to simulate correctly only up to termination, because termination may depend on the high input, and thus the choice of constants.

Our solution imposes further requirements that allow the application of a standard technique in computability: dovetailing (interleaving computations). If we require the set of values valid for the high inputs to be recursively enumerable, we can *test* the function on all possible inputs. For this test to succeed, we have to be able to simulate the function in a stepwise manner, e.g., as in a small-step semantics. We will interleave the simulations of the different input values, such that if there is at least one value that forces termination, we will find that case. As an example, assume that $f_k(x)$ denotes a computation of $f(x : \mathbb{N})$ for k steps. Then an interleaving could be $f_1(0)$, $f_2(0)$, $f_1(1)$, $f_3(0)$, $f_2(1)$, $f_1(2)$, ... If for any x, $f(x) = v$ is defined, there is a k such that $f_k(x) = v$, and the interleaving contains this computation.

Such an interleaving will terminate if there is at least one terminating high value. To complete correctness with respect to the original, we compute the original function in a high setting in sequence. This will ensure that the simulation does not terminate when it should not.

We demonstrate this approach in Figure 2. The first three blocks iteratively compute the values of the program for increasing values of y, where sim simulates the given program for t^{n} steps and assigns $\mathrm{t}^{\mathrm{s}} = 0$ if the program finished. If the loop terminates, a result for some y will be in $\mathrm{t}^{\mathrm{o}}_2$. Note that the loop only involves L variables and can thus be typed as L. The following three blocks compute an H version of the program for termination correctness. The last block assigns the result of the low simulation as the overall result.

5. Formalization

In this section we formalize the approach and requirements outlined in the previous section. We start by introducing generic notation for the security-typed language and its security-type system, and formally defining our requirements in the first subsection. In the second subsection, we formally show how these requirements lead to our revised hypothesis.

5.1 Definitions & Requirements

We assume a security-typed language $\mathcal{L}$ and its security-type system $\mathcal{T}$ with associated lattice $\mathcal{S}$. The languages provides a set of values, ranged over by v, a set of programs, ranged over by p, and state or input, ranged over by μ. The language has associated semantics that reduces a program and state to a value and state. We denote the semantics by $(p, \mu) \rightsquigarrow_s (v, \mu')$. We define $\Downarrow$ to include nontermination, such that $(p, \mu) \Downarrow (v, \mu')$ if $(p, \mu) \rightsquigarrow_s (v, \mu')$, and $(p, \mu) \Downarrow (\bot, \bot)$, if there is no such (v, μ').

We connect the semantics to a functional interpretation through two predicates defined by the language. A program p computes function $f(x_1, \ldots, x_n)$, if for all μ such that $in_{p,f}(x_1, \ldots, x_n, \mu)$, and $(p, \mu) \Downarrow (v, \mu')$, we have $f(x_1, \ldots, x_n) = res_{p,f}(v, \mu')$, where in and res abstract how a language defines input and output in program p with respect to function f[1]. We denote this by $comp(p, f)$.

[1] For an example, recall how in the example of Figure 1 the inputs were bound to variables x and y and the output to variable a.

a := x; while y $\neq$ 10 do { a := x; y := y + 1; }	$[\mathrm{x}: L,\ \mathrm{y}: H,\ \mathrm{a}: L]$
$\mathrm{t}_1^{\mathrm{x}} := \mathrm{x};\ \mathrm{t}_1^{\mathrm{y}} := \mathrm{y};\ \mathrm{t}_1^{\mathrm{o}} := \mathrm{t}_1^{\mathrm{x}}$	$[\mathrm{t}_1^{\mathrm{x}}: L,\ \mathrm{t}_1^{\mathrm{y}}: H,\ \mathrm{t}_1^{\mathrm{o}}: L]$ $\mathrm{t}_1^{\mathrm{o}} = \pi_1(x, y)$
$\mathrm{t}^{\mathrm{i}} := 0;\ \mathrm{t}^{\mathrm{s}} := 1;$	$[\mathrm{t}^{\mathrm{i}}: L,\ \mathrm{t}^{\mathrm{s}}: L]$
while $\mathrm{t}^{\mathrm{s}} > 0$ do {	
cantor$_1(\mathrm{t}^{\mathrm{i}}, \mathrm{t}_2^{\mathrm{y}})$; cantor$_2(\mathrm{t}^{\mathrm{i}}, \mathrm{t}^{\mathrm{n}})$;	$[\mathrm{t}_2^{\mathrm{y}}: L,\ \mathrm{t}^{\mathrm{n}}: L]$ $\mathrm{t}^{\mathrm{i}} \mapsto \langle \mathrm{t}_2^{\mathrm{y}}, \mathrm{t}^{\mathrm{n}} \rangle$
$\mathrm{t}_2^{\mathrm{x}} := \mathrm{t}_1^{\mathrm{o}}$; sim$(p^L, \mathrm{t}_2^{\mathrm{x}}, \mathrm{t}_2^{\mathrm{y}}, \mathrm{t}^{\mathrm{n}}, \mathrm{t}_2^{\mathrm{o}}, \mathrm{t}^{\mathrm{s}})$;	$[\mathrm{t}_2^{\mathrm{x}}: L,\ \mathrm{t}_2^{\mathrm{o}}: L]$ $p^L(\mathrm{t}_2^{\mathrm{x}}, \mathrm{t}_2^{\mathrm{y}}) \rightarrow^{(\mathrm{t}^{\mathrm{n}})} \mathrm{t}_2^{\mathrm{o}}$?
$\mathrm{t}^{\mathrm{i}} := \mathrm{t}^{\mathrm{i}} + 1;$ }	
$\mathrm{t}_3^{\mathrm{x}} := \mathrm{x};\ \mathrm{t}_3^{\mathrm{y}} := \mathrm{y};\ \mathrm{t}_3^{\mathrm{o}} := \mathrm{t}_3^{\mathrm{x}};$	$[\mathrm{t}_3^{\mathrm{x}}: L,\ \mathrm{t}_3^{\mathrm{y}}: H,\ \mathrm{t}_3^{\mathrm{o}}: H]$ $\mathrm{t}_3^{\mathrm{o}} = \pi_1(x, y)$
$\mathrm{t}_4^{\mathrm{x}} := \mathrm{x};\ \mathrm{t}_4^{\mathrm{y}} := \mathrm{y};\ \mathrm{t}_4^{\mathrm{o}} := \mathrm{t}_4^{\mathrm{y}};$	$[\mathrm{t}_4^{\mathrm{x}}: L,\ \mathrm{t}_4^{\mathrm{y}}: H,\ \mathrm{t}_4^{\mathrm{o}}: H]$ $\mathrm{t}_4^{\mathrm{o}} = \pi_2(x, y)$
$\mathrm{t}_5^{\mathrm{x}} := \mathrm{t}_3^{\mathrm{o}};\ \mathrm{t}_5^{\mathrm{y}} := \mathrm{t}_4^{\mathrm{o}};$ $\mathrm{t}_5^{\mathrm{o}} := \mathrm{t}_5^{\mathrm{x}}$; while $\mathrm{t}_5^{\mathrm{y}} \neq 10$ do { $\mathrm{t}_5^{\mathrm{o}} := \mathrm{t}_5^{\mathrm{x}};\ \mathrm{t}_5^{\mathrm{y}} := \mathrm{t}_5^{\mathrm{y}} + 1;$ }	$[\mathrm{t}_5^{\mathrm{x}}: H,\ \mathrm{t}_5^{\mathrm{y}}: H,\ \mathrm{t}_5^{\mathrm{o}}: H]$ $\mathrm{t}_5^{\mathrm{o}} = p^H(x, y)$
$\mathrm{a} := \mathrm{t}_2^{\mathrm{o}};$	

Figure 2. Example Pair-Result Program

The type system provides a set of types, ranged over by τ, and type judgements of the form $\Gamma \vdash_s p : \tau$, $\Gamma \vdash_s v : \tau$ and $\Gamma \vdash_s \mu$. Note that for our purposes, it is not necessary to explicitly include a program counter in the notation. Security completeness is about whole programs, at which point low side effects are permissible. We can extract a type level $l \in \mathcal{S}$ from a type τ through the function *top*. We use two predicates to connect a type judgment and function signature, similar to the semantic connection. A judgment $\Gamma \vdash_s p : \tau$ is typed according to f with signature $\tau_1 \times \cdots \times \tau_n \mapsto \tau_r$, if $in^t_{p,f}(\Gamma, \tau, \tau_1, \ldots, \tau_n)$ and $\tau_r = res^t_{p,f}(\Gamma, \tau)$. We denote this as $typed(p, f, \Gamma, \tau)$.

We define noninterference ni for a function f with respect to (security) signature $\tau_1 \times \cdots \times \tau_n \mapsto \tau$ in the following way:

$$ni(f, \tau_1 \times \cdots \times \tau_n \mapsto \tau) \iff \left(\begin{array}{l} \forall l \in \mathcal{S}.top(\tau) \sqsubseteq l \implies \\ \quad \forall x_1^1, x_1^2 : \tau_1, x_2^1, x_2^2 : \tau_2, \ldots . \\ \quad\quad (\forall i.top(\tau_i) \sqsubseteq l \implies x_i^1 = x_i^2) \implies \\ \quad\quad\quad f(x_1^1, \ldots) = f(x_1^2, \ldots) \end{array} \right)$$

A program p is noninterferent with respect to f and a signature $\tau_1 \times \cdots \times \tau_n \mapsto \tau$, if p computes f and f is noninterferent. The type system guarantees that a typable program is noninterferent with respect to all functions it computes and is typed accordingly[2]:

$$\begin{array}{l} \Gamma \vdash_s p : \tau \wedge comp(p, f) \wedge \\ \quad typed(p, f : \tau_1 \times \cdots \times \tau_n \mapsto \tau_r, \Gamma, \tau) \implies \\ \quad\quad ni(f, \tau_1 \times \cdots \times \tau_n \mapsto \tau_r) \end{array}$$

Associated with the security-typed versions we expect ground-typed versions, denoted by a g subscript or by $\lfloor \bullet \rfloor$ (which can be seen as an erasure function removing all security annotations), that is, the security-typed language is based on a regular language and type system with regular soundness guarantees, that is, ground-typed programs do not go wrong.

We require the following manipulation functions for annotations.

Requirement 3 (Erasure & Lift). *There exist an erasure function $\lfloor \bullet \rfloor$ and a lift function $\lceil \bullet \rceil^l$ such that*

$$\begin{array}{l} \forall p, v, \mu \in \mathcal{L}, \Gamma, \tau \in \mathcal{T}. \lfloor p \rfloor \in \lfloor \mathcal{L} \rfloor, \lfloor v \rfloor \in \lfloor \mathcal{L} \rfloor, \ldots \\ \forall p_g, v_g, \mu_g \in \lfloor \mathcal{L} \rfloor, \Gamma_g, \tau_g \in \lfloor \mathcal{T} \rfloor, l \in \mathcal{S}. \lceil p_g \rceil^l \in \mathcal{L}, \lceil v_g \rceil^l \in \mathcal{L}, . \\ \forall \tau_g, l \in \mathcal{S}. top(\lceil \tau_g \rceil^l) = l \end{array}$$

We define a complete relabeling $[\bullet]^l = \lceil \lfloor \bullet \rfloor \rceil^l$. The identity $\tau = [\tau]^{top(\tau)}$ is required to hold.

We use the requirements on relabeling to form a partial order on types lifted from their security levels.

$$\tau_1 \sqsubseteq \tau_2 \iff \exists \tau, l_1 \sqsubseteq l2. \tau_1 = [\tau]^{l_1} \wedge \tau_2 = [\tau]^{l_2}$$

Security and ground languages are suitably related:

Requirement 4 (Security to Ground.).

$$\begin{array}{l} \forall p, v, \mu, \mu', \Gamma, \tau. \\ \quad \Gamma \vdash_s p/v/\mu : \tau \implies \lfloor \Gamma \rfloor \vdash_g \lfloor p/v/\mu \rfloor : \lfloor \tau \rfloor \\ \quad (p, \mu) \rightsquigarrow_s (v, \mu') \implies (\lfloor p \rfloor, \lfloor \mu \rfloor) \rightsquigarrow_g (\lfloor v \rfloor, \lfloor \mu' \rfloor) \end{array}$$

Furthermore, it holds that

$$\begin{array}{l} typed(p, f : \tau_1 \times \cdots \times \tau_n \mapsto \tau, \Gamma, \tau) \implies \\ \quad typed(\lfloor p \rfloor, f : \lfloor \tau_1 \rfloor \times \cdots \times \lfloor \tau_n \rfloor \mapsto \lfloor \tau \rfloor, \lfloor \Gamma \rfloor, \lfloor \tau \rfloor) \end{array}$$

and $comp(p, f) \implies comp(\lfloor p \rfloor, \lfloor f \rfloor)$.

[2] The notion that a program might compute multiple functions might be surprising. But computation here is defined with respect to what parts of the output state are of interest. For example, consider projection $\pi_1(x, y) = x$ in a WHILE language.

Furthermore, we can gain security-type system judgments from ground-type judgments for any security level from $\mathcal{S}$.

Requirement 5 (Single-Level.).

$$\forall l \in \mathcal{S}.\Gamma_g \vdash_g p_g/v_g/\mu_g : \tau_g \implies \lceil\Gamma_g\rceil^l \vdash_s \lceil p_g/v_g/\mu_g\rceil^l : \lceil\tau_g\rceil^l$$
$$\forall l \in \mathcal{S}.(p_g, \mu_g) \rightsquigarrow_g (v_g, \mu'_g) \implies (\lceil p_g\rceil^l, \lceil\mu_g\rceil^l) \rightsquigarrow_s (\lceil v_g\rceil^l, \lceil\mu'_g\rceil^l)$$

Furthermore, it holds that

$$typed(p_g, f_g : \tau_1 \times \cdots \times \tau_n \mapsto \tau, \Gamma_g, \tau_g) \implies typed(\lceil p_g\rceil^l, f_g : \lceil\tau_1\rceil^l \times \cdots \times \lceil\tau_n\rceil^l \mapsto \lceil\tau\rceil^l, \lceil\Gamma_g\rceil^l, \lceil\tau_g\rceil^l)$$

and $comp(p_g, f_g) \implies comp(\lceil p_g\rceil^l, f_g)$.

We need programs that compute projection and constants.

Requirement 6 (Projection). *Let* $\pi_i^n(x_1, \ldots, x_n) = x_i$ *be the i-th projection function of n inputs. Let* $\pi_i^n : \tau_1 \times \cdots \times \tau_n \mapsto \tau_i$ *be a signature of* π_i^n. *Then there exists a program* p_i^n, *a* Γ *and* τ *such that*

$$\Gamma \vdash_s p_i^n : \tau \wedge comp(p_i^n, \pi_i^n) \wedge typed(p_i^n, \pi_i^n : \tau_1 \times \cdots \times \tau_n \mapsto \tau_i, \Gamma, \tau)$$

Requirement 7 (Constant Function). *Let* $c_i^{x,l}(x_1, \ldots, x_n) = x$ *be the x-constant function of n inputs. We have* $\tau_1 \times \cdots \times \tau_n \mapsto \tau_r$ *a signature of* $c_i^{x,l}$, *that is* $x : \tau_r$ *and* $\tau_r = \lceil\tau_i\rceil^l$. *Then there exists a program* p^x, *a* Γ *and* τ *such that*

$$\Gamma \vdash_s p^x : \tau \wedge comp(p^x, c_x) \wedge typed(p^x, c_i^{x,l} : \tau_1 \times \cdots \times \tau_n \mapsto \tau_r, \Gamma, \tau)$$

Note that this requirement is necessary. While it may seem that erasure and lifting of an arbitrary value of τ_i may fulfill the requirements, it does not guarantee the existence of a *program* that creates the value. This is important, since only programs need to be able to be composed. This restriction allows us to easily include imperative languages into the framework.

Finally, we want to compose typed programs. We decided to formulate a general composition requirement, instead of a special-cased one.

Requirement 8 (Composition).

$$\forall p_\bullet, p. \begin{pmatrix} \forall i.\Gamma_i \vdash_s p_i : \tau^i \wedge comp(p_i, f_i) \wedge \\ typed(p_i, f_i : \tau_1 \times \cdots \times \tau_n \mapsto \tau_r^i, \Gamma_i, \tau^i) \end{pmatrix} \wedge \begin{pmatrix} \Gamma \vdash p : \tau^p \wedge comp(p, f) \wedge \\ typed(p, f : \tau_r'^1 \times \cdots \times \tau_r'^m \mapsto \tau_r, \Gamma, \tau^p) \end{pmatrix} \wedge \forall i.\tau_r^i \sqsubseteq \tau_r'^i$$
$$\implies$$
$$\exists p_c, \Gamma_c, \tau_c. \begin{matrix} \Gamma_c \vdash_s p_c : \tau_c \wedge comp(p_c, f \circ \overrightarrow{f_i}) \wedge \\ typed(p_c, f \circ \overrightarrow{f_i} : \tau_1 \times \cdots \times \tau_n \mapsto \tau_r, \Gamma_c, \tau_c) \end{matrix}$$

where $(f \circ \overrightarrow{f_i})(x_1, \ldots, x_n) = f(f_1(x_1, \ldots, x_n), \ldots, f_m(x_1, \ldots, x_n))$.

5.2 Revised Theorem & Proof

Theorem 9 (Security-Typability Completeness). *Assume a language* $\mathcal{L}$ *and corresponding ground language that fulfill the requirements in the previous subsection. Such language is security-complete.*

Proof. Assume p a program that computes noninterferent $f : \tau_1 \times \cdots \times \tau_n \mapsto \tau$. Since p is ground-typable, we have $p_g = \lfloor p\rfloor$ such that there is a ground typing $\Gamma_g \vdash_g p_g : \tau_g$, such that $typed(p_g, f : \lfloor\tau_1\rfloor \times \cdots \times \lfloor\tau_n\rfloor \mapsto \lfloor\tau\rfloor, \Gamma_g, \tau_g)$ by requirement 4. Let $l = top(\tau)$. Define $g_\bullet$ as

$$g_i = \begin{cases} \pi_i^n : \tau_1 \ldots \tau_n \mapsto \tau_i & \text{if } top(\tau_i) \sqsubseteq l \\ c_i^{x_i,l} : \tau_1 \ldots \tau_n \mapsto \lceil\tau_i\rceil^l & \text{else, with arbitrary } x_i : \lceil\tau_i\rceil^l \end{cases}$$

which exist by requirements 6 and 7. Noninterference of f with respect to signature $\tau_1 \times \cdots \times \tau_n \mapsto \tau$ and level l states that

$$\forall x_1^1, x_1^2 : \tau_1, \ldots, x_n^1, x_n^2 : \tau_n. (\forall i.top(\tau_i) \sqsubseteq l \implies x_i^1 = x_i^2) \implies f(x_1^1, \ldots) = f(x_1^2, \ldots)$$

Take any set of inputs $x_\bullet$ for f. Let $y_\bullet$ be defined as $y_i = g_i(x_1, \ldots, x_n)$. Then $\forall i.top(\tau_i) \sqsubseteq l \implies x_i = y_i$ by construction. Now, by noninterference, we have

$$f(x_1, \ldots, x_n) = f(y_1, \ldots, y_n) = f(g_1(x_1, \ldots, x_n), \ldots, g_n(x_1, \ldots, x_n))$$

By requirements 6 and 7, there exist $p_\bullet$, $\Gamma_\bullet$ and $\tau_\bullet^f$ such that

$$\forall i.\Gamma_i \vdash_s p_i : \tau_i^g \wedge comp(p_i, g_i) \wedge typed(p_i, g_i : \tau_1 \ldots \tau_n \mapsto \tau^i, \Gamma_i, \tau_i^g).$$

Furthermore, by construction we have $\forall i.\tau^i \sqsubseteq \lceil\tau_i\rceil^l$, by requirements 3 and 7.

By the Single-level requirement, we can lift the typing of p_g such that $\lceil\Gamma_g\rceil^l \vdash_s \lceil p_g\rceil^l : \lceil\tau_g\rceil^l$ and $comp(\lceil p_g\rceil^l, f)$ and $typed(\lceil p_g\rceil^l, f : \lceil\tau_1\rceil^l \times \cdots \times \lceil\tau_n\rceil^l \mapsto \lceil\tau\rceil^l, \lceil\Gamma_g\rceil^l, \lceil\tau_g\rceil^l)$. This allows us to use the Composition requirement, composing $p_\bullet$ into $\lceil p_g\rceil^l$, which is functionally equivalent to composing $g_\bullet$ into f. This results in a program p_c and typing $\Gamma_c \vdash_s p_c : \tau_c$ such that $comp(p_c, f \circ \overrightarrow{g_i})$ and $typed(p_c, f \circ \overrightarrow{g_i} : \tau_1 \times \cdots \times \tau_n \mapsto \lceil\tau\rceil^l, \Gamma_c, \tau_c)$. Previous deductions and identity requirement on relabeling permit us to simplify this to $comp(p_c, f)$ and $typed(p_c, f : \tau_1 \times \cdots \times \tau_n \mapsto \tau, \Gamma_c, \tau_c)$. Thus, the program p_c is typable with the required signature and computes f, which concludes the proof. ☐

5.3 Sufficient vs. Necessary Conditions

Our derivation in the previous subsections concludes that the requirements established are sufficient for a language to be security-complete. However the reverse is not generally true. The leeway that the definition of security completeness allows us, i.e., that *another* equivalent program exists that is typable, makes a reverse deduction impossible in general.

6. Datatypes

We can extend the formalization of the previous section to data types. For security, compound values imply the possibility of more complicated indistinguishability relations, e.g., different parts of a value may have different security levels and need to be treated differently. A statement of noninterference may then use this complex indistinguishability both for inputs and outputs. That is, noninterferent programs create outputs that agree on low parts if the low input parts are equivalent. A simple case for demonstration follows. Assume that the language in questions supports *pairs*. Let $f(x, y) = \langle x, y+1 \rangle$, where x and the first component of the output pair are public, and y and the second component of the output pair are confidential. A sample noninterference statement for this function is

$$\begin{aligned}&\forall x, y_1, y_2, x_1', x_2', y_1', y_2'.\\ &\quad f(x, y_1) = \langle x_1', y_1' \rangle \wedge f(x, y_2) = \langle x_2', y_2' \rangle \implies\\ &\qquad\qquad \langle x_1', y_1' \rangle \sim \langle x_2', y_2' \rangle \equiv x_1' = x_2'.\end{aligned}$$

Notice that the construction in the previous subsection required the whole output to be equivalent, whereas now only the public part is. Also, the confidential output may depend on the confidential input, as in the given example function.

6.1 Assumptions

We assume some structure of complex values. First, complex values can be described as algebraic, that is, are of the form $v = c\ v_1, \ldots, v_n$ for an n-ary constructor c. Note that we require values to be made up of sub-values. To ensure termination of our recomputation, we require all treated values to be finite. We require typing to structurally match values: if a value $v = c\ v_1, \ldots, v_n$ can be typed as τ under Γ, then there are types $\tau_1, \ldots, \tau_n$ such that $v_1, \ldots, v_n$ are typed under Γ, and for all $v_1', \ldots, v_n'$ typable in that way, $c\ v_1', \ldots, v_n'$ can be typed as τ. This is a standard consequence in rule-based type systems.

Furthermore, we need functions to decompose values to their components. To unify product and variant treatment, we assume a matching construct in the language. Formally, if a type system can type values $v_i = c_i\ v_1^i, \ldots, v_{n_i}^i$ with $c_i \neq c_j$ (for $i \neq j$) as τ, where v_j^i can be typed with τ_j^i, then there exist matching functions with the signature $\mathrm{match} : \tau \mapsto (\tau_1^1 \times \cdots \times \tau_{n_1}^1 \mapsto \tau') \mapsto \ldots \mapsto \tau'$ for all τ', with the semantics that $\mathrm{match}(c_i\ \ v_1^i, \ldots, v_{n_i}^i, f_1, \ldots, f_m) = f_i(v_1^i, \ldots, v_{n_i}^i)$. This is standard for pattern-matching languages, and can be simulated in languages without explicit pattern matching (e.g., by branching on tag values encoding variants). We will use the common syntax, that is, "$\lambda x \ldots$" for functions and "$\mathrm{match}\ x\ \mathrm{with} \ldots$" for matching. Note that this existential requirement is very weak: to compute with datatypes, one form or another of matching is required.

We assume that each type τ involved has one immediate security-level annotation, which we denote by $tp(\tau)$. Multiple immediate annotations can be handled by complex security lattices. For matching, we require match to be typable, if $tp(\tau) \sqsubseteq tp(\tau_j^i)$ for all i and j, $tp(\tau) \sqsubseteq tp(\tau')$, and all f_i are typable according to the signature of match. This might seem restrictive, but is powerful enough to capture all cases outside the limitations outlined in the following subsection.

We also need to make minimum requirements on what indistinguishability means for values of a type τ and observer level ϕ. Our single requirement is that if two values v_1 and v_2 of type τ are indistinguishable at level ϕ, and $tp(\tau) \sqsubseteq \phi$, then both values have the same root constructor, and all immediate sub-values are indistinguishable with respect to their corresponding types at level ϕ.

6.2 Limitations

It turns out that Conjecture 2 is not provable in the generalized context anymore. As an example, take a language with pairs which have three security annotations: one for each component and one to signal the security level of the identity of the pair. Now take a pair that has a public and a private component, and is itself private. This leads to the public component not being accessible by an attacker (cf. [1, 12, 13]). Indistinguishability might thus be defined as:

$$\begin{aligned}\langle x_1, y_1 \rangle \sim \langle x_2, y_2 \rangle \text{ at } \langle \phi_1, \phi_2 \rangle^{\phi_3} &\iff\\ \phi_3 = H \vee &\begin{pmatrix} (\phi_1 = L \implies x_1 = x_2) \wedge \\ (\phi_2 = L \implies y_1 = y_2) \end{pmatrix}\end{aligned}$$

With this, the following computation is noninterferent:

$$\texttt{if h>0 then } \langle 3,5 \rangle \texttt{ else } \langle 4,5 \rangle \ : \ H \mapsto \langle L, H \rangle^H$$

However, this computation has a dependency between high input h and the low output component. In our companion technical report [4] we formally show that FlowML, a practical non-trivial language, cannot type any program that computes this function. We thus limit the theorems to security types such that levels of sub-types are at least as high as those of enclosing types.

6.3 Approach

The intuition behind our approach is to split computations by output level, allowing a level-separated computation. The final result then needs to be composed from the parts. Separability is a known result for trace-based security. We re-use and extend it to complex datastructures.

In a language-based environment, directly separating by security level is complicated. Since levels are connected to types, which are connected to the structure of values, we instead separate structurally, which implies a level separation. E.g., with the example above, we will find a program that represents $f(x, y)$ as a composition of computations for each pair component:

$$f(x, y) = \mathrm{match}\ f^L(x, y)\ \mathrm{with}\ \langle x_t, y_t \rangle \Rightarrow \langle f^1(x, y), f^2(x, y) \rangle$$

where $f^1(x, y) = \pi_1(f(x, y))$ and $f^2(x, y) = \pi_2(f(x, y))$. Intuitively, the matching will compute a single (sub-)value

$\text{if } y = 0 \text{ then } a := \langle x, y\rangle \qquad [x : L,\ y : H,\ a : L \times H]$
$\quad \text{else } a := \langle x + 0, y + 1\rangle;$

$t_1^x := x;\ t_1^y := y;\ t_1^o := t_1^x \qquad [t_1^x : L,\ t_1^y : H,\ t_1^o : L]$
$\qquad t_1^o = \pi_1(x, y)$

$t_2^x := x;\ t_2^y := y;\ t_2^o := 0; \qquad [t_2^x : L,\ t_2^y : H,\ t_2^o : L]$
$\qquad t_2^o = c_0(x, y)$

$t_3^x := t_1^o;\ t_3^y := t_2^o; \qquad [t_3^x : L,\ t_3^y : L,\ t_3^o : L \times L]$
$\text{if } t_3^y = 0 \text{ then } t_3^o := \langle t_3^x, t_3^y\rangle \qquad t_3^o = p^L(t_1^o, t_2^o)$
$\quad \text{else } t_3^o := \langle t_3^x + 0, t_3^y + 1\rangle;$

$t_4^o := \pi_1\ t_3^o; \qquad [t_4^o : L]$

$t_5^x := x;\ t_5^y := y;\ t_5^o := t_5^y; \qquad [t_5^x : L,\ t_5^y : H,\ t_5^o : H]$
$\qquad t_5^o = \pi_2(x, y)$

$t_6^x := t_1^o;\ t_6^y := t_5^o; \qquad [t_6^x : H,\ t_6^y : H,\ t_6^o : H \times H]$
$\text{if } t_6^y = 0 \text{ then } t_6^o := \langle t_6^x, t_6^y\rangle \qquad t_6^o = p^H(t_1^o, t_5^o)$
$\quad \text{else } t_6^o := \langle t_6^x + 0, t_6^y + 1\rangle;$

$t_7^o := \pi_2\ t_6^o; \qquad [t_7^o : H]$

$a := \langle t_6^o, t_7^o\rangle;$

Figure 3. Example Pair-Result Program

at the level of the immediate annotation of that type. Noninterference will enforce that at least the variant chosen is correctly computed at this level. The corresponding matched case will re-compute all sub-values, at their correct levels, and reconstruct the correct value in a typable fashion.

An example of this construction is given in Figure 3. The program p on top computes $f(x, y) = \langle x, y + 1\rangle$, but is not typable. In the transformed program, for brevity we use π to extract components of a pair. The first four blocks compute the low component, while the next three blocks compute the high component, and finally the pair is reconstituted. Note the conceptual similarity to [3]. They perform a similar process at runtime to enforce noninterference, compared to our approach of showing typability in the case when noninterference is given.

6.4 Nonrecursive Datatypes

For nonrecursive datatypes, a type τ can be matched statically to any value v it types. We will recompute a (sub-)value corresponding to the structure of its (sub-)type, ensuring typability along the way.

We can recursively generate a function for this whole computation. Note that underlined functions are meta-level functions defining a language-level construct - in a sense they are macros to construct the language-level computation. Assume that f is noninterferent with respect to signature $\tau^i \mapsto \tau$. Here, we assume τ^i is not complex to simplify the presentation. Also, let f^ϕ denote the function that results from single-level typing as outlined in the previous section. We start with the actual computation, modeled with $\underline{\text{match}}$:

$$\underline{\text{match}}(p, \tau) = \lambda x : \tau^i.\ \underline{\text{extract}}(p, \tau)\ f^{tp(\tau')}(x)$$
`// if τ' is not a datatype`
$$\underline{\text{match}}(p, \tau) = \lambda x : \tau^i.$$
$$\quad \text{match } (\underline{\text{extract}}(p, \tau)\ f^{tp(\tau')}(x)) \text{ with}$$
$$\vdots$$
$$c_i\ t_1^i, \ldots, t_{n_i}^i \Rightarrow c_i\ (\underline{\text{match}}(p + +(i, 1), \tau)\ x), \ldots,$$
$$(\underline{\text{match}}(p + +(i, n_i), \tau)\ x)$$
`// else`

Here, p is a path the a sub-value/sub-type, which is encoded by a list of pairs for the choice of constructor and immediate sub-value. We denote the type in τ relative to path p by τ'. Note that the concept of paths is purely meta-level, since nonrecursive types can be fully statically described - we only need it to describe the computation recursively.

The key point of $\underline{\text{match}}$ is the recomputation of f at the level of the currently inspected sub-value denoted by p. To avoid inspection of f, we do a full recomputation, which then requires to extract the sub-value in question - this is the job of $\underline{\text{extract}}$. With the restrictions on τ and indistinguishability, it follows that this recomputation is correct up to the choice of constructor, but not necessarily the sub-values $t_1^i, \ldots, t_{n_i}^i$. We thus recompute the sub-values recursively by extending the path for $\underline{\text{match}}$.

Extraction itself does not need to recompute at each step. To be typable as needed, $\underline{\text{extract}}$ refers to a default value v_{def} for type τ' when the given path does not lead to such a case (we use "default" to stand for the finite number of other cases).

$$\underline{\text{extract}}((), \tau) = \lambda x : \tau.\ x$$
$$\underline{\text{extract}}((i, j) :: p, \tau) = \lambda x : \tau.\ \text{match } x \text{ with}$$
$$c_i\ t_1^i, \ldots, t_{n_i}^i \Rightarrow \underline{\text{extract}}(p, \tau_j^i)\ t_j^i$$
$$\text{default} \Rightarrow v_{def}$$

We can now formalize our conjecture for nonrecursive datatypes.

Theorem 10 (Nonrecursive Datatypes). *Assume a language $\mathcal{L}$ and corresponding ground language that fulfill all the requirements of the previous section, as well as the requirements in this section. This language is security-complete with the mentioned restrictions.*

The proof proceeds by induction over the structure of types and paths and can be found in [4].

6.5 Recursive Datatypes

The approach of the previous section can be extended to recursive datatypes, but for space reasons we only sketch our solution. The key difference is that now the path in a value needs to be handled dynamically. We can model the path with a list of integers, which is a recursive type and thus allowed by the language in question. We use μ types to guide the construction of the corresponding code. μ types allow a binding construct $\mu x.\tau$, where x may appear in τ.

For each binder a recomputation function is generated that assumes that the current path leads to a place in the value that corresponds to the binder. Furthermore, to minimize typing requirements, e.g., not require polymorphism, we create extraction functions for each start and end binder, e.g., $\text{extract}_{x \mapsto y}$ assumes a value corresponding to binder x, and a path that will lead to binder y.

With this setup we can state a theorem corresponding to Theorem 10. The details of the construction, exact statement and proof are available in [4].

7. References

References introduce additional constructs that need to be handled. This complicates matters and requires further restrictions on languages that our technique can support. For one, most languages with references only allow limited interactions with references. Allocation of new locations can usually not be influenced directly on the language level. This makes exact recomputation impossible. Our technique can thus only simulate correctly up to renaming of heap locations. This also means that computations exhibiting identity behaviour cannot be simulated correctly. We see this as a minor disadvantage. We want to use the simulation to replace an embedded program that is cleanly separated from the host. It seems reasonable to require that any objects returned from the embedded program are independent of the inputs. This is usually the case when the embedded program cannot "call back" into the host program.

Any recomputation in parts will repeatedly invoke the original computation at certain levels. This may create several temporary locations polluting the heap, which, of course, do not appear in the original computation. Our technique is thus only correct up to locations reachable from the result of the function.

Also, computation with references allows side effects. In this case, a side effect may change the input values. We can contain side effects if we can create temporary "clones" of the relevant inputs and use those for computations. This means that the language needs to guarantee that two suitably related inputs, e.g., clones, compute suitably related outputs. We formalize this as the shape of the part of the heap reachable from the inputs, which corresponds to the first restriction. This, however, forbids any reflective language constructs.

7.1 Heaps

We formalize state through the concept of heaps. Heaps, denoted by $\mathcal{H}$, are mappings of locations, denoted by ℓ, to values. Values are extended to include locations. nil is a special value that is not mapped by any heap. Typings may contain a heap typing that assigns types to locations. Reference types are composed of the type of values that can be stored at the location, as well as the security level of location value itself.

7.2 Reachability, Equivalence & Indistinguishability

As outlined above, we restrict our attention to languages that restrict computation to reachable values. We formalize reachability as a set parameterized over a heap and starting location in said heap. The reachable set $\mathcal{R}$ of $\mathcal{H}$ and ℓ is the smallest set closed under the following rules: (1) $\ell \in \mathcal{R}$ and (2) if $\ell \in \mathcal{R}$ and $\mathcal{H}(\ell) = o$ a value of a type τ, then for all location-typed sub-values o' of o we have $o' \in \mathcal{R}$. For our treatment, we require $\mathcal{R}$ to be finite.

We define two pairs of heap and start locations to be equivalent if there exists a bijection ρ between the locations of the reachable sets such that non-reference values in related locations are identical, and reference values are related by the bijection. We denote equivalence by $\equiv$.

If two locations are indistinguishable with respect to bijection ρ and level ϕ and their level is at most ϕ, then they are in relation with respect to ρ. This is standard. Now, along the lines of datatypes we require that if two references to values of type τ are indistinguishable with respect to ϕ and ρ, and the security annotation is at most ϕ, then the potential variants of both objects are identical. We require that indistinguishability for heaps is with respect to its reachable part. That is $(\mathcal{H}_\infty, o_1)$ is indistinguishable to $(\mathcal{H}_\in, o_2)$ at level ϕ if there exists a bijection ρ between the reachable sets and o_1 and o_2 are indistinguishable with respect to ρ.

7.3 Computation

We define as a computation a function from a heap $\mathcal{H}$ and location in the heap, to a result heap $\mathcal{H}'$ and result object. A program computes f if reduction of the main fragment with variables bound to the input object and given heap results in the result heap and result object. As mentioned above, we assume correct executions. Thus we will leave typing constraints implicit here. All definitions are predicated on heaps and input objects correct with respect to f, that is $\mathcal{H}$ etc. range only over valid input states for f.

We formalize our requirements on the treated programs in the following way. A function f is *ok*, if:

- $\forall \mathcal{H}, \mathcal{H}', o, o'. f(\mathcal{H}, o) = (\mathcal{H}', o') \implies \mathcal{R}_{\mathcal{H},o} \cap \mathcal{R}_{\mathcal{H}',o} = \emptyset$
- $\forall \mathcal{H}_1, o_1, \mathcal{H}_2, o_2. (\mathcal{H}_1, o_1) \equiv (\mathcal{H}_2, o_2) \implies f(\mathcal{H}_1, o_1) \equiv f(\mathcal{H}_2, o_2)$

A simulation g is correct for f, if $\forall \mathcal{H}, o. f(\mathcal{H}, o) \equiv g(\mathcal{H}, o)$.

7.4 Approach

Treatment of references generalizes the approach of recursive data types. In this case, a heap walking approach is used. At each location in the heap, inputs need to be duplicated. Note that this is typable due to the single level necessary for the current computation. Non-location values can be immediately computed when a location is reached. Otherwise, references are resolved recursively, extending the current path from the starting location. Since the reachable part of the heap is required to be finite, the workload is finite.

A complication arises from the potential for cyclic paths in the heap. The process is complicated by the fact that the original result will be recomputed in every step. Our solution is to store a list of objects seen when extracting the current object from the result along the current path. This list can be typed with a single level, since the result object and heap are typed at a single level. A "back edge" is detected when the current extracted object is present in the list. To also detect "cross edges", we must also walk all completed paths again. This can be implemented through a deterministic processing order of fields in objects. To break the cycle, we return the object constructed earlier. This is the main reason why the treatment of datatypes (value is created late) differs from references (value is created early). Retrieval can be encoded with single-level integer lists describing paths to stored objects. If we update locations early, that is, a child adds itself to its parent, and have access to the root, we can use the path to retrieve the recomputed object in a typable way.

For space reasons, we omit a formalization of the construction, which can be found in the technical report, and only state the resulting theorem.

Theorem 11 (References). *Assume a language $\mathcal{L}$ and corresponding ground language that fulfill all the requirements of the previous sections, as well as the requirements in this section. Such a language is security-complete with the mentioned restrictions.*

8. Example Languages

This section briefly describes three case studies which demonstrate that our formalization and requirements permit such different paradigms as imperative, functional and object-oriented languages. A more detailed analysis can be found in the technical report.

8.1 Volpano, Smith & Irvine

VSI [16] is based on a simple WHILE language based on integers. It fits the development in Section 5. Erasure and lifting functions are straightforward for VSI, since only types are annotated. Requirement 5 follows from the polymorphic setup of the type rules and can be formally proved by induction on the ground typing. Variable assignment represents the projection function of requirement 6, typable by the assignment rule. Assignment of an integer literal represents the constant function of requirement 7, and can be typed at the output variable level.

The only complicated requirement is composition. In a WHILE language, composition is basically sequencing the components, with possible assignments to connect the components. Composition actually necessitates renaming of variables and connecting assignments to allow typing, but satisfies the requirements.

8.2 FlowML

FlowML [13] is based on a core functional ML fragment including references, pairs, sums and exceptions. For simplicity of the functional interpretation we do not treat exceptions and references here. FlowML fits the development in Section 6.4. Lifting, erasure and single-level typing follow from the polymorphic setup of the rules. Projection is provided by a simple variable, while constants can be freely formed. Composition is provided by variable substitution, which may be combined with renaming and weakening to fulfill the requirements. Extraction for pairs is provided by typed projection, and a `case` construct allows to distinguish variants. However, basic noninterference cannot be lifted to abstractions, so that we cannot support arrow types (c.f. [6]).

8.3 Banerjee & Naumann

It is easy to extend the work in Section 7 to a class-based setting. We study the work in [1]. Additional treatment over pure references is necessary for encapsulation, which we solve by making all fields accessible through accessor methods. This does not change the computation. Single-level requirements can be ensured by complete copies of all classes and setting all annotations at the requested level. Projection, constant functions, and composition can be handled as in VSI. Furthermore, we need a matching construct to match objects to their respective classes. This can be realized with `instanceof` and dynamic casts provided by the language. Note that these constructs have the same security level as their inputs, so that they are typable as required.

9. Related Work

Completeness To the best of our knowledge, this is the first work to formally investigate completeness in the context of security-typed languages. Kahrs [7, 8] studied completeness for basic type systems, where the question is if all computable functions that are "well-going" can be typed. Kahrs formalized languages and type systems as transition systems and used the product and reachability to define soundness. In comparison, our goal is to permit easy adoption of existing languages, which usually have rule-based designs for both semantics and type systems. As demonstrated, the requirements usually easily follow from the modular nature of judgments, and can be derived for both imperative and functional security-typed languages.

Traditional work in security-typed languages attempts to broaden the permissibility of the type system, that is, accept more programs as typed and thus certified secure. For an overview we refer to [15]. Our work is orthogonal to such efforts. We show that, under certain constraints formulated in our requirements, there are always programs that compute a given noninterferent function.

Language Composition To the best of our knowledge, this is the first work to consider composing two different security-typed languages. Composition has been studied in the security field for trace-based systems (e.g., [11]), in the setting of process algebras ([14] for an overview), and security-typed languages ([10] for an overview). In all these, multiple programs (or fragments) of *one* formal system are composed, and the question is if all programs are secure, is the composition secure. In contrast, our fragments are derived from different security-typed languages, exhibiting different semantics that are interfaced through an additional host statement.

Approach Our approach of level separation to establish security completeness is similar to the runtime effort in [3]. Devriese and Piessens enhance the semantics of a language to allow for level-separated computation to ensure noninterference at runtime, potentially changing the meaning of a program. We achieve typing through the use of single-level typing and also separating computations, without changing semantics or meaning of a program. Furthermore, we study the approach also for complex datatypes, nondeterminism and termination-insensitive noninterference, whereas Devriese and Piessens only speculate on the first and avoid the second and third.

10. Conclusion & Future Work

In this paper we have shown an approach, under certain restrictions, to show security of a language composition if the composed components themselves are secure. The approach is based on a simulation of component behavior, and accompanying proof that the noninterference of the component computation guarantees that there exists a typable program for the simulation, thus deducing noninterference for the composed language from noninterference for the host language.

This result allows us to develop separate type systems for languages, and lift the results to compositions. It thus significantly reduces the burden of showing security in modern programs that employ many programming languages for different tasks like data retrieval and modification.

Acknowledgments We would like to thank our shepherd Nikhil Swamy and the anonymous referees for their helpful comments improving the presentation of this paper.

This work was supported by the National Science Foundation under grants CCF-0846010 and CNS-0964710.

References

[1] A. Banerjee and D. A. Naumann. Stack-based access control and secure information flow. *J. Funct. Program.*, 15(2):131–177, Mar. 2005.

[2] D. E. Denning. A lattice model of secure information flow. *Commun. ACM*, 19:236–243, May 1976. ISSN 0001-0782.

[3] D. Devriese and F. Piessens. Noninterference through secure multi-execution. In *Proceedings of the 2010 IEEE Symposium on Security and Privacy*, SP '10, pages 109–124, Washington, DC, USA, 2010. IEEE Computer Society.

[4] A. Gampe and J. Von Ronne. Towards noninterference in composed languages. Technical Report CS-TR-2012-014, Department of Computer Science, The University of Texas at San Antonio, 2012.

[5] J. A. Goguen and J. Meseguer. *Security Policies and Security Models*, volume pages, pages 11–20. IEEE, 1982.

[6] N. Heintze and J. G. Riecke. The slam calculus: programming with secrecy and integrity. In *Proceedings of the 25th ACM SIGPLAN-SIGACT symposium on Principles of programming languages*, POPL '98, pages 365–377, New York, NY, USA, 1998. ACM.

[7] S. Kahrs. Limits of ml-definability. In *Proceedings of the 8th International Symposium on Programming Languages: Implementations, Logics, and Programs*, PLILP '96, pages 17–31, London, UK, UK, 1996. Springer-Verlag.

[8] S. Kahrs. Well-going programs can be typed. In *Proceedings of the 6th international conference on Typed lambda calculi and applications*, TLCA'03, pages 167–179, Berlin, Heidelberg, 2003. Springer-Verlag.

[9] J. Liu, M. D. George, K. Vikram, X. Qi, L. Waye, and A. C. Myers. Fabric: a platform for secure distributed computation and storage. In *SOSP '09: Proceedings of the ACM SIGOPS 22nd symposium on Operating systems principles*, pages 321–334, New York, NY, USA, 2009. ACM.

[10] H. Mantel, D. Sands, and H. Sudbrock. Assumptions and guarantees for compositional noninterference. In *Proceedings of the 2011 IEEE 24th Computer Security Foundations Symposium*, CSF '11, pages 218–232, Washington, DC, USA, 2011. IEEE Computer Society.

[11] D. McCullough. Specifications for multi-level security and a hook-up. *Security and Privacy, IEEE Symposium on*, 0:161, 1987.

[12] A. C. Myers. Jflow: Practical mostly-static information flow control. In *In Proc. 26th ACM Symp. on Principles of Programming Languages (POPL)*, pages 228–241, 1999.

[13] F. Pottier and V. Simonet. Information flow inference for ML. In *POPL '02: Proceedings of the 29th ACM SIGPLAN-SIGACT symposium on Principles of programming languages*, pages 319–330, New York, NY, USA, 2002. ACM.

[14] P. Y. A. Ryan and S. A. Schneider. Process algebra and non-interference. *J. Comput. Secur.*, 9(1-2):75–103, Jan. 2001.

[15] A. Sabelfeld and A. Myers. Language-based information-flow security. *Selected Areas in Communications, IEEE Journal on*, 21(1):5 – 19, Jan. 2003. ISSN 0733-8716. doi: 10.1109/JSAC.2002.806121.

[16] D. Volpano, C. Irvine, and G. Smith. A sound type system for secure flow analysis. *J. Comput. Secur.*, 4:167–187, January 1996.

[17] S. Zdancewic and A. C. Myers. Secure information flow and cps. In *ESOP '01: Proceedings of the 10th European Symposium on Programming Languages and Systems*, pages 46–61, London, UK, 2001. Springer-Verlag.

Position Paper: Sapper — A Language for Provable Hardware Policy Enforcement

Xun Li Vineeth Kashyap Jason K. Oberg* Mohit Tiwari† Vasanth Ram Rajarathinam
Ryan Kastner* Timothy Sherwood Ben Hardekopf Frederic T. Chong

Department of Computer Science
University of California, Santa Barbara
Santa Barbara, CA
{xun,vineeth,vasanthram,sherwood,benh,chong}@cs.ucsb.edu

*Department of Computer Science and Engineering
University of California, San Diego
La Jolla, CA
{jkoberg,kastner}@cs.ucsd.edu

†Department of Electrical Engineering and Computer Science
University of California, Berkeley
Berkeley, CA
{tiwari@eecs.berkeley.edu}

Abstract

We describe Sapper, a language for creating critical hardware components that have provably secure information flow. Most systems that enforce information flow policies place the hardware microarchitecture within the trusted computing base, and also assume that the observable behavior of that microarchitecture is fully and correctly documented. However, the reality is that this behavior is incompletely (and sometimes incorrectly) specified, and that the microarchitecture itself often contains implementation bugs. This fact means that all such systems are vulnerable to attack by exploiting undocumented or buggy hardware features. Sapper addresses this problem by enabling flexible and efficient hardware design that is provably secure with respect to a given information flow policy. Sapper uses a hybrid approach that leverages unique language features and static analysis to determine a set of dynamic checks that are automatically inserted into the hardware design. These checks are provably sufficient to guarantee that the resulting hardware prevents all explicit, implicit, and timing channels even if the hardware is otherwise buggy or poorly documented.

Categories and Subject Descriptors B.5.2 [*Design Aids*]: Hardware description languages

General Terms Security, Languages

Keywords Hardware Description Language, non-interference, information flow

1. Introduction

In this paper we present our ongoing work towards designing hardware components with strong security properties, specifically with respect to information flow. Information flow control mechanisms enforce privacy and integrity security policies by tracking and constraining the propagation of data through a system. This tracking is accomplished by associating *labels* with the data, and propagating these labels appropriately. A wide spectrum of techniques for enforcing information flow policies have been proposed, ranging from language support [26], to operating system support [15, 35], to hardware support [34]. While these techniques are effective in a variety of scenarios, they make the critical assumption that the hardware documentation correctly and fully describes the behavior of the machine with respect to information flow. Unfortunately, even the most widely examined and used processors fail to meet this fundamental assumption.

Modern microprocessors ship with a significant number of bugs, despite being one of the most tested products brought to market today. To create these microprocessor designs, hardware engineers use design tools ranging from synthesis tools that can convert a subset[1] of hardware description languages such as Verilog into low-level netlists,[2] testing tools [9], model checking tools [6], and even verification tools to prove the correctness of *subcomponents* with respect to a reference [14]. However, hardware can have just as many "moving parts" as a fully featured operating system and full verification is a practical impossibility [1]. The size and complexity of these designs mean that real production systems ship with bugs with software level ramifications. While these bugs may not occur in commonplace execution, a motivated attacker will find unique ways to exploit these undocumented behaviors to leak information and circumvent security policies [11, 13].

1.1 Our Approach

The core of our approach is a security-aware hardware design synthesis language called *Sapper*. Sapper uses a hybrid approach that leverages unique language features and static analysis to determine a set of dynamic checks that are automatically inserted into the hardware design. These checks translate runtime *security policy violations* into *safe operations*, and they are provably sufficient to

PLAS'13, June 20, 2013, Seattle, WA, USA.

[1] Unlike software compilers, HDL compilers typically handle only a subset of the language and/or only specific types of constructs that infer certain types of hardware. In this respect they are quite unlike traditional programming languages.

[2] A netlist is a directed graph of circuit elements (e.g. logic gates) and interconnects (i.e. wires) that can be mapped onto a physical substrate (e.g. an FPGA or custom hardware implementation).

guarantee that the resulting hardware prevents all explicit, implicit, and timing channels. Sapper wraps around existing Verilog Hardware Description Language (HDL) code. The Sapper compiler automatically derives and inserts security checks into the system at critical latches; these checks operate in parallel with the logic they analyze. During design testing but before fabrication[3], the inserted checks will detect actions that violate security and translate those actions into pre-specified (by the hardware designer) non-violating actions. In other words, policy violations will show up during the design testing phase as functional bugs. Through careful design, the hardware engineers ensure that the system will operate as intended in the vast majority of cases even with these checks in place (as covered by traditional testing/verification techniques). Once testing is complete the second function of the inserted checks comes into play, as they will remain in the fabricated design. The checks serve as the last line of defense against run-time violations in conditions never encountered during testing and verification. Both undiscovered hardware bugs and rarely occurring combinations of events may provide opportunities to attack an unprotected system; however, hardware designed with Sapper will automatically capture and prevent any runtime violations.

2. Motivation

Sapper enforces a timing-sensitive *noninterference* security policy, where the security principles and relations between principles are defined by the hardware designer. Noninterference means that data tagged with a lower-level security label cannot influence the values of data tagged with a higher-level security label.[4] Timing-sensitive noninterference means that we take into account not only *explicit* (data-dependency related) information flow and *implicit* (control-dependency related) information flow, but also information flow related to *when* events happen. Timing-sensitivity is extremely difficult to enforce at the software level (see, e.g., Kashyap et al [12]), because timing variations generated by hardware components are abstracted away from the software programming model. For example, a memory access instruction can take widely varying amounts of time depending on the cache status, and code with branches can take varying amounts of time depending on branch predictor status. However, timing-sensitivity is important for critical systems: these timing characteristics can be exploited to create covert channels that break security systems with a reasonable level of practicality [10]. One might consider exposing to the software level a low-level model of the microarchitecture that includes timing information, as proposed by previous work [36]. However, the complexity of modern processors prohibits deriving a sound abstraction model for the hardware without digging into every logic gate in the design. Even hardware designers themselves might not be able to figure out the set of hardware components that are responsible for the timing of each instruction. Sound enforcement of information flow security policies demands tools that are tightly integrated into the hardware design process.

Hardware is designed using programming languages known as hardware description languages (HDL). Examples of HDLs include Verilog and VHDL. Intuitively, it might seem that one could apply information flow techniques from software languages directly to HDLs. However, HDLs are different from software languages in many aspects, and information flow analysis techniques for HDLs must be invented from scratch. In particular, there are three major difference between software programming languages and HDLs:

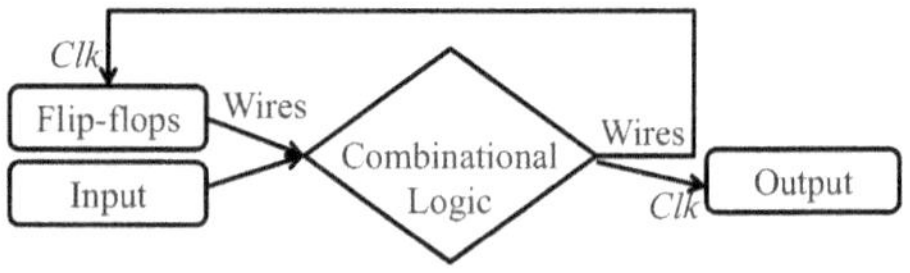

Figure 1. Structure of a synchronous circuit design used by typical modern processors. Flip-flops (e.g. registers) are controlled by a global clock (Clk). Inputs and values of flip-flops are fed into combinational logic, which finishes computation within a clock cycle and writes to output or back to flip-flops on clock edges.

Timing Model. In (most) software programming languages, programs are defined as a sequence of commands that each translate to a series of ISA instructions. The timing of each command in the language depends upon a number of factors, including the compiler implementation and hardware implementation as well as the current state of the hardware. It is almost impossible to determine the precise timing of software programs. On the other hand, hardware designs for modern processors are synchronous circuits based on a global clock. Data coming from inputs or flip-flops (i.e., hardware registers) are wired into a combinational logic circuit for computation, and the results are written to outputs or back to flip-flops as shown in Figure 1. By definition of synchronous circuits, state changes (i.e., changes to outputs and flip-flops) occurr only at clock edges. Under this model, commands written in HDL, no matter how complex, will become part of the combinational logic and the results will not take effect until the next clock edge. All forms of information flow in hardware designs are compressed into a single clock cycle.

It might seem that this timing model makes information flow analysis easier, due to centralized information and strict timing, however it in fact makes hardware designs highly susceptible to taint explosion when typical information flow analysis techniques are applied. Specifically, any input to the combinational logic that is tainted will potentially taint the entire hardware. Thus, it is not hard to see that pure static analysis based on static type systems as used in most software-based information flow mechanisms [26, 33] will unavoidably lead to duplication of all hardware resources in order to be statically verified for noninterference. The economic cost of this duplication is not acceptable, and thus conventional techniques are not adequate for our purpose.

Output Channels. Output channels are interfaces through which attackers are able to observe data. For software programs, output is usually implemented by well-defined library calls. In these programs, information flow policies can be enforced by checking that the security level of users who can observe the output is at least the same as that of the data being output. In hardware designs, there are no predefined "library calls" for I/O operations. Assuming that attackers cannot wire-tap the circuits themselves, output can be observed through a set of ports on the bus. Although enforcing information flow policies on those ports is sound, it is a challenging task to recover the system when violations are captured since the rest of the system would have been largely tainted at the time of output. This setup also makes it difficult to debug the source of violations. Sapper aims at securing the system in a way that is not only recoverable at runtime violations but also useful as a hardware testing tool.

ISA Support. The ultimate goal of enforcing security policies for HDLs is not to make the hardware itself more secure, but to protect systems and applications running on top of the hardware. This extra level of hierarchy makes HDLs different from software

[3] Typically such tests are performed through a combination of hardware simulation and prototyping on reconfigurable hardware.

[4] Non-interference is may be too strong of a property for general purpose systems, but is useful both in the context of crypto systems and safety critical designs, and it matches closely with the existing design goals expressed by both Intel [5] and ARM [3].

programming languages in nature. In designing secure hardware, not only do we need to ensure that the hardware design enforces noninterference, but the hardware also needs to provide a corresponding ISA interface for systems to interact with the security mechanisms. Designing those ISAs in a formal and secure manner can be a significant challenge.

The philosophy of Sapper is to reinvent information flow analysis techniques for hardware description languages, incorporating all of the distinct characteristics and challenges of HDLs, to enable the creation of efficient, flexible, practical and provably secure computer architectures.

3. Overview of Sapper

We show that modern programming language techniques, when applied in the new domain of hardware description languages (HDLs), can provide static guarantees at design time along with precise control of information flow. Specifically we propose Sapper, a hardware description language that operates at the abstraction of a high-level HDL while enforcing security policies through statically-inserted logic for dynamic tracking and enforcement. A compiler is be responsible for statically analyzing the program in order to generate dynamic tracking and checking logic when translating the program into Verilog, thereby delivering provable guarantees. The generated logic will help eliminate most of the security bugs in the hardware design during testing, and remain in the design to prevent any runtime violations.

A typical Verilog program consists of three parts: signal declarations that define registers and wires (i.e., variables), a synchronous block in which all operations are triggered at the clock edge, and a combinational logic block containing all of the computation that will finish within a clock cycle. The synchronous block is responsible for writing data back to flip-flops at clock edges. The combinational logic blocks contain commands that are similar to those in software programming languages, including assignments, branches and switch/cases. Sapper keeps most of the Verilog syntax and requires minimum changes to the source code. In this section we sketch the details of Sapper. For convenience we assume that the security policy being enforced has two levels, Low and High, such that High information should never affect Low information. Sapper can handle arbitrary finite security lattices in practice.

3.1 Security Tags

Variables (i.e. signals, wires, etc.) in Sapper are associated with security tags that are tracked and checked for security policy violations at runtime. Checking *every* data movement in hardware for violations of noninterference would be extremely expensive, both in terms of additional hardware and performance overhead. We observe that in most hardware designs only certain outputs are exposed and observable by software/programmers and thus require strict enforcement. Many variables, such as internal pipeline registers and wires used to hold intermediate results, are only for temporary storage and are not directly observable. Those non-observable variables only require security tags to be correctly tracked dynamically so that their security level is correctly reflected at runtime. However, if we only enforce security policies for those small set of output ports, it may be extremely difficult for the system to "roll back" from violations or to debug the cause of violations. To this end, we propose Staged Enforcement, in which not only the end output ports are enforced for security policies, but also a set of architectural components that lie on the critical path of data movement are enforced. For example, data movement to the memory can be enforced for noninterference, such that the system can capture violations immediately at the point when data touches the memory. Based on the above observations, Sapper allows designers to declare data variables as one of the following two categories:

- **Enforced Tagged:** Variables having enforced tags will be declared with a default security tag at the beginning, and such security tag will not change until it is *explicitly* modified in the design through provided commands. Information flowing into enforced tagged variables will always be checked for noninterference.
- **Dynamic Tagged:** Variables with dynamic tags are not enforced by security policies, but their tags are dynamically tracked at runtime. Since most of the variables in typical hardware designs are dynamic tagged, variables that are declared without any initial security tags will be dynamic tagged by default.

This dichotomy requires designers to make decisions on what data should be tracked versus enforced, but it is often an easy decision to make since typical architectures only consist of a small portion of components exposed to users or central to data movement. In many architectures, selecting enforced tags for all the bus output ports, the memory and the cache will be sufficient. Note that as long as the I/O ports are enforced, not enforcing policies on some of the other components does not lead to unsoundness, but rather makes the system less precise and thus harder to use. The Sapper compiler is responsible for generating dynamic tracking logic and inserting dynamic checks depending on the tag of the target variable. Below we describe the details of tracking and enforcement.

3.1.1 Tracking

Assignments to dynamic tagged variables will trigger the tracking of security levels: the maximum security level of information that may affect the assigned value shall be propagated to the target variable. Instead of generating tracking logic for every single logic gate as in some previous work [31], Sapper takes advantage of static analysis on the HDL code and inserts tracking logic aggregately at the granularity of expressions and code blocks. Implicit flows (i.e. conditionals) are also derived by the compiler, which inserts logic to ensure sound security label propagation.

Furthermore, unlike previous work that must track information through each bit because it lacks language-level information about the hardware design and thus requires complex but precise tag propagation logic, Sapper tracks information at the register level[5] and uses simple logic to compute security levels (each variable has an n-bit tag independent of its width and the security level of the output is the least upper bound of the security levels of the inputs). In theory, Sapper may be less precise (but still sound) compared to bit-level tracking due to the coarser tracking granularity and relaxed tag propagation. However we observe that the major purpose of using precise bit-level tracking in previous work is to avoid label creep and allow a secure switch from a High to Low context. In the next section we will describe how the "nested states" feature we use in Sapper provides exactly what is needed to satisfy this requirement. In fact, there is nothing that prohibits bit-level tracking in Sapper, but we believe this is not necessary because the state transforms can be expressed in the language itself rather than needing to be inferred from the generated logic. Hence Sapper achieves sufficient precision for security enforcement with significantly less overhead while retaining a high degree of flexibility.

3.1.2 Enforcement

Any assignment to a variable with enforced tags needs to be enforced for noninterference. Specifically, the security level of the target variable can never be lower than the maximum security level of information that may affect the assigned value. The necessary

[5] Note that we do not mean only architectural registers here (like %eax), we mean register-transfer-level register, which is any set of bits used as a group in the hardware description language.

	Sapper	Verilog

CHECK	reg[7:0] a : L,
	reg[7:0] b, c;
	a <= b & c;
		reg[7:0] a,b,c;
		reg a_tag,b_tag,c_tag;
		if (a_tag>=(b_tag|c_tag))
		  a <= b & c;

TRACK	reg[7:0] a, b, c;
	a <= b & c;
		reg[7:0] a,b,c;
		reg a_tag,b_tag,c_tag;
		a <= b & c;
		a_tag <= b_tag | c_tag;

Figure 2. An 8-bit adder written in Sapper along with the generated Verilog code. There are two cases: in the first case register *a* is enforced tagged hence the assignment needs to be checked for noninterference; in the second case *a* is dynamic tagged hence only tracking is needed.

enforcement conditions will be derived by the compiler and the security checks will be automatically inserted into the resulting logic. These assignments will take effect only when they are guaranteed to be secure. Sapper also provides some flexibility for designers to deal with potential violations, which will be described in 3.4. Figure 2 shows the generated Verilog code for an *8-bit-and* design written in Sapper. There are two different cases shown in the figure, one with enforcement (CHECK) while another with tracking (TRACK) only. Note that both the tracking and enforcement logic are automatically generated by the compiler and there is no need for designers to manually specify anything except the initial enforced tags.

3.2 State Machines

Timing in most synchronous hardware designs is strictly aligned to clock edges, and registers are only updated at clock edges. To capture the notion of hardware timing, Sapper explicitly models hardware designs as *state machines*. During a clock cycle the hardware can only be in one of the machine's logical states, and all the logic from that state will be executed within the clock cycle. State transitions take effect at clock edges. Another important motivation behind modeling hardware as state machines is that state machines are a common pattern used by hardware designers, and most hardware designs are already written in or can be easily transformed to state machines.

Since state transitions can be conditional, to catch implicit leaks states must also have security tags and these tags must be correctly propagated or checked during state transitions. In the same manner as variables, states can be declared with enforced or dynamic tags. The security level of states with dynamic tags will be tracked dynamically at runtime, while states with enforced tags will be enforced for noninterference and their security level will not change until it is explicitly modified. An immediate advantage of Sapper is that the same state (if dynamic tagged) can act at different security levels dynamically, and hence the same piece of code can be reused as long as context switches are securely controlled.

Additionally, state transitions carry information by definition. To uphold noninterference, a transition from some state *A* to some state *B* should only occur if A is lower than B. In the case of a state machine diagram that is strongly connected (i.e. every state can reach every other state), the existence of any High state will require all states to be High (label creep). Sapper uses the concept of *nested states* proposed by Li et. al [19] in previous work to solve this problem. States can be organized hierarchically as a tree structure. Within each clock cycle, before executing the logic of any state, its parent state has to be executed first (recursively applied till the root). To give parent states complete control of child states and decide whether/when to fall into them, **fall** commands are used as an indication of transfer from parent state to child state. By having

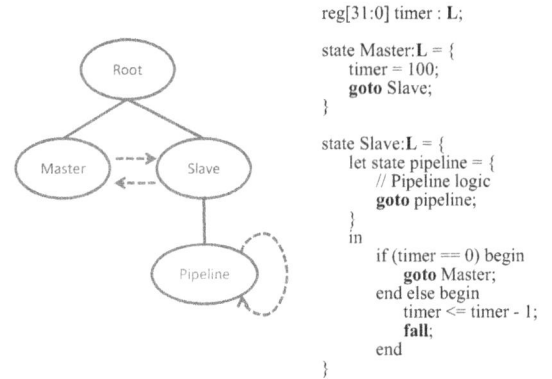

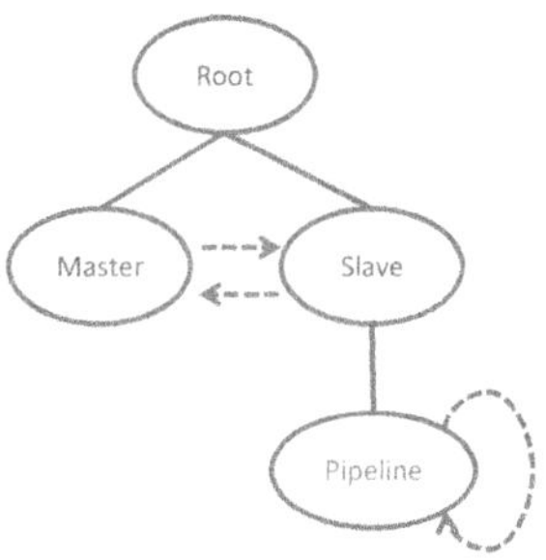


```
reg[31:0] timer : L;

state Master:L = {
    timer = 100;
    goto Slave;
}

state Slave:L = {
    let state pipeline = {
        // Pipeline logic
        goto pipeline;
    }
    in
        if (timer == 0) begin
            goto Master;
        end else begin
            timer <= timer - 1;
            fall;
        end
}
```

Figure 3. State Machine Diagram example of a secure hardware controller, along with its corresponding implementation in Sapper. Noninterference is achieved by having a trusted timer controlling the behavior of the computation logic.

parent states with Low security levels and child states with High security levels, Low states have the freedom to decide when to terminate High states, without violating security.

Figure 3 shows an example of a state machine diagram for a secure hardware design based on TDMA (Time Division Multiple Access), which is a common design pattern used by secure systems. A trusted timer (Low) is used to control the execution of untrusted components. In particular, the Master state (trusted, labeled with Low, enforced tagged) sets up a timer and transits to the Slave state (also trusted, Low), which falls into its child state (potentially untrusted, dynamic tagged) and executes the computation logic. At the beginning of every cycle, the Slave State is always executed first and the timer is checked. If the timer expires control will transfer back to the Master State. The security level of the child state (i.e. Pipeline State in the diagram) can be either High of Low at runtime depending on the data it is dealing with. No matter what level it is, it will never affect its parent states, thus enforcing noninterference. The corresponding implementation in Sapper is also shown on the side. The timer variable, Master state and Slave state are provided with default types L (Low), indicating they are enforced tagged; while the Pipeline State does not have any default type, indicating it is dynamic tagged. When the code is compiled down to Verilog, tracking and checking logic will be generated based on a formal semantics. Although the runtime security level of the Pipeline State is dynamically changing, the generated checking logic will guarantee that the Master State is always trusted.

3.3 Manipulating Tags

One important advantage of Sapper compared to purely static mechanisms is that security labels can be read, reacted upon and updated at runtime. As we have defined earlier, the security level of enforced tagged registers will not change until they are explicitly modified through the language provided interface. This feature can be used by system kernels to efficiently and securely share memory among different security levels. Although we allow security tags to be modified explicitly, they cannot be modified arbitrarily otherwise information can be leaked through the labels. Sapper provides pre-defined commands to allow modification of the security tags of enforced tagged variables and states. Sapper language rules will ensure that no information can be leaked: a) the security level of any data can only be changed under a context whose level is not higher than the data's (e.g. Low data cannot be hoisted under a High context), thus no information can flow from High to Low by manipulating tags; b) When data is downgraded (e.g., changed from High to Low) the data is automatically *zeroed* instantly to avoid leakage.

The logic for checking, changing the tag and zeroing the data is generated by the Sapper compiler.

3.4 Violation Handling

To give hardware designers full flexibility to decide how to react to runtime security violations, Sapper provides a language interface for specifying the behavior when violation is *about* to happen. The syntax is: [*command*] *otherwise* [*actions*]; which specifies that if there exists any security violation in *command*, *actions* will be executed in replace of *command*. Our compiler will analyze every command that requires enforcement, derive necessary checks (in the form of security tag comparisons) that guarantees noninterference, and insert them into the design. The above code will become the following after compilation: *if* (*derived condition*) [*command*] *else* [*actions*].

Note that *command* will never be speculatively executed, instead, only one of *actions* and *command* will get executed depending on the value of condition. In the case when designers do not provide "otherwise" for commands that require enforcement, our compiler will automatically insert default "otherwise" actions that are guaranteed to be secure (e.g., disabling the operation to make it a noop). These *otherwise* rules can be defined recursively, meaning that the action in the otherwise branch can itself have an otherwise clause. These nested otherwise clauses are terminated by the default, guaranteed safe action; thus all commands in the program are guaranteed to be secure even if designers provide buggy otherwise clauses.

4. Related Work

Denning and Denning were one of the first to show that high level programming language techniques aided by static analysis can be used to enforce information flow policies [8]. This approach was formalized by Volpano [33] and is often implemented as language extensions to existing languages [22, 28]. A more comprehensive study of programming language techniques related to information flow security is found in the survey by Sabelfeld and Myers [26]. Other systems have explored tradeoffs between static and dynamic approaches [29], exploring the space between these two extremes—for example, inserting dynamic checks into the program and then using static analysis to verify that the program will be secure at runtime [4, 21, 25, 27].

While language-level techniques provide strong guarantees inside applications, security enforcement between applications relies on an underlying operating system. There are many approaches tackling this problem from different angles [15–17, 24, 35]. Security mechanisms at the OS level cannot provide full hardware / software system security guarantees in the face of adversaries that take advantage of information leakage in the underlying hardware implementation, such as through caches [23] and branch predictors [2]. Specific secure hardware component designs have been proposed to defend against existing covert channel attacks [34]. More systematic approaches have also been proposed to control timing channels through software/hardware contracts [36], quantitative measurements [7] or fuzzing mechanisms [20]. Towards this end, various approaches have been proposed in previous work towards analyzing and enforcing information flow security in hardware designs, including Gate Level Information Flow Tracking (GLIFT) [31] (and its extensions Execution Lease [30] and Star Logic [32]) and Caisson [18, 19].

GLIFT tracks every single bit of information in the system through each logic gate. Every bit in the system is associated with a shadow bit to represent its security label (either *High* or *Low*), and for every logic gate, a shadow logic is used to calculate the resulting security level based on the security level of inputs as well as the value of inputs. Despite GLIFT's pure dynamic nature, the tracking technique is guaranteed to be complete, i.e. it covers both implicit flows and timing channels, since all forms of information flow become explicit at the gate level. Being a fine-grained dynamic tracking technique, GLIFT can result in a substantial hardware overhead. To reduce this overhead, the authors reworked their method to be used for static analysis in the form of *Star Logic* [32]. It is important to see that Star Logic does not provide assistance or early feedback for hardware designers attempting to create secure hardware; instead it allows for the *after-the-fact static verification of a coordinated processor and kernel design*, which is not the same problem Sapper is solving.

In an attempt to bring a notion of security into hardware design languages, Caisson takes techniques from information flow security at the language level and applies them to HDLs, making it possible to verify hardware security policies during design. In Caisson, registers and wires are declared with static security types, and typing rules are used to enforce security policies. To avoid having to treat the design as simply a network of gates (as in GLIFT) and to allow secure switching between High states and Low states, Caisson requires an explicit state-machine-based model for designing hardware. Despite the simplicity of static type checking, it comes with two major problems: a) statically verifying those properties requires that resources be hard partitioned or even duplicated, resulting in large area overheads; and b) there is no way for the system to ever examine, react to, or affect the flow of program metadata (i.e., security labels). Labels are strictly a concept used for analysis, and have no physical manifestation in the final design.

While these past approaches represent a first generation of secure hardware design tools, both the expressiveness of those techniques (the class of hardware systems that could be shown to be secure) and the efficiency of their implementations (the amount of extra logic required to perform checks) can be prohibitively poor.

5. Conclusions and Future Work

As the current technology trends point to increasingly complex hardware platforms and more special-purpose functionality, it is time to reexamine the common assumptions that hardware is both unchangeable and always completely correct with respect to the documentation. While hardware security is a large area to explore, information flow properties are one important aspect of any secure design. This paper is a step towards a new class of tools that inform hardware designers of the information flow ramifications of their design choices and assist them in guarding against unforeseen exploits. We prototype a novel hardware description language that automatically augments a hardware design with appropriate security checks so that it is impossible to violate secrecy or integrity as defined by a policy lattice. The formal semantics and compilation tool-chain is still under development.

There are still many details to be filled in and open questions remaining, such as what kind of hardware and systems can be built using Sapper. We are aiming at using Sapper to design fully functional processors that contain modern architectural components and that are able to run realistic applications.

Acknowledgments

This research was supported by NSF CCF-1117165. The views and conclusions contained herein are those of the authors and should not be interpreted as necessarily representing the official policies or endorsements, either expressed or implied, of the sponsoring agencies.

References

[1] OpenSPARC: World's first free 64-bit microprocessors. http://www.opensparc.net.

[2] O. Accigmez, J. pierre Seifert, and C. K. Koc. Predicting secret keys via branch prediction. In *The Cryptographers' Track at the RSA Conference*, 2007.

[3] T. Alves. Trustzone: Integrated hardware and software security. *ARM white paper*, 3(4), 2004.

[4] T. H. Austin and C. Flanagan. Efficient purely-dynamic information flow analysis. In *Proceedings of the ACM SIGPLAN Fourth Workshop on Programming Languages and Analysis for Security*, PLAS '09, pages 113–124, New York, NY, USA, 2009. ACM.

[5] R. Benadjila, O. Billet, S. Gueron, and M. J. Robshaw. The intel aes instructions set and the sha-3 candidates. In *Proceedings of the 15th International Conference on the Theory and Application of Cryptology and Information Security: Advances in Cryptology*, ASIACRYPT '09, pages 162–178, Berlin, Heidelberg, 2009. Springer-Verlag.

[6] E. Clarke, O. Grumberg, and D. Peled. *Model checking*. MIT press, 2000.

[7] J. Demme, R. Martin, A. Waksman, and S. Sethumadhavan. Side-channel vulnerability factor: a metric for measuring information leakage. In *Proceedings of the 39th Annual International Symposium on Computer Architecture*, ISCA '12, pages 106–117, Washington, DC, USA, 2012. IEEE Computer Society.

[8] D. E. Denning and P. J. Denning. Certification of programs for secure information flow. *Communications of the ACM*, 20(7):504–513, 1977.

[9] A. Gattiker. An overview of integrated circuit testing methods. *Microelectronics Failure Analysis Desk Reference*, page 190, 2011.

[10] D. Gullasch, E. Bangerter, and S. Krenn. Cache games – bringing access-based cache attacks on aes to practice. In *Security and Privacy*, 2011.

[11] Intel Corporation. AAJ1 Clarification of TRANSLATION LOOKASIDE BUFFERS, Intel® Core^{TM} i7-900 Desktop Processor Extreme Edition Series and Intel® Core^{TM} i7–900 Desktop Processor Series Datasheet. May 2011.

[12] V. Kashyap, B. Wiedermann, and B. Hardekopf. Timing- and termination-sensitive secure information flow: Exploring a new approach. In *IEEE Symposium on Security and Privacy*, 2011.

[13] K. Kaspersky and A. Chang. Remote code execution through Intel CPU bugs. In *Hack In The Box (HITB) 2008 Malaysia Conference*.

[14] C. Kern and M. Greenstreet. Formal verification in hardware design: a survey. *ACM Transactions on Design Automation of Electronic Systems (TODAES)*, 4(2):123–193, 1999.

[15] G. Klein, K. Elphinstone, G. Heiser, J. Andronick, D. Cock, P. Derrin, D. Elkaduwe, K. Engelhardt, R. Kolanski, M. Norrish, T. Sewell, H. Tuch, and S. Winwood. sel4: formal verification of an os kernel. In *Proceedings of the ACM SIGOPS 22nd symposium on Operating systems principles*, SOSP '09, pages 207–220, New York, NY, USA, 2009. ACM.

[16] M. Krohn and E. Tromer. Noninterference for a practical difc-based operating system. In *Security and Privacy*, 2009.

[17] M. Krohn, A. Yip, M. Brodsky, N. Cliffer, M. F. Kaashoek, E. Kohler, and R. Morris. Information flow control for standard os abstractions. In *Proceedings of twenty-first ACM SIGOPS symposium on Operating systems principles*, SOSP '07, pages 321–334, New York, NY, USA, 2007. ACM.

[18] X. Li, M. Tiwari, B. Hardekopf, T. Sherwood, and F. T. Chong. Secure information flow analysis for hardware design: using the right abstraction for the job. In *Proceedings of the 5th ACM SIGPLAN Workshop on Programming Languages and Analysis for Security*, PLAS '10, pages 8:1–8:7, New York, NY, USA, 2010. ACM.

[19] X. Li, M. Tiwari, J. K. Oberg, V. Kashyap, F. T. Chong, T. Sherwood, and B. Hardekopf. Caisson: a hardware description language for secure information flow. In *Proceedings of the 32nd ACM SIGPLAN conference on Programming language design and implementation*, PLDI '11, pages 109–120, New York, NY, USA, 2011. ACM.

[20] R. Martin, J. Demme, and S. Sethumadhavan. Timewarp: rethinking timekeeping and performance monitoring mechanisms to mitigate side-channel attacks. In *Proceedings of the 39th Annual International Symposium on Computer Architecture*, ISCA '12, pages 118–129, Washington, DC, USA, 2012. IEEE Computer Society.

[21] S. Moore and S. Chong. Static analysis for efficient hybrid information-flow control. In *Proceedings of the 2011 IEEE 24th Computer Security Foundations Symposium*, CSF '11, pages 146–160, Washington, DC, USA, 2011.

[22] A. C. Myers, N. Nystrom, L. Zheng, and S. Zdancewic. Jif: Java information flow. Software release. http://www.cs.cornell.edu/jif, 2001.

[23] C. Percival. Cache missing for fun and profit. In *Proc. of BSDCan*, 2005.

[24] I. Roy, D. E. Porter, M. D. Bond, K. S. McKinley, and E. Witchel. Laminar: practical fine-grained decentralized information flow control. In *Proceedings of the 2009 ACM SIGPLAN conference on Programming language design and implementation*, PLDI '09, pages 63–74, New York, NY, USA, 2009. ACM.

[25] A. Russo and A. Sabelfeld. Dynamic vs. static flow-sensitive security analysis. In *Proceedings of the 2010 23rd IEEE Computer Security Foundations Symposium*, CSF '10, pages 186–199, Washington, DC, USA, 2010. IEEE Computer Society.

[26] A. Sabelfeld and A. C. Myers. Language-based information-flow security. *IEEE Journal on Selected Areas in Communications*, 21(1), Jan. 2003.

[27] A. Sabelfeld and A. Russo. From dynamic to static and back: Riding the roller coaster of information-flow control research. In *Ershov Memorial Conference*, 2009.

[28] V. Simonet. Flow Caml in a nutshell. In *Proceedings of the first APPSEM-II workshop*, 2003.

[29] G. E. Suh, J. W. Lee, D. Zhang, and S. Devadas. Secure program execution via dynamic information flow tracking. In *Proceedings of the 11th international conference on Architectural support for programming languages and operating systems*, ASPLOS XI, pages 85–96, New York, NY, USA, 2004. ACM.

[30] M. Tiwari, X. Li, H. M. G. Wassel, F. T. Chong, and T. Sherwood. Execution leases: a hardware-supported mechanism for enforcing strong non-interference. In *Proceedings of the 42nd Annual IEEE/ACM International Symposium on Microarchitecture*, MICRO 42, pages 493–504, New York, NY, USA, 2009. ACM.

[31] M. Tiwari, H. M. Wassel, B. Mazloom, S. Mysore, F. T. Chong, and T. Sherwood. Complete information flow tracking from the gates up. In *Proceedings of the 14th international conference on Architectural support for programming languages and operating systems*, ASPLOS XIV, pages 109–120, New York, NY, USA, 2009. ACM.

[32] M. Tiwari, J. K. Oberg, X. Li, J. Valamehr, T. Levin, B. Hardekopf, R. Kastner, F. T. Chong, and T. Sherwood. Crafting a usable microkernel, processor, and i/o system with strict and provable information flow security. In *Proceedings of the 38th annual international symposium on Computer architecture*, ISCA '11, pages 189–200, New York, NY, USA, 2011. ACM.

[33] D. Volpano, C. Irvine, and G. Smith. A sound type system for secure flow analysis. *J. Comput. Secur.*, 4, 1996.

[34] Z. Wang and R. B. Lee. A novel cache architecture with enhanced performance and security. In *Proceedings of the 41st annual IEEE/ACM International Symposium on Microarchitecture*, MICRO 41, pages 83–93, Washington, DC, USA, 2008. IEEE Computer Society.

[35] N. Zeldovich, S. Boyd-Wickizer, E. Kohler, and D. Mazières. Making information flow explicit in histar. In *Proceedings of the 7th USENIX Symposium on Operating Systems Design and Implementation - Volume 7*, OSDI '06, pages 19–19, Berkeley, CA, USA, 2006. USENIX Association.

[36] D. Zhang, A. Askarov, and A. C. Myers. Language-based control and mitigation of timing channels. In *Proceedings of the 33rd ACM SIGPLAN conference on Programming Language Design and Implementation*, PLDI '12, pages 99–110, New York, NY, USA, 2012. ACM.

Trusted JavaScript Semantics

Philippa Gardner
Imperial College London
London, UK
pg@doc.ic.ac.uk

Type-based Dependency Analysis for JavaScript

Matthias Keil Peter Thiemann
Institute for Computer Science
University of Freiburg
Freiburg, Germany
{keilr,thiemann}@informatik.uni-freiburg.de

Abstract

Dependency analysis is a program analysis that determines potential data flow between program points. While it is not a security analysis per se, it is a viable basis for investigating data integrity, for ensuring confidentiality, and for guaranteeing sanitization. A noninterference property can be stated and proved for the dependency analysis.

We have designed and implemented a dependency analysis for JavaScript. We formalize this analysis as an abstraction of a tainting semantics. We prove the correctness of the tainting semantics, the soundness of the abstraction, a noninterference property, and the termination of the analysis.

Categories and Subject Descriptors F.3.2 [*LOGICS AND MEANINGS OF PROGRAMS*]: Semantics of Programming Languages—Program analysis; D.3.1 [*PROGRAMMING LANGUAGES*]: Formal Definitions and Theory—Semantics ; D.4.6 [*OPERATING SYSTEMS*]: Security and Protection—Information flow controls

General Terms Security

Keywords Type-based Analysis, Dependency, JavaScript

1. Introduction

Security Engineering is one of the challenges of modern software development. The connected world we live in consists of interacting entities that process distributed private data. This data has to be protected against illegal usage, tampering, and theft.

Web applications are one popular example of such interacting entities. They run in the web browser and consist of program fragments from different sources (e.g., mashups). Such fragments should not be entrusted with sensitive information. However, if a fragment's input data can be shown not to depend on confidential data, then it cannot divulge this data or tamper with it.

A Web application may also be vulnerable to an injection attack. Such an attack arises when data is stored in a database or in the DOM without proper escaping. If an analysis can determine that the input to the database never depends directly on a data source (like an HTML input field), but rather is always filtered by a suitable sanitizer, then many kinds of injection attacks can be avoided.

Dependency analysis is a program analysis that can help in both situations, because it determines potential data flow between program points. Intuitively, there is a dependency between the value in variable x and the value of an expression $e[x]$ containing the variable if substituting different expressions e' for x may change the value of $e[e']$. In our application we label data sources (e.g., as confidential) in a JavaScript program and are interested in identifying the potential sinks reachable from these data sources. For sanitization, we instrument sanitizers with a relabeling operation that modifies the dependency on the original data source to a sanitized dependency. We consider a data sink safe, if it only depends on data that passed through a sanitizer. Other uses of dependency information for optimization or parallelization are possible, but not considered in this work.

We designed and implemented our dependency analysis as an extension of TAJS [15], a type analyzer for JavaScript. The implementation allows us to label data sources with a $\mathbf{trace}^{\ell}$ marker and to indicate relabelings with an $\mathbf{untrace}^{(\mathcal{A} \hookrightarrow \mathcal{A}')}$ marker. The analysis performs an abstract interpretation to approximate the flow of the markers throughout the program. The marker is part of the analyzed type and propagated to all program points that depend on a marked value.

Part of our work consists in establishing the formal underpinnings of the implemented analysis. Thus, we outline a correctness proof for the dependency part of the analysis. For conducting the proofs, we have simplified the domains with respect to the implementation to avoid an overly complex formal system. To this end, we formalize the dynamic semantics of a JavaScript core language, extend that with marker propagation, and then formalize the abstract inter-

PLAS'13, June 20, 2013, Seattle, WA, USA.

pretation of this extended semantics. Both, concrete and abstract semantics are given as big-step semantics. We prove sound marker propagation, sound approximation of the dynamic semantics by its abstract counterpart, noninterference, and the termination of the analysis.

Contributions

- Design and implementation of a type-based dependency analysis based on TAJS [15].
- Formalization of the analysis.
- Proofs of correctness and termination.
- Extension of the analysis for sanitization (Section 7).
- A noninterference theorem (Section 8).

Overview Section 2 considers some example scenarios of our implemented system. Section 3 formalizes a core language, its dynamic semantics, and defines noninterference semantically. Section 4 extends this semantics with tainting. Section 5 defines the corresponding abstraction, Section 6 gives some example applications, and Section 7 defines the extension for sanitization. Section 8 contains our theorems of soundness, noninterference, and termination. Section 9 briefly describes the implementation. Related work is discussed in Section 10 followed by a conclusion.

A technical report [18] is available with all technical details including the proofs.

2. Application Scenario

Web developers rely on third-party libraries for calendars, maps, social networks, and so on. To create a trustworthy application, they should ensure that these libraries do not leak sensitive information of their users.

One way to avoid such leaks is to detect information flow from confidential data sources to untrusted sinks by program analysis and take measures to avoid this flow. Sometimes, this approach is too restrictive, because the data arriving at the sink has been sanitized on the way from the source. Sanitization can take many forms: data may have been encrypted or a username/password combination may have been reduced to a boolean. In such cases, the resulting data still depends on the confidential source, but it can be safely declassified and passed on to an untrusted sink.

An analogous scenario is the avoidance of injection attacks where direct dependencies of database queries or DOM contents from input fields in a Web form should be avoided. However, an indirect dependency via a sanitizer that, in this case, escapes the values suitably is acceptable.

Our dependency analysis addresses both scenarios as illustrated with the following examples.

2.1 Cookies

A web developer might want to ensure that the code does not read sensitive data from cookies and sends it to the net. Technically, it means that data that is passed to network send operations must not depend on document.cookie. This dependency can be checked by our analysis.

```
var userHandler = function(uid) {
   var userData = {name:''};
   var onSuccess = function(response) {
      userData = response;
   };

   if (Cookie.isset(uid)) {
      Cookie.request(uid, onSuccess);
   } else {
      Ajax.request('http:\\example.org', {
         content : uid
      }, onSuccess);
   }

   return {
      getName : function() {
         return userData.name;
      }
   }
};
var name1 = userHandler(trace("uid1")).getName();
var name2 = userHandler(trace("uid2")).getName();
```

Figure 1. Loading sensitive data.

To label data sources, our implementation reads a configuration file with a list of JavaScript objects that are labeled with a dependency mark before starting the analysis. Any predefined value or function can be marked in this way. For this example, the analyzer is to label document.cookie with t0.

Values that are written to a cookie are labeled by wrapping them in a trace expression. The analysis determines that values returned from cookies are influenced by document.cookie. Furthermore, after writing a marked value to a cookie, each subsequent read operation returns a value that depends on it.

The following code snippet uses a standard library for reading and writing cookies. The comments show the analyzed dependencies of the respective values.

```
var val1 = readCookie('test');  // d(val1)={t0}
var val2 = trace(4711);         // d(val2)={t1}
writeCookie('test', val2);
var val3 = readCookie('test');  // d(val3)={t0,t1}
```

Thus, the read value in val1 is influenced by document.cookie. The value in val2 is labeled by a fresh mark t1. Later, this value is written to the cookie. Hence, the result val3 of the last read operation is influenced by document.cookie and val2.

2.2 Application: Sensitive Data

The next example is to illustrate the underpinnings of our analysis and to point out differences to other techniques. Figure 1 shows a code fragment to request the user name corresponding to a user id. This data is either read from a cookie or obtained by an Ajax request.

The function userHandler returns an interface to a user's personal data. The implementation abstracts from the data source by using a callback function onSuccess to handle the results. The code ignores the problem that userData may not be valid before completion of the Ajax request.

To detect all values depending on user information, a developer would mark the id. This mark should propagate to

```
loadForeignCode = trace(function() {
   Array.prototype.foreach = function(callback) {
      for ( var k = 0; k < this.length; k++) {
         callback(k, this[k]);
      }
   };
});
loadForeignCode();
// [..]
var array = new Array(4711, 4712);
array.foreach(function(k, v) {
   result = k + v;
});
```

Figure 2. Using foreign Code.

values returned from Cookie.request() and Ajax.request(). Because we are interested in values depending on Cookie.request() and Ajax.request() the interfaces also get marked.

The conditional in line 7 depends on Cookie.isset(uid) and thus on uid and on the cookie interface. The value in userData (line 4) depends on uid, on the cookie interface, and on Cookie.isset(uid) from the Ajax interface. The result name1 depends on userData.name and therefore on the user id, the cookie interface, and potentially on the Ajax interface.

Standard security analyses label values with marks drawn from a security lattice, often just *Low* and *High*. If both sources, the cookie interface and the Ajax interface, are labeled with the same mark, there is no way to distinguish these sources. Dependencies allow us a to formulate security properties on a fine level of granularity that distinguishes different sources without changing the underlying lattice.

Second, our analysis is flow-sensitive. Dependencies are bound to values instead of variable names or parameters. A variable may containt different values depending on different sources during evaluation. In addition, the underlying TAJS implementation already handles aliasing and polyvariant analysis in a satisfactory way.

In the example, the values in name1 and name2 result from the same function but may depend on different sources. The flow-sensitive model retains the independence of the value in name1 and trace("uid2"). Section 6.1 discusses the actual outcome of the analysis.

2.3 Application: Foreign Code

The second scenario (Figure 2) illustrates one way a library can extend existing functionality. This example extends the prototype of Array by a foreach function. Later on, this function is used to iterate over elements.

The goal here is to protect code from being compromised by the libraries used. The function loadForeignCode encapsulates foreign code and is labeled as a source. In consequence, all values created or modified by calling loadForeignCode depend on this function and contain its mark. Because the function in the foreach property gets marked, the values in result also get marked. Therefore, result may be influenced by loading foreign code. See Section 6.2 for the results of the analysis.

```
1  $ = function(id) {
2    return trace(document.getElementById(id).value, "#DOM");
3  }
4  function sanitizer(value) {
5    /* clean up value ... */
6    return untrace(value, "#DOM");
7  }
8  // [...]
9  var input = $("text");
10 var secureInput = sanitizer(input);
11 consumer(secureInput);
```

Figure 3. Analyzing sanitization.

2.4 Application: Sanitization

Noninterference is not the only interesting property that can be investigated with the dependency analyzer. To avoid injection attacks, programmers should ensure that only escaped values occur in a database query or become part of an HTML page. Also, a dependency on a secret data source may be acceptable if the data is encrypted before being published. These examples illustrate the general idea of sanitization where a suitable function needs to be interposed in the dataflow between certain sources and sinks.

The concrete example in Figure 3 applies our analysis to the problem. The input is labeled with mark #DOM (line 2). The function in line 4 performs some (unspecified) sanitization and finally applies the untrace function to mark the dependency on the marks identified with #DOM as a sanitized, safe dependency. The argument of the consumer can now be checked for dependencies on unsanitized values. In the example code, the analysis determines that the argument depends on the DOM, but that the dependency is sanitized.

Changing line 10 as indicated below leaves the argument of the consumer with a mixture of sanitized and unsanitized dependencies. This mixture could be flagged as an error.

```
var secureInput =
  i_know_what_i_do ? sanitizer(input) : input;
```

3. Formalization

This section presents the JavaScript core calculus λ_J along with a semantic definition of independence.

3.1 Syntax of λ_J

λ_J is inspired by JavaScript core calculi from the literature [11, 14]. A λ_J expression (Figure 4) is either a constant c (a boolean, a number, a string, **undefined**, or **null**), a variable x, a lambda expression, an application, a primitive operation, a conditional, an object creation, a property reference, a property assignment, or a trace expression.

The trace expression is novel to our calculus. It creates marked values that can be tracked by our dependency analysis. The expression $\mathbf{new}^{\ell}\ e$ creates an object whose prototype is the result of e. The lambda expression, the new expression, and the trace expression carry a unique mark ℓ.

$$
\begin{aligned}
e \quad ::= \quad & c \mid x \mid \lambda^\ell x.e \mid e(e) \mid \mathbf{op}(e,e) \\
\mid \quad & \mathbf{if}\,(e)\; e,\; e \mid \mathbf{new}^\ell\; e \mid e[e] \mid e[e] = e \mid \mathbf{trace}^\ell(e)
\end{aligned}
$$

$$
\begin{array}{llll}
\textit{Location} & \ni \xi^\ell & & \\
\textit{Value} & \ni v & ::= & c \mid \xi^\ell \\
\textit{Prototype} & \ni p & ::= & v \\
\textit{Closure} & \ni f & ::= & \emptyset \mid \langle \rho, \lambda^\ell x.e \rangle \\
\textit{Object} & \ni o & ::= & \emptyset \mid o[\textit{str} \mapsto v] \\
\textit{Storable} & \ni s & ::= & \langle o, f, p \rangle \\
\textit{Environment} & \ni \rho & ::= & \emptyset \mid \rho[x \mapsto v] \\
\textit{Heap} & \ni \mathcal{H} & ::= & \emptyset \mid \mathcal{H}[\xi^\ell \mapsto s]
\end{array}
$$

Figure 4. Syntax and semantic domains of λ_J.

$$
\begin{array}{lll}
\langle o, f, p \rangle(\textit{str}) & ::= & \begin{cases} v, & o = o'[\textit{str} \to v] \\ o'(\textit{str}), & o = o'[\textit{str}' \to v] \\ \mathcal{H}(\xi^\ell)(\textit{str}), & o = \emptyset \wedge p = \xi^\ell \\ \textbf{undefined}, & o = \emptyset \wedge p = c \end{cases} \\
\langle o, f, p \rangle[\textit{str} \mapsto v] & ::= & \langle o[\textit{str} \mapsto v], f, p \rangle \\
\langle o, f, p \rangle_f & ::= & f \\
\mathcal{H}[\xi^\ell, \textit{str} \mapsto v] & ::= & \mathcal{H}[\xi^\ell \mapsto \mathcal{H}(\xi^\ell)[\textit{str} \mapsto v]] \\
\mathcal{H}[\xi^\ell \mapsto \emptyset] & ::= & \mathcal{H}[\xi^\ell \mapsto \langle \emptyset, \emptyset, \textbf{null} \rangle] \\
\mathcal{H}[\xi^\ell \mapsto o] & ::= & \mathcal{H}[\xi^\ell \mapsto \langle o, \emptyset, \textbf{null} \rangle] \\
\mathcal{H}[\xi^\ell \mapsto f] & ::= & \mathcal{H}[\xi^\ell \mapsto \langle \emptyset, f, \textbf{null} \rangle] \\
\mathcal{H}[\xi^\ell \mapsto p] & ::= & \mathcal{H}[\xi^\ell \mapsto \langle \emptyset, \emptyset, p \rangle]
\end{array}
$$

Figure 5. Abbreviations.

3.2 Semantic domains

Figure 4 also defines the semantic domains of λ_J. A heap maps a location ξ^ℓ to a storable s, which is a triple consisting of an object o, potentially a function closure f (only for function objects), and a value p, which serves as the prototype. The superscript ℓ refers the expression causing the allocation. An object o maps a string to a value. A closure consists of an environment ρ and an expression e. The environment ρ maps a variable to a value v, which may be a base type constant or a location.

Program execution is modeled by a big-step evaluation judgment of the form $\mathcal{H}, \rho \vdash e \Downarrow \mathcal{H}' \mid v$. The evaluation of expression e in an initial heap $\mathcal{H}$ and environment ρ results in the final heap $\mathcal{H}'$ and the value v. We omit its standard definition for space reasons, but show excerpts of an augmented semantics in Section 4.

Figure 5 introduces some abbreviated notation. A property lookup or a property update on a storable $s = \langle o, f, p \rangle$ is relayed to the underlying object. The property access $s(\textit{str})$ returns **undefined** by default if the accessed string is not defined in o and the prototype of s is not a location ξ^ℓ. We write s_f for the closure in s. The notation $\mathcal{H}[\xi^\ell, \textit{str} \mapsto v]$ updates a property of storable $\mathcal{H}(\xi^\ell)$, $\mathcal{H}[\xi^\ell \mapsto o]$ initializes an object, and $\mathcal{H}[\xi^\ell \mapsto f]$ defines a function.

3.3 Independence

The $\mathbf{trace}^\ell$ expression serves to mark a program point as a source of sensitive data. An expression e is independent from that source if the value of the $\mathbf{trace}^\ell$ expression does not influence the final result of e. The first definition formalizes replacing the argument of a $\mathbf{trace}^\ell$ expression.

Definition 1. *The substitution $e[\ell \mapsto \tilde{e}]$ of ℓ in e by $\tilde{e}$ is defined as the homomorphic extension of*

$$
\textit{trace}^\ell(e')[\ell \mapsto \tilde{e}] \equiv \textit{trace}^\ell(\tilde{e}) \tag{1}
$$

Definition 2 (incomplete first attempt)**.** *The expression e is independent from ℓ iff all possible substitutions of ℓ are unobservable.*

$$
\begin{aligned}
\forall e_1, e_2 :\ & \mathcal{H}, \rho \vdash e[\ell \mapsto e_1] \Downarrow \mathcal{H}_1 \mid v \\
\leftrightarrow\ & \mathcal{H}, \rho \vdash e[\ell \mapsto e_2] \Downarrow \mathcal{H}_2 \mid v
\end{aligned} \tag{2}
$$

This definition covers both, the terminating and the non-terminating cases. Furthermore, we consider direct dependencies, indirect dependencies, and transitive dependencies, similar to the behavior described by Denning [8, 9]. In Section 8, we complete this definition to make it amenable to proof.

4. Dependency Tracking Semantics

To attach marker propagation for upcoming values we apply definition 2 to the λ_J calculus. The later on derived abstract interpretation is formalized on this extended calculus.

This section extends the semantics of λ_J with mark propagation. The resulting calculus $\lambda_J^{\mathcal{D}}$ *only* provides a baseline calculus for subsequent static analysis. $\lambda_J^{\mathcal{D}}$ is *specifically not* meant to perform any kind of dynamic analysis, where the presence or absence of a mark in a value guarantees some dependency related property.

The calculus extends *Value* to *Tainted Value* $\ni \omega ::= v : \kappa$ where $\kappa ::= \emptyset \mid \ell \mid \kappa \bullet \kappa$ is a dependency annotation. *Tainted Value* replaces *Value* in objects and environments. The operation $\bullet$ joins two dependencies. If $\omega = v : \kappa_v$ then write $\omega \bullet \kappa$ for $v : \kappa_v \bullet \kappa$ to apply a dependency annotation to a value.

The big-step evaluation judgment $\mathcal{H}, \rho, \kappa \vdash e \Downarrow \mathcal{H}' \mid \omega$ for $\lambda_J^{\mathcal{D}}$ extends the one for λ_J by a new component κ which tracks the context dependency for expression e. Figure 6 contains its defining inference rules.

The evaluation rules (DT-CONST), (DT-VAR), and (DT-ABS) are trivial. Their return values depend on the context. (DT-OP) calculates the result on the value part and combines the dependencies of the involved values. $\Downarrow_{\mathbf{op}}^v$ stands for the application of operator **op**. The rule (DT-NEW) binds the dependency of the evaluated prototype to the returned location. During (DT-APP) the dependency of the value referencing the function is bound to the sub-context. In a similar

(DT-CONST)

$$\frac{}{\mathcal{H}, \rho, \kappa \vdash c \Downarrow \mathcal{H} \mid c : \kappa}$$

(DT-VAR)

$$\frac{}{\mathcal{H}, \rho, \kappa \vdash x \Downarrow \mathcal{H} \mid \rho(x) \bullet \kappa}$$

(DT-ABS)

$$\frac{\xi^\ell \notin dom(\mathcal{H})}{\mathcal{H}, \rho, \kappa \vdash \lambda^\ell x.e \Downarrow \mathcal{H}[\xi^\ell \mapsto \langle \rho, \lambda^\ell x.e \rangle] \mid \xi^\ell : \kappa}$$

(DT-OP)

$$\frac{\begin{array}{c}\mathcal{H}, \rho, \kappa \vdash e_0 \Downarrow \mathcal{H}' \mid v_0 : \kappa_0 \\ \mathcal{H}', \rho, \kappa \vdash e_1 \Downarrow \mathcal{H}'' \mid v_1 : \kappa_1 \\ v_{op} = \Downarrow^v_{\mathbf{op}} (v_0, v_1)\end{array}}{\mathcal{H}, \rho, \kappa \vdash \mathbf{op}(e_0, e_1) \Downarrow \mathcal{H}'' \mid v_{op} : \kappa_0 \bullet \kappa_1}$$

(DT-NEW)

$$\frac{\mathcal{H}, \rho, \kappa \vdash e \Downarrow \mathcal{H}' \mid v : \kappa_v \qquad \xi^\ell \notin dom(\mathcal{H})}{\mathcal{H}, \rho, \kappa \vdash \mathbf{new}^\ell\, e \Downarrow \mathcal{H}'[\xi^\ell \mapsto v] \mid \xi^\ell : \kappa_v}$$

(DT-APP)

$$\frac{\begin{array}{c}\mathcal{H}, \rho, \kappa \vdash e_0 \Downarrow \mathcal{H}' \mid \xi^\ell : \kappa_0 \\ \langle o, \langle \dot\rho, \lambda^\ell x.e \rangle, p \rangle = \mathcal{H}'(\xi^\ell) \\ \mathcal{H}', \rho, \kappa \vdash e_1 \Downarrow \mathcal{H}'' \mid v_1 : \kappa_1 \\ \mathcal{H}'', \dot\rho[x \mapsto v_1 : \kappa_1], \kappa \bullet \kappa_0 \vdash e \Downarrow \mathcal{H}''' \mid v : \kappa_v\end{array}}{\mathcal{H}, \rho, \kappa \vdash e_0(e_1) \Downarrow \mathcal{H}''' \mid v : \kappa_v}$$

(DT-IFTRUE)

$$\frac{\begin{array}{c}\mathcal{H}, \rho, \kappa \vdash e_0 \Downarrow \mathcal{H}' \mid v_0 : \kappa_0 \\ v_0 = true \qquad \mathcal{H}', \rho, \kappa \bullet \kappa_0 \vdash e_1 \Downarrow \mathcal{H}''_1 \mid v_1 : \kappa_1\end{array}}{\mathcal{H}, \rho, \kappa \vdash \mathbf{if}\,(e_0)\, e_1,\, e_2 \Downarrow \mathcal{H}''_1 \mid v_1 : \kappa_1}$$

(DT-IFFALSE)

$$\frac{\begin{array}{c}\mathcal{H}, \rho, \kappa \vdash e_0 \Downarrow \mathcal{H}' \mid v_0 : \kappa_0 \\ v_0 \neq true \qquad \mathcal{H}', \rho, \kappa \bullet \kappa_0 \vdash e_2 \Downarrow \mathcal{H}''_2 \mid v_2 : \kappa_2\end{array}}{\mathcal{H}, \rho, \kappa \vdash \mathbf{if}\,(e_0)\, e_1,\, e_2 \Downarrow \mathcal{H}''_2 \mid v_2 : \kappa_2}$$

(DT-GET)

$$\frac{\begin{array}{c}\mathcal{H}, \rho, \kappa \vdash e_0 \Downarrow \mathcal{H}' \mid \xi^\ell : \kappa_{\xi^\ell} \\ \mathcal{H}', \rho, \kappa \vdash e_1 \Downarrow \mathcal{H}'' \mid str : \kappa_{str}\end{array}}{\mathcal{H}, \rho, \kappa \vdash e_0[e_1] \Downarrow \mathcal{H}'' \mid \mathcal{H}''(\xi^\ell)(str) \bullet \kappa_{\xi^\ell} \bullet \kappa_{str}}$$

(DT-PUT)

$$\frac{\begin{array}{c}\mathcal{H}, \rho, \kappa \vdash e_0 \Downarrow \mathcal{H}' \mid \xi^\ell : \kappa_{\xi^\ell} \\ \mathcal{H}', \rho, \kappa \vdash e_1 \Downarrow \mathcal{H}'' \mid str : \kappa_{str} \\ \mathcal{H}'', \rho, \kappa \vdash e_2 \Downarrow \mathcal{H}''' \mid v : \kappa_v \\ \mathcal{H}'''' = \mathcal{H}'''[\xi^\ell, str \mapsto v : \kappa_v \bullet \kappa_{\xi^\ell} \bullet \kappa_{str}]\end{array}}{\mathcal{H}, \rho, \kappa \vdash e_0[e_1] = e_2 \Downarrow \mathcal{H}'''' \mid v : \kappa_v}$$

(DT-TRACE)

$$\frac{\mathcal{H}, \rho, \kappa \bullet \ell \vdash e \Downarrow \mathcal{H}' \mid v : \kappa_v}{\mathcal{H}, \rho, \kappa \vdash \mathbf{trace}^\ell\,(e) \Downarrow \mathcal{H}' \mid v : \kappa_v}$$

Figure 6. Inference rules of $\lambda_J^{\mathcal{D}}$.

Undefined		::=	$\wp(\{\texttt{undefined}\})$
Null		::=	$\wp(\{\texttt{null}\})$
Bool		::=	$\wp(\{\texttt{true}, \texttt{false}\})$
Num		::=	$NUM^\top_\bot$
String		::=	$STRING^\top_\bot$
Lattice Value	$\ni \mathcal{L}$	::=	*Undefined* × *Null* × *Bool* × *Num* × *String*

Figure 7. Base Type Value Lattice.

Label	$\ni \Xi$	::=	$\{\ell \ldots\}$
Abstract Closure	$\ni \Lambda^\ell$	::=	$\langle \sigma, \lambda^\ell x.e \rangle$
Abstract Object	$\ni \Delta$	::=	$\emptyset \mid \Delta[\mathcal{L} \mapsto \vartheta]$
Abstract Value	$\ni \vartheta$	::=	$\langle \mathcal{L}, \Xi, \mathcal{D} \rangle$
Abstract Storable	$\ni \theta$	::=	$\langle \Delta, \Lambda^\ell, \Xi \rangle$
FunctionStore	$\ni \mathcal{F}$	::=	$\emptyset \mid \mathcal{F}[\ell \mapsto \langle \Gamma, \vartheta, \Gamma, \vartheta \rangle]$
Scope	$\ni \sigma$	::=	$\emptyset \mid \sigma[x \mapsto \vartheta]$
ObjectStore	$\ni \Sigma$	::=	$\emptyset \mid \Sigma[\ell \mapsto \theta]$
State	$\ni \Gamma$	::=	$\langle \Sigma, \mathcal{D} \rangle$
Dependency	$\ni \mathcal{D}$	::=	$\emptyset \mid \ell \mid \mathcal{D} \sqcup \mathcal{D}$

Figure 8. Abstract Semantic Domains.

way (DT-IFTRUE) and (DT-IFFALSE) bind the dependency of the condition to the sub-context. The rule (DT-GET) combines the dependencies of heap location and property reference to the returned value. The rule (DT-PUT) combines these dependencies to the assigned value because the evaluated location and property references affect the write operation and further the value which is accessible at this location.

The trace expression $\mathbf{trace}^\ell\,(e)$ (DT-TRACE) adds the ℓ annotation to the context of expression e. This addition causes all values created or modified in e to be marked with ℓ (e.g. to detect side effects) as stated by the following context dependency lemma.

Lemma 1. *$\mathcal{H}, \rho, \kappa \vdash e \Downarrow \mathcal{H}' \mid v : \kappa_v$ implies that $\kappa \subseteq \kappa_v$.*

The proof is by induction on the relation $\Downarrow$.

5. Abstract Analysis

The analysis is an abstraction of the $\lambda_J^{\mathcal{D}}$ calculus. Its basis is the lattice for base type values (Figure 7), which is a simplified adaptation of the lattice of TAJS [15]. *NUM* is the set of floating point numbers, *STRING* the set of string literals, and the annotation $\cdot^\top_\bot$ turns a set into a flat lattice by adding a bottom and top element. An element of the analysis lattice is a tuple like $\langle \bot, \bot, \texttt{true}, \bot, \text{"x"} \rangle$ which represents a value which is either the boolean value `true` or the string "x". Further, $\langle \bot, \bot, \bot, \top, \bot \rangle$ represents all possible number values. The abstract semantic domains (Figure 8) are similar to the domains arising from the $\lambda_J^{\mathcal{D}}$ calculus except that a set of marks Ξ abstracts a set of concrete locations ξ^ℓ where $\ell \in \Xi$. An abstract value $\vartheta = \langle \mathcal{L}, \Xi, \mathcal{D} \rangle$ is a triple of a lattice element $\mathcal{L}$, object marks Ξ, and dependency $\mathcal{D}$.

Hence, each abstract value represents a set of base type values and a set of objects. We write $\mathcal{L}_\vartheta$ for the analysis lattice, Ξ_ϑ for the marks, and $\mathcal{D}_\vartheta$ for the dependency component of the abstract value ϑ. Each abstract object is identified by the mark ℓ corresponding to the **new**$^\ell$ e expression creating the object. An abstract storable consists of an abstract object, a function closure, and a set of locations representing the prototype. Unlike before, the abstract object maps a lattice element to a value. This mechanism reduces the number of merge operations during the abstract analysis.

The abstract state is a pair $\Gamma = \langle \Sigma, \mathcal{D} \rangle$ where Σ is the mapping from marks to abstract storables. We write Σ_Γ for the object store, and $\mathcal{D}_\Gamma$ for the dependency in Γ. $\Gamma(\Xi)$ provides a set of storables, denoted by Θ. The substitution of $\mathcal{D}$ in Γ written $\Gamma[\mathcal{D} \mapsto \mathcal{D}'] \equiv \langle \Sigma_\Gamma, \mathcal{D}' \rangle$ replaces the state dependency.

To handle recursive function calls we introduce a global function store $\mathcal{F}$, which maps a mark ℓ to two pairs of state Γ and value ϑ. Functions are also identified by marks ℓ. The function store contains the merged result of the last evaluation for each function. The first pair $\Gamma_{In}, \vartheta_{In}$ represents the input state and input parameter of all heretofore taken function calls, the second one $\Gamma_{Out}, \vartheta_{Out}$ the output state and return value. For further use we write $\mathcal{F}(\ell)_{In}$ to select the input, and $\mathcal{F}(\ell)_{Out}$ for the output. The substitutions $\mathcal{F}[\ell, In \mapsto \langle \Gamma, \vartheta \rangle]$ and $\mathcal{F}[\ell, Out \mapsto \langle \Gamma, \vartheta \rangle]$ denotes the store update operation on input or output pairs.

Its inference is stated by the following lemma.

Lemma 2 (Function Store). $\forall \mathcal{F}, \Lambda^\ell, \Gamma, \vartheta$: *If* $\langle \Gamma, \vartheta \rangle \sqsubseteq \mathcal{F}(\ell)_{In}$ *and* $\Lambda^\ell = \langle \dot{\sigma}, \lambda^\ell x.e \rangle$ *then* $\Gamma, \dot{\sigma}[x \mapsto \vartheta] \vdash e \Downarrow \Gamma' \mid \vartheta'$ *and* $\langle \Gamma', \vartheta' \rangle \sqsubseteq \mathcal{F}(\ell)_{Out}$.

The proof is by induction on the derivation of $\Gamma''[\mathcal{D} \mapsto \mathcal{D}_{\Gamma''} \sqcup \mathcal{D}_0] \vdash^{\Theta}_{\text{APP}} \Gamma''(\Xi_0), \vartheta_1 \Downarrow \Gamma''' \mid \vartheta$.

The **trace**$^\ell$ expression registers the dependency from ℓ on all values that pass through it.

The abstraction is defined as relation between $v \in$ *Tainted Value* and $\vartheta \in$ *Abstract Value*.

Definition 3 (Abstraction). *The abstraction* α : *Tainted Value* $\rightarrow$ *Abstract Value is defined as:*

$$\alpha(v : \kappa) ::= \begin{cases} \langle \bot, \{\ell\}, \{\ell | \ell \in \kappa\} \rangle & v = \xi^\ell \\ \langle c, \emptyset, \{\ell | \ell \in \kappa\} \rangle & v = c \end{cases} \tag{3}$$

Definition 4 (Abstract Operation). *The abstract operation* $\Downarrow^\vartheta_{op}$ *is defined in terms of the concrete operation* $\Downarrow^v_{op}$ *as usual:*

$$\begin{aligned} &\Downarrow^\vartheta_{op} (\vartheta_0, \vartheta_1) ::= \\ &\bigsqcup \{ \Downarrow^v_{op} (v_0, v_1) \mid v_0 \in \vartheta_0, v_1 \in \vartheta_1 \} \end{aligned} \tag{4}$$

(A-PROGRAM)

$$\frac{\Gamma_\bot, \sigma_\bot \vdash e \Downarrow \Gamma \mid \vartheta \qquad \vdash^{\mathcal{R},\mathcal{Q}}_{\mathbf{P}} \langle \mathcal{F}_\bot, \Gamma_\bot, \vartheta_\bot \rangle, \langle \mathcal{F}, \Gamma, \vartheta \rangle, e \Downarrow \Gamma' \mid \vartheta'}{\vdash e \Downarrow \Gamma' \mid \vartheta'}$$

(P-ITERATION-NOTEQUALS)

$$\frac{\Gamma_\bot, \sigma_\bot \vdash e \Downarrow \Gamma' \mid \vartheta' \qquad \vdash^{\mathcal{R},\mathcal{Q}}_{\mathbf{P}} \mathcal{R}', \langle \mathcal{F}, \Gamma', \vartheta' \rangle, e \Downarrow \mathcal{Q}}{\vdash^{\mathcal{R},\mathcal{Q}}_{\mathbf{P}} \mathcal{R}, \mathcal{R}', e \Downarrow \mathcal{Q}}$$

(P-ITERATION-EQUALS)

$$\frac{}{\vdash^{\mathcal{R},\mathcal{Q}}_{\mathbf{P}} \mathcal{R}, \mathcal{R}, e \Downarrow \mathcal{R}}$$

Figure 9. Inference rules for program interpretation.

(APP-ITERATION)

$$\frac{\Gamma \vdash^{\Lambda^\ell}_{\text{APP}} \Lambda^\ell, \vartheta \Downarrow \Gamma' \mid \vartheta' \qquad \Gamma' \vdash^{\Theta}_{\text{APP}} \Theta, \vartheta \Downarrow \Gamma'' \mid \vartheta''}{\Gamma \vdash^{\Theta}_{\text{APP}} \langle \Delta, \Lambda^\ell, \Xi \rangle; \Theta, \vartheta \Downarrow \Gamma'' \mid \vartheta' \sqcup \vartheta''}$$

(APP-ITERATION-EMPTY)

$$\frac{}{\Gamma \vdash^{\Theta}_{\text{APP}} \emptyset, \vartheta \Downarrow \Gamma \mid \vartheta_\bot}$$

(APP-STORE-SUBSET)

$$\frac{\langle \Gamma, \vartheta \rangle \sqsubseteq \mathcal{F}(\ell)_{In} \qquad \langle \Gamma', \vartheta' \rangle = \mathcal{F}(\ell)_{Out}}{\Gamma \vdash^{\Lambda^\ell}_{\text{APP}} \Lambda^\ell, \vartheta \Downarrow \Gamma' \mid \vartheta'}$$

(APP-STORE-NONSUBSET)

$$\frac{\begin{array}{ll} \langle \Gamma, \vartheta \rangle \not\sqsubseteq \mathcal{F}(\ell)_{In} & \langle \dot{\sigma}, \lambda^\ell x.e \rangle = \Lambda^\ell \\ \langle \bar{\Gamma}, \bar{\vartheta} \rangle = \mathcal{F}(\ell)_{In} \sqcup \langle \Gamma, \vartheta \rangle & \mathcal{F}[\ell, In \mapsto \langle \bar{\Gamma}, \bar{\vartheta} \rangle] \\ \bar{\Gamma}, \dot{\sigma}[x \mapsto \bar{\vartheta}] \vdash e \Downarrow \bar{\Gamma}' \mid \bar{\vartheta}' & \mathcal{F}[\ell, Out \mapsto \langle \bar{\Gamma}', \bar{\vartheta}' \rangle] \end{array}}{\Gamma \vdash^{\Lambda^\ell}_{\text{APP}} \Lambda^\ell, \vartheta \Downarrow \bar{\Gamma}' \mid \bar{\vartheta}'}$$

Figure 11. Inference rules for function application.

This definition implies that:

$$\begin{aligned} &\Downarrow^v_{op} (v_0, v_1) = v_{op} \rightarrow \\ &\Downarrow^\vartheta_{op} (\alpha(v_0), \alpha(v_1)) \sqsupseteq \alpha(v_{op}) \end{aligned} \tag{5}$$

Figures 9, 10, 11, 12, and 13 show the inference rules for the big-step evaluation judgment of the abstract semantics. It has the form $\Gamma, \sigma \vdash e \Downarrow \Gamma' \mid \vartheta$. State Γ and scope σ analyze expression e and result in state Γ' and value ϑ. We use notations similar to Figure 5.

The global program rule (A-PROGRAM) (Figure 9) relies on two auxiliary rules to repeatedly evaluate the program until the analysis state, an element of *Analysis Lattice* consisting of $\mathcal{F}$, Γ and ϑ, becomes stable. In the figure, $\mathcal{R}$, $\mathcal{Q}$ range over *Analysis Lattice* and write $\mathcal{F}_\bot$, $\Gamma_\bot$ and $\sigma_\bot$ for the empty instances of the components.

In Figure 10, the rules for constants (A-CONST) and variables (A-VAR) work similarly as in $\lambda^{\mathcal{D}}_J$.

$$\text{(A-CONST)}\quad \frac{}{\Gamma, \sigma \vdash c \Downarrow \Gamma \mid \langle c, \emptyset, \mathcal{D}_\Gamma \rangle}$$

$$\text{(A-VAR)}\quad \frac{}{\Gamma, \sigma \vdash x \Downarrow \Gamma \mid \sigma(x) \sqcup \mathcal{D}_\Gamma}$$

$$\text{(A-OP)}\quad \frac{\Gamma, \sigma \vdash e_0 \Downarrow \Gamma' \mid \vartheta_0 \quad \Gamma', \sigma \vdash e_1 \Downarrow \Gamma'' \mid \vartheta_1 \quad \langle \mathcal{L}, \Xi \rangle = \Downarrow^{\vartheta}_{\mathbf{op}} (\vartheta_0, \vartheta_1)}{\Gamma, \sigma \vdash \mathbf{op}(e_0, e_1) \Downarrow \Gamma'' \mid \langle \mathcal{L}, \Xi, \mathcal{D}_{\vartheta_0} \sqcup \mathcal{D}_{\vartheta_1} \rangle}$$

$$\text{(A-NEW-NONEXISTING)}\quad \frac{\ell \notin dom(\Gamma) \qquad \Gamma, \sigma \vdash e \Downarrow \Gamma' \mid \langle \mathcal{L}, \Xi, \mathcal{D} \rangle}{\Gamma, \sigma \vdash \mathbf{new}^\ell\ e \Downarrow \Gamma'[\ell \mapsto \Xi] \mid \langle \mathcal{L}_\bot, \{\ell\}, \mathcal{D}_\Gamma \sqcup \mathcal{D} \rangle}$$

$$\text{(A-NEW-EXISTING)}\quad \frac{\ell \in dom(\Gamma) \qquad \Gamma, \sigma \vdash e \Downarrow \Gamma' \mid \langle \mathcal{L}, \Xi, \mathcal{D} \rangle}{\Gamma, \sigma \vdash \mathbf{new}^\ell\ e \Downarrow \Gamma'[\ell \mapsto \Gamma(\ell) \sqcup \langle \emptyset, \Lambda^\ell_\bot, \Xi \rangle] \mid \langle \mathcal{L}_\bot, \{\ell\}, \mathcal{D}_\Gamma \sqcup \mathcal{D} \rangle}$$

$$\text{(A-ABS-NONEXISTING)}\quad \frac{\ell \notin dom(\Gamma) \qquad \mathcal{F}[\ell \mapsto \langle \Gamma_\bot, \vartheta_\bot, \Gamma_\bot, \vartheta_\bot \rangle]}{\Gamma, \sigma \vdash \lambda^\ell x.e \Downarrow \Gamma[\ell \mapsto \langle \sigma, \lambda^\ell x.e \rangle] \mid \langle \mathcal{L}_\bot, \{\ell\}, \mathcal{D}_\Gamma \rangle}$$

$$\text{(A-ABS-EXISTING)}\quad \frac{\ell \in dom(\Gamma) \qquad \langle \dot{\sigma}, \lambda^\ell x.e \rangle = \Gamma(\ell)_{\Lambda^\ell}}{\Gamma, \sigma \vdash \lambda^\ell x.e \Downarrow \Gamma[\ell \mapsto \langle \sigma \sqcup \dot{\sigma}, \lambda^\ell x.e \rangle] \mid \langle \mathcal{L}_\bot, \{\ell\}, \mathcal{D}_\Gamma \rangle}$$

$$\text{(A-APP)}\quad \frac{\Gamma, \sigma \vdash e_0 \Downarrow \Gamma' \mid \langle \mathcal{L}_0, \Xi_0, \mathcal{D}_0 \rangle \quad \Gamma', \sigma \vdash e_1 \Downarrow \Gamma'' \mid \vartheta_1 \quad \Gamma''[\mathcal{D} \mapsto \mathcal{D}_{\Gamma''} \sqcup \mathcal{D}_0] \vdash^{\Theta}_{\text{APP}} \Gamma''(\Xi_0), \vartheta_1 \Downarrow \Gamma''' \mid \vartheta}{\Gamma, \sigma \vdash e_0(e_1) \Downarrow \langle \Sigma_{\Gamma'''}, \mathcal{D}_\Gamma \rangle \mid \vartheta}$$

$$\text{(A-GET)}\quad \frac{\Gamma, \sigma \vdash e_0 \Downarrow \Gamma' \mid \langle \mathcal{L}_0, \Xi_0, \mathcal{D}_0 \rangle \quad \Gamma', \sigma \vdash e_1 \Downarrow \Gamma'' \mid \langle \mathtt{str}, \Xi_1, \mathcal{D}_1 \rangle \quad \Gamma'' \vdash^{\Theta}_{\text{GET}} \Gamma''(\Xi_0), \mathtt{str} \Downarrow \vartheta}{\Gamma, \sigma \vdash e_0[e_1] \Downarrow \Gamma'' \mid \langle \mathcal{L}_\vartheta, \Xi_\vartheta, \mathcal{D}_0 \sqcup \mathcal{D}_1 \sqcup \mathcal{D}_\vartheta \rangle}$$

$$\text{(A-PUT)}\quad \frac{\Gamma, \sigma \vdash e_0 \Downarrow \Gamma' \mid \langle \mathcal{L}_0, \Xi_0, \mathcal{D}_0 \rangle \quad \Gamma', \sigma \vdash e_1 \Downarrow \Gamma'' \mid \langle \mathtt{str}, \Xi_1, \mathcal{D}_1 \rangle \quad \Gamma'', \sigma \vdash e_2 \Downarrow \Gamma''' \mid \vartheta \quad \Gamma''' \vdash^{\Xi}_{\text{PUT}} \Xi_0, \mathtt{str}, \langle \mathcal{L}_\vartheta, \Xi_\vartheta, \mathcal{D}_0 \sqcup \mathcal{D}_1 \sqcup \mathcal{D}_\vartheta \rangle \Downarrow \Gamma''''}{\Gamma, \sigma \vdash e_0[e_1] = e_2 \Downarrow \Gamma'''' \mid \vartheta}$$

$$\text{(A-IFTRUE)}\quad \frac{\Gamma, \sigma \vdash e_0 \Downarrow \Gamma' \mid \langle \mathcal{L}_0, \Xi_0, \mathcal{D}_0 \rangle \quad \mathcal{L}_0 = \mathtt{true} \qquad \Gamma'[\mathcal{D} \mapsto \mathcal{D}_{\Gamma'} \sqcup \mathcal{D}_0], \sigma \vdash e_1 \Downarrow \Gamma'' \mid \vartheta_1}{\Gamma, \sigma \vdash \mathbf{if}\,(e_0)\, e_1,\ e_2 \Downarrow \langle \Sigma_{\Gamma''}, \mathcal{D}_\Gamma \rangle \mid \vartheta_1}$$

$$\text{(A-IFFALSE)}\quad \frac{\Gamma, \sigma \vdash e_0 \Downarrow \Gamma' \mid \langle \mathcal{L}_0, \Xi_0, \mathcal{D}_0 \rangle \quad \mathcal{L}_0 = \mathtt{false} \qquad \Gamma'[\mathcal{D} \mapsto \mathcal{D}_{\Gamma'} \sqcup \mathcal{D}_0], \sigma \vdash e_2 \Downarrow \Gamma'' \mid \vartheta_2}{\Gamma, \sigma \vdash \mathbf{if}\,(e_0)\, e_1,\ e_2 \Downarrow \langle \Sigma_{\Gamma''}, \mathcal{D}_\Gamma \rangle \mid \vartheta_2}$$

$$\text{(A-IF)}\quad \frac{\Gamma, \sigma \vdash e_0 \Downarrow \Gamma' \mid \langle \mathcal{L}_0, \Xi_0, \mathcal{D}_0 \rangle \quad \mathcal{L}_0 \neq \mathtt{true} \wedge \mathcal{L}_0 \neq \mathtt{false} \quad \Gamma'[\mathcal{D} \mapsto \mathcal{D}_{\Gamma'} \sqcup \mathcal{D}_0], \sigma \vdash e_1 \Downarrow \Gamma''_1 \mid \vartheta_1 \quad \Gamma'[\mathcal{D} \mapsto \mathcal{D}_{\Gamma'} \sqcup \mathcal{D}_0], \sigma \vdash e_2 \Downarrow \Gamma''_2 \mid \vartheta_2}{\Gamma, \sigma \vdash \mathbf{if}\,(e_0)\, e_1,\ e_2 \Downarrow \langle \Sigma_{\Gamma''_1} \sqcup \Sigma_{\Gamma''_2}, \mathcal{D}_\Gamma \rangle \mid \vartheta_1 \sqcup \vartheta_2}$$

$$\text{(A-TRACE)}\quad \frac{\Gamma[\mathcal{D} \mapsto \mathcal{D}_\Gamma \sqcup \ell], \sigma \vdash e \Downarrow \Gamma' \mid \vartheta}{\Gamma, \sigma \vdash \mathbf{trace}^\ell\ (e) \Downarrow \langle \Sigma_{\Gamma'}, \mathcal{D}_\Gamma \rangle \mid \vartheta}$$

Figure 10. Inference rules for abstract interpretation.

The object and function creation rules are also omitted. They check if an object or function, referenced by ℓ, already exists. In this case the object or function creation has to merge the prototypes or scopes.

The rule (A-OP) is also standard. As in $\lambda_J^{\mathcal{D}}$ the **trace**$^\ell$ expression (A-TRACE) assigns mark ℓ to the sub-state. The rules for the conditional (A-IF), (A-IFTRUE), and (A-IFFALSE) have to handle the case that it is not possible to distinguish between *true* and *false*. In this case both branches have to be evaluated and the results merged.

Similar problems arise in function application, property reference, and property assignment. Each value can refer to a set of objects including a set of prototypes. Therefore each referenced function has to be evaluated (A-APP) and a property has to be read from (A-GET) or written to (A-PUT) all objects. Results have to be merged. The auxiliary rules are shown in figure 11, 12, and 13.

The rules (APP-ITERATION) and (APP-ITERATION-EMPTY) iterate over all referenced functions. Function application relies on the function store $\mathcal{F}$. Before evaluating the function body, the analyzer checks if the input, consisting of Γ and parameter ϑ, is already subsumed by the stored input. In that case (APP-STORE-SUBSET), the stored result, consisting of output state Γ and return value ϑ, is used.

(GET-ITERATION)

$$\frac{\Gamma \vdash^{\Delta}_{\text{GET}} \Delta, \mathcal{L} \Downarrow \vartheta \quad \Gamma \vdash^{\Theta}_{\text{GET}} \Theta, \mathcal{L} \Downarrow \vartheta' \quad \Gamma \vdash^{\Theta}_{\text{GET}} \Gamma(\Xi), \mathcal{L} \Downarrow \vartheta''}{\Gamma \vdash^{\Theta}_{\text{GET}} \langle \Delta, \Lambda^{\ell}, \Xi \rangle; \Theta, \mathcal{L} \Downarrow \vartheta \sqcup \vartheta' \sqcup \vartheta''}$$

(GET-ITERATION-EMPTY)

$$\frac{}{\Gamma \vdash^{\Theta}_{\text{GET}} \emptyset, \mathcal{L} \Downarrow \vartheta_{\bot}}$$

(GET-INTERSECTION)

$$\frac{\mathcal{L} \sqcap \mathcal{L}_i \neq \bot \quad \Gamma \vdash^{\Theta}_{\text{GET}} \Delta, \mathcal{L} \Downarrow \vartheta'}{\Gamma \vdash^{\Delta}_{\text{GET}} (\mathcal{L}_i : \vartheta_i); \Delta, \mathcal{L} \Downarrow \vartheta_i \sqcup \vartheta'}$$

(GET-NONINTERSECTION)

$$\frac{\mathcal{L} \sqcap \mathcal{L}_i = \bot \quad \Gamma \vdash^{\Theta}_{\text{GET}} \Delta, \mathcal{L} \Downarrow \vartheta'}{\Gamma \vdash^{\Delta}_{\text{GET}} (\mathcal{L}_i : \vartheta_i); \Delta, \mathcal{L} \Downarrow \vartheta'}$$

(GET-EMPTY)

$$\frac{}{\Gamma \vdash^{\Delta}_{\text{GET}} \emptyset, \mathcal{L} \Downarrow \langle \langle \top, \bot, \bot, \bot, \bot \rangle, \emptyset, \emptyset \rangle}$$

Figure 12. Inference rules for property reference.

(PUT-ITERATION)

$$\frac{\Gamma \vdash^{\ell}_{\text{PUT}} \ell, \mathcal{L}, \vartheta \Downarrow \Gamma' \quad \Gamma' \vdash^{\Xi}_{\text{PUT}} \Xi, \mathcal{L}, \vartheta \Downarrow \Gamma''}{\Gamma \vdash^{\Xi}_{\text{PUT}} \ell; \Xi, \mathcal{L}, \vartheta \Downarrow \Gamma''}$$

(PUT-ITERATION-EMPTY)

$$\frac{}{\Gamma \vdash^{\Xi}_{\text{PUT}} \emptyset, \mathcal{L}, \vartheta \Downarrow \Gamma}$$

(PUT-ASSIGNMENT-INDOM)

$$\frac{\mathcal{L} \in dom(\Gamma(\ell))}{\Gamma \vdash^{\ell}_{\text{PUT}} \ell, \mathcal{L}, \vartheta \Downarrow \Gamma[\ell, \mathcal{L} \mapsto \Gamma(\ell)(\mathcal{L}) \sqcup \vartheta]}$$

(PUT-ASSIGNMENT-NOTINDOM)

$$\frac{\mathcal{L} \notin dom(\Gamma(\ell))}{\Gamma \vdash^{\ell}_{\text{PUT}} \ell, \mathcal{L}, \vartheta \Downarrow \Gamma[\ell, \mathcal{L} \mapsto \vartheta]}$$

Figure 13. Inference rules for property assignment.

Otherwise the function body is evaluated (APP-STORE-NONSUBSET) and the store is updated with the result.

For read and write operations the rules (GET-ITERATION), (GET-ITERATION-EMPTY), (PUT-ITERATION) and (PUT-ITERATION-EMPTY) iterate in a similar way over all references. An abstract object maps a lattice element to a value in case a reference is not a singleton value. All entries having an intersection with the reference are affected by the read operation. The prototype-set has to be involved. (GET-INTERSECTION), (GET-NONINTERSECTION) and (GET-EMPTY) shows its inference. Before writing a property, the analyser checks if the property already exists. In this case (PUT-ASSIGNMENT-INDOM), the values get merged. Otherwise (PUT-ASSIGNMENT-NOTINDOM) the value gets assigned. The actual implementation uses a more refined lattice to improve precision.

The abstract interpretation over-approximates the dependencies. The merging of results in (A-IF), (A-APP), (A-GET), and (A-PUT) may cause false positives. While some marked values may be independent from the mark's source, unmarked values are guaranteed to be independent.

6. Applying the Analysis

This section reconsiders the examples Sensitive Data (Section 2.2) and Foreign Code (Section 2.3) from the introduction from an abstract analysis point of view.

6.1 Application: Sensitive Data

Given the newly created mark ℓ_1, the function userHandler is initially called with $\langle\langle\bot,\bot,\bot,\bot,\texttt{uid1}\rangle,\emptyset,\ell_1\rangle$. If the result of calling Cookie.isset can be determined to be `false`, then the dependencies associated with `false` (ℓ_1 and ℓ_c — resulting from the cookie interface) are bound to the conditional's context.

The Ajax request cannot be evaluated. So, response in onSuccess is a value containing the location of an unspecified object like $\emptyset[\langle\bot,\bot,\bot,\bot,\top\rangle \mapsto \langle\langle\bot,\bot,\bot,\bot,\top\rangle,\emptyset,\ell_a\rangle]$ augmented with ℓ_a. In this case, all further calls to onSuccess are already covered by the first input.

By calling the userHandler with "uid2" a new mark ℓ_2 is introduced. This call is not covered by the first one so that the function is reanalyzed with the merged value $\langle\langle\bot,\bot,\bot,\bot, \mathit{String}\rangle,\emptyset,\{\ell_1,\ell_2\}\rangle$. After the analysis has stabilized, name1 also depends on ℓ_2.

The example illustrates that merging functions can result in conservative results. The implementation has a more refined function store which is indexed by a pair of scope σ and source location ℓ to prevent such inaccuracies.

6.2 Application: Foreign Code

The trace expression in line 1 (Section2.3) marks the subcontext for creating the foreach function. The resulting location that points to the function is augmented with this mark. By calling loadForeigenCode the mark is bound to the callees context and finally to the value referencing the foreach function.

By iterating over the array elements (line 11) the dependency annotation is forwarded to the value occurring in result.

Unlike many other security analyses, the objects Array and Array.prototype do not receive marks. If the analysis can determine the updated property exactly, as is the case with foreach, then no other properties can be affected by the update (expect the length). Such an abstract update occurs if the property name is independent from the input. Otherwise, the update happens on a approximated set of property names, all of which are marked by this update.

$$e \ ::= \ \ldots \mid \textbf{trace}^{\ell,\mathcal{A}}(e,\ c) \mid \textbf{untrace}^{(\mathcal{A}\hookrightarrow\mathcal{A}')}(e,\ c)$$

Figure 14. Extended syntax of $\lambda_J^{\mathcal{A}}$.

(DT-TRACE-CLASSIFIED)
$$\frac{\mathcal{H}, \rho, \kappa \bullet \ell^c \vdash e \Downarrow \mathcal{H}' \mid v : \kappa_v}{\mathcal{H}, \rho, \kappa \vdash \textbf{trace}^{\ell,\mathcal{A}}\ (e,\ c) \Downarrow \mathcal{H}' \mid v : \kappa_v}$$

(DT-UNTRACE)
$$\frac{\mathcal{H}, \rho, \kappa \vdash e \Downarrow \mathcal{H}' \mid v : \kappa_v \qquad \kappa' = \kappa_v[\ell^{\mathcal{A},c} \mapsto \ell^{\mathcal{A}',c}]}{\mathcal{H}, \rho, \kappa \vdash \textbf{untrace}^{(\mathcal{A}\hookrightarrow\mathcal{A}')}\ (e,\ c) \Downarrow \mathcal{H}' \mid v : \kappa'}$$

Figure 15. Inference rules of $\lambda_J^{\mathcal{A}}$.

(A-TRACE-CLASSIFIED)
$$\frac{\Gamma[\mathcal{D} \mapsto \mathcal{D}_\Gamma \sqcup \ell^{\mathcal{A},c}], \sigma \vdash e \Downarrow \Gamma' \mid \vartheta}{\Gamma, \sigma \vdash \textbf{trace}^{\ell,\mathcal{A}}\ (e,\ c) \Downarrow \langle \Sigma_{\Gamma'}, \mathcal{D}_\Gamma \rangle \mid \vartheta}$$

(A-UNTRACE)
$$\frac{\Gamma, \sigma \vdash e \Downarrow \Gamma' \mid \vartheta \qquad \mathcal{D}'_\vartheta = \mathcal{D}_\vartheta[\ell^{\mathcal{A},c} \mapsto \ell^{\mathcal{A}',c}]}{\Gamma, \sigma \vdash \textbf{untrace}^{(\mathcal{A}\hookrightarrow\mathcal{A}')}\ (e,\ c) \Downarrow \langle \Sigma_{\Gamma'}, \mathcal{D}_\Gamma \rangle \mid \langle \mathcal{L}_\vartheta, \Xi_\vartheta, \mathcal{D}'_\vartheta \rangle}$$

Figure 16. Inference rules for abstract trace.

6.3 Further sample applications

We also applied our analysis to real-world examples like the *JavaScript Cookie Library with jQuery bindings and JSON support*[1] (version 2.2.0) and the *Rye*[2] library (version 0.1.0), a JavaScript library for DOM manipulation.

These libraries were augmented by wrapping several functions and objects using the trace function. The analysis successfully tracks the flow of the thus marked values, which pop up in the expected places.

7. Dependency Classification

To cater for dependency classification, the accompanying formal framework $\lambda_J^{\mathcal{A}}$ extends $\lambda_J^{\mathcal{D}}$ (Figure 14). In $\lambda_J^{\mathcal{A}}$ marks are classified according to a finite set of modes. They are further augmented by an identifier that can be referred to in the trace and untrace expressions. The operator $\textbf{trace}^{\ell,\mathcal{A}}$ generates a mark in mode $\mathcal{A}$ and the untrace operator changes the mode of all ℓ-marks according to the sanitization method applied (this distinction is ignored in the example). In the calculus, this change is expressed by the $\textbf{untrace}^{(\mathcal{A}\hookrightarrow\mathcal{A}')}$ expression, where $\mathcal{A}$ ranges over an unspecified set of modes.

[1] http://code.google.com/p/cookies/

[2] http://ryejs.com/

Marks $\kappa ::= \ldots \mid \ell^{\mathcal{A},c}$ are extended by an new mark-type, a location classified with a class $\mathcal{A}$ and identifier c.

The mark propagation is like in Section 4 (see Figure 15). Rule (DT-TRACE-CLASSIFIED) augments the sub-context with the new classified mark. (DT-UNTRACE) substitutes location $\ell^{\mathcal{A},c}$ by a declassified location $\ell^{\mathcal{A}',c}$.

In the analysis, $\tau ::= \ell \mid \ell^{\mathcal{A},c}$ replaces ℓ in $\mathcal{D}$. Rule (A-TRACE-CLASSIFIED) (Figure 16) generates new dependencies and (A-UNTRACE) substitutes $\mathcal{A}$ by $\mathcal{A}'$ in all locations ℓ labeled with c.

8. Technical Results

To prove the soundness of our abstract analysis we show termination insensitive noninterference. The required steps are proving noninterference for the $\lambda_J^{\mathcal{D}}$ calculus, showing that the abstract analysis provides a correct abstraction of the $\lambda_J^{\mathcal{D}}$ calculus, and that the abstract analysis terminates.

8.1 Noninterference

Proving noninterference requires relating different substitution instances of the same expression. As they may evaluate differently, we need to be able to cater for differences in the heap, for example, with respect to locations.

Definition 5. *A renaming* $\flat ::= \emptyset \mid \flat[\xi^\ell \mapsto \xi^{\ell\prime}]$ *is a partial mapping on locations where* $\flat(\xi^\ell)$ *carries the same mark* ℓ *as* ξ^ℓ.

It extends to values by $\flat(c) = c$.

In the upcoming definitions, the dependency annotation κ contains the marks created by the selected $\textbf{trace}^\ell$ expression, the body of which may be substituted.

Further, we introduce equivalence relations for each element affected by the ℓ substitution.

Definition 6. *Two marked values are* $\flat,\kappa$*-equivalent* $v_0 : \kappa_0 \equiv_{\flat,\kappa} v_1 : \kappa_1$ *if they are equal as long as their marks are disjoint from* κ.

$$\kappa \cap \kappa_0 = \emptyset \ \wedge \ \kappa \cap \kappa_1 = \emptyset \ \Rightarrow \ \flat(v_0) = v_1 \tag{6}$$

Definition 7. *Two environments* ρ_0, ρ_1 *are* $\flat,\kappa$*-equivalent* $\rho_0 \equiv_{\flat,\kappa} \rho_1$ *if* $R := dom(\rho_0) = dom(\rho_1)$ *and they contain equivalent values.*

$$\forall x \in R : \ \rho_0(x) \equiv_{\flat,\kappa} \rho_1(x) \tag{7}$$

Definition 8. *Two expressions* e_0, e_1 *are* $\flat,\kappa$*-equivalent* $e_0 \equiv_{\flat,\kappa} e_1$ *iff they only differ in the argument of* $\textbf{trace}^\ell(e')$ *subexpressions with* $\ell \in \kappa$.

$$\begin{aligned} &\kappa = \{\ell_0, \ldots, \ell_n\} \ \Rightarrow \\ &\exists e'_0 \ldots \exists e'_n : \ e_0 \ = \ e_1[\ell_0 \mapsto e'_0] \ldots [\ell_n \mapsto e'_n] \end{aligned} \tag{8}$$

Definition 9. *Two storables* s_0, s_1 *are* $\flat,\kappa$*-equivalent* $\langle o_0, \langle \rho_0, \lambda^\ell x.e_0 \rangle, p_0 \rangle \equiv_{\flat,\kappa} \langle o_1, \langle \rho_1, \lambda^\ell x.e_1 \rangle, p_1 \rangle$ *if* $S :=$

$dom(o_0) = dom(o_1)$ *and they only differ in values* $c : \kappa_c$ *with any intersection with* κ.

$$\forall str \in S : o_0(str) \equiv_{\flat,\kappa} o_1(str) \quad (9)$$

$$\rho_0 \equiv_{\flat,\kappa} \rho_1 \wedge \lambda^\ell x.e_0 \equiv_{\flat,\kappa} \lambda^\ell x.e_1 \quad (10)$$

$$\flat(p_0) = p_1 \quad (11)$$

Definition 10. *Two heaps* $\mathcal{H}_0, \mathcal{H}_1$ *are* $\flat$, κ*-equivalent* $\mathcal{H}_0 \equiv_{\flat,\kappa} \mathcal{H}_1$ *if they only differ in values* $x : \kappa_x$ *with any intersection with* κ *or in one-sided locations.*

$$\forall \xi^\ell \in dom(\flat) : \mathcal{H}_0(\xi^\ell) \equiv_{\flat,\kappa} \mathcal{H}_1(\flat(\xi^\ell)) \quad (12)$$

Now, the noninterference theorem can be stated as follows.

Theorem 1. *Suppose* $\mathcal{H}, \rho, \kappa \vdash e \Downarrow \mathcal{H}' \mid v : \kappa_v$. *If* $\ell \notin \bar{\kappa}$ *and* $\mathcal{H} \equiv_{\flat,\{\ell|\ell\notin\bar{\kappa}\}} \tilde{\mathcal{H}}$ *and* $\rho \equiv_{\flat,\{\ell|\ell\notin\bar{\kappa}\}} \tilde{\rho}$ *then* $\tilde{\mathcal{H}}, \tilde{\rho}, \kappa \vdash \bar{e} \Downarrow \tilde{\mathcal{H}}' \mid \tilde{v} : \tilde{\kappa}_v$ *with* $\bar{e} = e[\ell \mapsto \tilde{e}]$ *and* $e \equiv_{\flat,\{\ell|\ell\notin\bar{\kappa}\}} \bar{e}$ *and* $\mathcal{H}' \equiv_{\flat',\{\ell|\ell\notin\bar{\kappa}\}} \tilde{\mathcal{H}}'$ *and* $v : \kappa_v \equiv_{\flat',\{\ell|\ell\notin\bar{\kappa}\}} \tilde{v} : \tilde{\kappa}_v$, *for some* $\flat'$ *extending* $\flat$.

The proof is by induction on the evaluation $\Downarrow$.

8.2 Correctness

The abstract analysis is a correct abstraction of the $\lambda_J^{\mathcal{D}}$ calculus. To formalize correctness, we introduce a consistency relation that relates semantic domains of the concrete dependency tracking semantics of $\lambda_J^{\mathcal{D}}$ with the abstract domains.

Definition 11. *The consistency relation* $\prec_C$ *is defined by:*

$$
\begin{array}{lcl}
\kappa \prec_C \mathcal{D} & \Leftrightarrow & \kappa \subseteq \mathcal{D} \\
c \prec_C \mathcal{L} & \Leftrightarrow & c \in \mathcal{L} \\
\xi^\ell \prec_C \Xi & \Leftrightarrow & \ell \in \Xi \\
v \prec_C \vartheta & \Leftrightarrow & \begin{cases} \xi^\ell \prec_C \Xi_\vartheta, & v = \xi^\ell \\ c \prec_C \mathcal{L}_\vartheta, & v = c \end{cases} \\
v : \kappa \prec_C \vartheta & \Leftrightarrow & \kappa \prec_C \mathcal{D}_\vartheta \wedge v \prec_C \vartheta \\
o \prec_C \Delta & \Leftrightarrow & \forall str \in dom(o) : \exists \mathcal{L} \in dom(\Delta) : \\
& & str \prec_C \mathcal{L} \wedge o(str) \prec_C \Delta(\mathcal{L}) \wedge \\
& & \forall str \notin dom(o) : \textbf{\textit{undefined}} \prec_C \Delta(\mathcal{L}) \\
\rho \prec_C \sigma & \Leftrightarrow & \forall x \in dom(\rho) : x \in dom(\sigma) \\
& & \wedge \rho(x) \prec_C \sigma(x) \\
f \prec_C \Lambda^\ell & \Leftrightarrow & \langle \rho, \lambda^\ell x.e_f \rangle = f \wedge \langle \sigma, \lambda^\ell x.e_{\Lambda^\ell} \rangle = \Lambda^\ell \\
& & \to \rho \prec_C \sigma \wedge \lambda^\ell x.e_f = \lambda^\ell x.e_{\Lambda^\ell} \\
s \prec_C \theta & \Leftrightarrow & \langle o, f, p \rangle = s \wedge \langle \Delta, \Lambda^\ell, \Xi \rangle = \theta \\
& & \to o \prec_C \Delta \wedge f \prec_C \Lambda^\ell \wedge p \prec_C \Xi \\
\mathcal{H} \prec_C \Gamma & \Leftrightarrow & \forall \xi^\ell \in dom(\mathcal{H}) : \ell \in \Sigma_\Gamma \\
& & \wedge \mathcal{H}(\xi^\ell) \prec_C \Sigma_\Gamma(\ell)
\end{array}
$$

Showing adherence to the inference of $\lambda_J^{\mathcal{D}}$ requires to proof that consistent heaps, environments, and values produce a consistent heap and value.

Lemma 3 (Program). $\forall e : \emptyset, \emptyset, \emptyset \vdash e \Downarrow \mathcal{H} \mid \omega$ *and* $\vdash e \Downarrow \Gamma \mid \vartheta$ *implies that* $\langle \mathcal{H}, \omega \rangle \prec_C \langle \Gamma, \vartheta \rangle$

Given by theorem (2) and definition (11).

Lemma 4 (Property Reference). $\forall \mathcal{H}, \xi^\ell, str, \Gamma, \Xi, \mathcal{L} : \mathcal{H} \prec_C \Gamma$, $\xi^\ell \prec_C \Xi$, $str \prec_C \mathcal{L}$, *and* $\vdash^{\Theta}_{\text{GET}} \Gamma(\Xi), \mathcal{L} \Downarrow \vartheta$ *implies* $\mathcal{H}(\xi^\ell)(str) \prec_C \vartheta$

The proof is by definition (11) and by induction on the derivation of $\Gamma'' \vdash^{\Theta}_{\text{GET}} \Gamma''(\Xi_0), \texttt{str} \Downarrow \vartheta$.

Lemma 5 (Property Assignment). $\forall \mathcal{H}, \xi^\ell, str, \omega, \Gamma, \Xi, \mathcal{L}, \vartheta :$ $\mathcal{H} \prec_C \Gamma$, $\xi^\ell \prec_C \Xi$, $str \prec_C \mathcal{L}$, $\omega \prec_C \vartheta$ *and* $\Gamma \vdash^{\Xi}_{\text{PUT}} \Xi, \mathcal{L}, \vartheta \Downarrow \Gamma'$ *implies* $\mathcal{H}[\xi^\ell, str \mapsto \omega] \prec_C \Gamma'$

The proof is by definition (11) and by induction on the derivation of $\Gamma''' \vdash^{\Xi}_{\text{PUT}} \Xi_0, \texttt{str}, \langle \mathcal{L}_\vartheta, \Xi_\vartheta, \mathcal{D}_0 \sqcup \mathcal{D}_1 \sqcup \mathcal{D}_\vartheta \rangle \Downarrow \Gamma''''$.

The following correctness theorem relates the concrete semantics to the abstract semantics.

Theorem 2. *Suppose that* $\mathcal{H}, \rho, \kappa \vdash e \Downarrow \mathcal{H}' \mid x$ *then* $\forall \Gamma, \sigma$ *with* $\mathcal{H} \prec_C \Gamma$, $\rho \prec_C \sigma$ *and* $\kappa \prec_C \mathcal{D}_\Gamma$: $\Gamma, \sigma \vdash e \Downarrow \Gamma' \mid \vartheta$ *with* $\mathcal{H}' \prec_C \Gamma'$ *and* $x \prec_C \vartheta$.

The proof is by induction on the evaluation of e.

8.3 Termination

Finally, we want to guarantee termination of our analysis.

Theorem 3. *For each* Γ, σ, *and* e, *there exist* Γ' *and* ϑ *such that* $\Gamma, \sigma \vdash e \Downarrow \Gamma' \mid \vartheta$.

For the proof, we observe that all rules of the abstract system in Section 5 are monotone with respect to all their inputs. As the analysis lattice for Γ has finite height, all fixpoint computations in the abstract semantics terminate.

9. Implementation

The implementation extends TAJS[3], the type analyzer for JavaScript. TAJS accepts standard JavaScript [14] .

The abstract interpretation of values and the analysis state are extended by a set of dependency annotations, according to the description in Section 5. As shown in Section 3.1 values can be marked by using the **trace**$^\ell$ expression, which is implemented as a built-in function. A configuration file can be used to trace values produced by JavaScript standard operations or DOM functions. The DOM environment gets constructed during the initialization of TAJS and is available as as normal code would be. The functionality and the dependency propagation for these operations is hard coded.

The extended dependency set has no influence on the lattice structure and does not compromise the precision of the type analyzer. Some notes about the precision can be found in the original work of TAJS [15].

The functions **trace**$^\ell$ and **untrace**$^{(\mathcal{A} \hookrightarrow \mathcal{A}')}$ have to be defined as identity functions before the instrumented code can run in a standard JavaScript engine.

TAJS handles all language features like prototypes, iterations, and exceptions. The specification in Figure 10 simplifies the implementation in several respects. To support the

[3] `http://www.brics.dk/TAJS/`

Benchmark	TAJS	TbDA
Richards (539 lines)	1596	2890
DeltaBlue (880 lines)	3471	4031
Crypto (1689 lines)	3637	7527
RegExp (4758 lines)	3710	4104
Splay (394 lines)	1598	2521
Navier Stokes (387 lines)	2794	3118

Figure 17. Google V8 Benchmark Suite.

conditional to properly account for indirect information flow, the control flow graph had to be extended with special dependency push and pop nodes to encapsulate sub-graphs and to add or remove state dependencies.

The type analyzer provides an over-approximation according to the principles described in Section 3. The analysis result shows the set of traced values and the set of values, which are potentially influenced by them.

There are several ways to use the analyzer. First, a value can be marked and its influence and usage can be determined. This feature can be used to prevent private data from illegal usage and theft. Second, the $\mathbf{trace}^{\ell}$ function may be used to encapsulate foreign code. As a result of this encapsulation each value which is modified due to the foreign code is highlighted by the analysis. An inspection of the results can show breaches of integrity.

Our implementation is based on an early version of TAJS. The current TAJS version includes support for further language features including `eval` [16]. The dependency analysis can benefit from these extensions by merging it into the current development branch of TAJS.

9.1 Runtime Evaluation

We evaluated the performance impact of our extension by analyzing programs from the Google V8 Benchmark Suite[4]. The programs we selected range from about 400 to 5000 lines of code and perform tasks like an OS kernel simulation, constraint solving, or extraction of regular expressions. The tests were run on a MacBook Pro with 2 GHz Intel Core i7 processor with 8 GB memory.

Figure 17 shows the particular benchmarks together with the averaged time (in milliseconds) to run the analysis and to print the output. The **TAJS** column shows the timing of the original type analyzer without dependency extension. The **TbDA** column shows the timing of our extended version. The figures demonstrate that the dependency analysis leads to a slowdown between 12% and 106%. Two further benchmarks (*RayTrace* and *EarleyBoyer*) did not run to completion because of compatibility problems caused by the outdated version of TAJS underlying our implementation.

[4] `http://v8.googlecode.com/svn/data/benchmarks/v7/run.html`

10. Related Work

Information flow analysis was pioneered by Denning's work [8, 9] which models different security levels as values in a lattice containing elements like *High* and *Low* and which suggests an analysis as an abstract interpretation of the propagation of these levels through the program. Zanioli and others [24] present a recent example of such an analysis with an emphasis on constructing an expressive analysis domain.

Many authors have taken up this approach and transposed it to type theoretic and logical settings [1, 3, 13, 21, 23].

In these systems, input value types are enhanced with security levels. Well-typed programs guarantee that no *High* value flows into a *Low* output and thus noninterference between high inputs and low outputs [10]. Similar to the soundness property of our dependency analysis changes on *High* inputs are unobservable in *Low* outputs. Dependencies are related to security types, but more flexible [2]. They can be analyzed before committing to a fixed security lattice.

Security aspects of JavaScript programs have received much attention. Different approaches focus on static or dynamic analysis techniques, e.g. [6, 12, 17], or attempt to make guarantees by reducing the functionality [20]. The analysis for dependencies is no security analysis per se, but the analysis results express information that is relevant for confidentiality and integrity concerns.

Dependency analysis can be seen as the static counterpart to data tainting (e.g., [7]). Tainting relies on augmenting the run-time representation of a value with information about its properties (like its confidentiality level). Users of the value first check at run time if that use is granted according to some security policy. Dynamic tainting approaches have been successfully used to address security attacks, including buffer overruns, format string attacks, SQL and command injections, and cross-site scripting. Tainting semantics are also used for automatic sanitizer placement [5, 19]. There are also uses in program understanding, software testing, and debugging. Tainting can also be augmented with static analysis to increase its effectiveness [22].

Dynamic languages like JavaScript have many peculiarities that make program analysis and the interpretation of its results challenging [4]. TAJS [15] and hence our analysis can handle almost all dynamic features of JavaScript.

11. Conclusion

We have designed a type-based dependency analysis for JavaScript, proved its soundness and termination, and demonstrated that independence ensures noninterference. We have implemented the analysis as an extension of the open-source JavaScript analyzer TAJS. This approach ensures that our analysis can be applied to real-world JavaScript programs.

While a dependency analysis is not a security analysis, it can form the basis for investigating noninterference. This way, its results can be used to ensure confidentiality and integrity, as well as verify the correct placement of sanitizers.

References

[1] M. Abadi. Access control in a core calculus of dependency. *Electron. Notes Theor. Comput. Sci.*, 172:5–31, April 2007.

[2] M. Abadi, A. Banerjee, N. Heintze, and J. Riecke. A core calculus of dependency. In A. :Aiken, editor, *Proceedings 26th Annual ACM Symposium on Principles of Programming Languages*, pages 147–160, San Antonio, Texas, USA, Jan. 1999. ACM Press.

[3] T. Amtoft and A. Banerjee. Information flow analysis in logical form. In *Proc. 11th Static Analysis Symposium, SAS'04*, pages 33–36. Springer, 2004.

[4] A. Askarov and A. Sabelfeld. Tight enforcement of information-release policies for dynamic languages. In *Computer Security Foundations Symposium, 2009. CSF '09. 22nd IEEE*, pages 43 –59, july 2009. doi: 10.1109/CSF.2009.22.

[5] D. Balzarotti, M. Cova, V. Felmetsger, N. Jovanovic, E. Kirda, C. Kruegel, and G. Vigna. Saner: Composing static and dynamic analysis to validate sanitization in web applications. In *IEEE Symposium on Security and Privacy*, pages 387–401, Oakland, California, USA, May 2008. IEEE Computer Society.

[6] R. Chugh, J. A. Meister, R. Jhala, and S. Lerner. Staged information flow for javascript. In *Proceedings of the 2009 ACM SIGPLAN conference on Programming language design and implementation*, PLDI '09, pages 50–62, New York, NY, USA, 2009. ACM.

[7] J. Clause, W. Li, and A. Orso. Dytan: A generic dynamic taint analysis framework. In *Proc. 2007 Symposium on Software Testing and Analysis*, ISSTA '07, pages 196–206, New York, NY, USA, 2007. ACM.

[8] D. E. Denning. A lattice model of secure information flow. *Commun. ACM*, 19:236–243, May 1976.

[9] D. E. Denning and P. J. Denning. Certification of programs for secure information flow. *Commun. ACM*, 20:504–513, July 1977.

[10] J. A. Goguen and J. Meseguer. Security policies and security models. In *IEEE Symposium on Security and Privacy*, pages 11–20, 1982.

[11] A. Guha, C. Saftoiu, and S. Krishnamurthi. The essence of JavaScript. In *Proc. 24th European Conference on Object-oriented Programming*, ECOOP'10, pages 126–150, Berlin, Heidelberg, 2010. Springer-Verlag.

[12] D. Hedin and A. Sabelfeld. Information-flow security for a core of javascript. In *Computer Security Foundations Symposium (CSF), 2012 IEEE 25th*, pages 3–18. IEEE, 2012.

[13] N. Heintze and J. G. Riecke. The SLam calculus: Programming with secrecy and integrity. In *Proc. 25th ACM SIGPLAN-SIGACT Symposium on Principles of Programming Languages*, POPL '98, pages 365–377, New York, NY, USA, 1998. ACM.

[14] E. International. *Standard ECMA-262*, volume 3. 1999.

[15] S. H. Jensen, A. Møller, and P. Thiemann. Type analysis for JavaScript. In *Proc. 16th Static Analysis Symposium, SAS'09*, volume 5673 of *LNCS*. Springer-Verlag, August 2009.

[16] S. H. Jensen, P. A. Jonsson, and A. Møller. Remedying the eval that men do. In *Proc. 21st International Symposium on Software Testing and Analysis (ISSTA)*, July 2012.

[17] S. Just, A. Cleary, B. Shirley, and C. Hammer. Information flow analysis for javascript. In *Proceedings of the 1st ACM SIGPLAN international workshop on Programming language and systems technologies for internet clients*, PLASTIC '11, pages 9–18, New York, NY, USA, 2011. ACM.

[18] M. Keil and P. Thiemann. Type-based dependency analysis for javascript. Technical report, Institute for Computer Science, University of Freiburg, 2013.

[19] B. Livshits and S. Chong. Towards fully automatic placement of security sanitizers and declassifiers. In *Proceedings of the 40th annual ACM SIGPLAN-SIGACT symposium on Principles of programming languages*, POPL '13, pages 385–398, New York, NY, USA, 2013. ACM.

[20] M. S. Miller, M. Samuel, B. Laurie, I. Awad, and M. Stay. Safe active content in sanitized javascript. Technical report, Tech. Rep., Google, Inc, 2008.

[21] A. Sabelfeld and A. C. Myers. Language-based information-flow security. *IEEE Journal on Selected Areas in Communications*, 21:2003, 2003.

[22] P. Vogt, F. Nentwich, N. Jovanovic, E. Kirda, C. Kruegel, and G. Vigna. Cross-site scripting prevention with dynamic data tainting and static analysis. In *Proc. Network and Distributed System Security Symposium (NDSS)*, volume 42, 2007.

[23] D. Volpano, C. Irvine, and G. Smith. A sound type system for secure flow analysis. *J. Comput. Secur.*, 4:167–187, January 1996.

[24] M. Zanioli, P. Ferrara, and A. Cortesi. Sails: Static analysis of information leakage with Sample. In *Proc. 27th Annual ACM Symposium on Applied Computing*, SAC '12, pages 1308–1313, New York, NY, USA, 2012. ACM.

WEBLOG: A Declarative Language for Secure Web Development

Timothy L. Hinrichs, Daniele Rossetti, Gabriele Petronella, V. N. Venkatakrishnan,
A. Prasad Sistla, Lenore D. Zuck
University of Illinois at Chicago
Computer Science Department
hinrichs@uic.edu, daniele.rossetti@me.com, gabriele.petronella@gmail.com, venkat@uic.edu,
sistla@cs.uic.edu, lenore@cs.uic.edu

Abstract

WEBLOG is a declarative language for web application development designed to automatically eliminate several security vulnerabilities common to today's web applications. In this paper, we introduce WEBLOG, detail the security vulnerabilities it eliminates, and discuss how those vulnerabilities are eliminated. We then evaluate WEBLOG's ability to build and secure real-world applications by comparing traditional implementations of 3 existing small- to medium-size web applications to WEBLOG implementations.

Categories and Subject Descriptors D.3.3 [*Programming Languages*]: Language Constructs and Features; D.4.6 [*Security and Protection*]: Access Controls; K.6.5 [*Security and Protection*]: Unauthorized access

General Terms Languages, Security, Verification, Design

Keywords web security; correct-by-construction; declarative language

1. Introduction

While many programming languages and frameworks have been designed specifically to develop software for the World Wide Web, they widely differ in addressing security concerns. Some languages simply provide a library of countermeasures that a developer may apply at will, such as taint-tracking (e.g. Perl) and auto-sanitization (in Google Closure Templates) of user-provided data. Such languages provide no real guarantees for the developer but simply reduce her manual effort. Other languages are more ambitious and are designed to eliminate security vulnerabilities automatically, *e.g.*, by ensuring that a type-safe program is not vulnerable to a specific class of attacks [12, 19]. Such languages typically eliminate one or two classes of vulnerabilities; extending such approaches to address a wide range of Web vulnerabilities is hard because of fundamental computational limits on how much analysis can be performed on the underlying language (*e.g.*, analyzing arbitrary loops is undecidable).

The limitations of current-day, language-based web security are rooted in the fact that today's web development languages are designed primarily for rapid prototyping — for a developer to achieve a certain functionality quickly. In contrast, the web development language introduced in this paper, WEBLOG, was designed primarily for security—for protecting applications from today's most prevalent vulnerabilities. In fact, we began with a list of prevalent web security vulnerabilities (the OWASP Top-10 [21]) and designed a language just expressive enough that the compiler and runtime can automatically eliminate those vulnerabilities correctly, comprehensively, and automatically. Not surprisingly, we discovered that the language must be significantly less expressive than traditional programming languages, meaning that not all possible web applications can be expressed. One of the main questions we are trying to answer in this paper is whether such a language is expressive *enough* to be used for real-world applications.

WEBLOG supports two conceptually different kinds of defenses. It includes automatic defenses for some of the most critical web application security risks as ranked in the OWASP Top-10. These defenses are cutting-edge, leveraging the recent advances in web security. Because they are incorporated into the compiler, developers can always leverage the most recent countermeasures by simply updating their compiler and recompiling their applications.

A second, more compelling, class of defenses are those that require weaving a separately written security policy throughout the application. For example, controlling which users can access resources in which ways (access control) is something that can only be implemented by changing all of the application fragments that access sensitive resources. For these defenses, the developer writes a separate security policy, and the compiler generates code that simultaneously implements the application's functionality while respecting the developer's policy.

We view this work as a first step in a long-term research project aimed at developing a multi-layer web development programming language. WEBLOG serves as the core of the language; any application expressible in WEBLOG is automatically protected against a plethora of security vulnerabilities. Each layer built on top of WEBLOG could add additional expressiveness at the cost of some number of security guarantees. At the top level is a fully-expressive, traditional programming language that provides no absolute security guarantees but is outfitted with a library of common countermeasures. A developer can then weigh the use of additional expressiveness either for functionality or convenience against the loss of automatic security.

PLAS'13, June 20, 2013, Seattle, WA, USA.

This paper makes the following technical contributions:

- WebLog *design* We present the design rationale and conceptual basis for WebLog[1]. We show how WebLog is a minimal, yet powerful framework for web development.
- *Practical Defenses for Common Attack Vectors* WebLog includes cutting edge defenses for most of the OWASP security errors. An important characteristic of WebLog is that the security of the application is less reliant on the programmer. Except for problems with the logic of the application, the burden of eliminating security weaknesses lies with the framework.
- *Evaluation* We show that WebLog is sufficiently expressive to implement an entire, real world web application. We also discuss how common web application features can be realized efficiently and securely through WebLog. Finally, we report on development experiences and the security of two implementations of the same application: one in WebLog and one in Sinatra (a Ruby-based web development framework).

This paper is organized as follows. Section 2 provides a running example and illustrates the motivation behind the design of WebLog. Section 3 gives an overview of WebLog. Section 4 describes how WebLog automatically eliminates a number of prevalent security vulnerabilities by leveraging recent results from web security research. Section 5 discusses our evaluation of WebLog. In Section 6, we discuss related work. Section 7 concludes.

2. Background

Web Applications Web applications are based on the client-server architecture, where the client and server communicate using the Hypertext transfer protocol (HTTP) or its encrypted variant (HTTPS). The client must be written in one of a handful of programming languages the web browser understands, *e.g.*, usually some combination of HTML, JavaScript, Flash, and Silverlight. Servers can be written in any programming language, though most applications today are written using web-specific languages, such as PHP, or web-development frameworks built on top of general-purpose languages, such as Java Servlets, Ruby-on-Rails, or Django (a framework for Python).

Running Example The example we use throughout the paper is a real-world online auction application called WeBid [3]. WeBid allows people to create new auctions, search through a myriad of existing auctions, and place bids on merchandise of interest. Figure 1 shows a simplified version of the user registration page where a new user chooses a login ID and password and provides some basic personal information like first and last name, address, and email.

Once the user fills out the form, the browser encodes the form's data as a collection of key-value pairs in an HTTP request, and sends that request to the server. The server accepts the HTTP request, checks the data for errors, updates its backend relational database to store the user's profile data, and responds with another HTTP message whose payload is the client code describing whether or not the registration succeeded. Sometimes the browser will send auxiliary information to the server by embedding *cookies* within that initial HTTP request—information that typically tells the server something about the user sending the data. The server may also maintain additional information in an in-memory *session* object to improve performance, so named because it is typically used to group several distinct HTTP requests into a single user session.

Web Security An attacker could attempt to compromise this web application in numerous ways. If the attacker includes SQL commands within the Last Name field, she might fool the application into executing those commands on the server's backend database, an attack referred to as SQL Injection (SQLi). If the attacker includes malicious JavaScript code within one of the fields, she might convince the application to create a client page that executes that code when loaded by another user, an attacked referred to as cross-site scripting (XSS). If the attacker changes the value of a hidden field called *admin* on the form, she might convince the application to grant her administrative rights, an attack called parameter tampering.

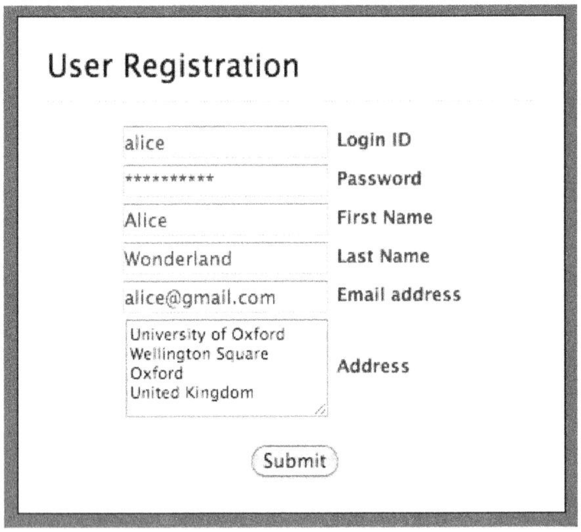

Figure 1. Running example: WeBid user registration

The attacker could also simply type URLs into the browser that the web developer did not expect and in so doing circumvent the application's intended access control policy. For example, in WeBid, there are "premier" auctions that are only visible to registered users. All of WeBid's search functions delete premier auctions from their results unless the user performing the search is logged in. But if an unregistered user asks the application for the details of a premier auction by providing that auction's ID directly, she gains access to that auction, thereby violating the application's intended access control policy.

Motivation Securing an application like WeBid is difficult for several reasons. First, the developer must understand the security defenses to put in place to defend against each kind of attack. Second, defenses must be deployed comprehensively and consistently across the application. Third, because applications are always undergoing bug fixes and feature improvements, the task of hardening the application against attack must be revisited each time the application is updated. Finally, security is still a secondary goal of many web developers (and managers) and hence in practice devoting the necessary time and energy to protecting applications is difficult.

The above challenges are not easy to meet as illustrated by the vast numbers of SQL injection and XSS attacks on applications (still the top two as reported by Common Weaknesses Enumeration (CWE) [2]). A web development language where cutting-edge security defenses are installed by the compiler would address all of the concerns above. The developer would not need to keep up to date with the intricacies of web security defenses; the defenses would be deployed completely and automatically; maintenance of web applications would require no additional hardening phase; and resource-limited organizations could still build secure, functional web applications.

[1] Implemented as part of the CLICL library available at `https://code.google.com/p/clicl/`

Scope In this paper we focus on developing a language for programming the server component of a web application and leave client-side programming to future work (though we discuss a placeholder client-side language for the sake of completeness). This means that our testing and development of WEBLOG has focused on Web 1.0 applications; however, WEBLOG has been designed with Web 2.0 applications in mind (where the client asynchronously communicates with the server). We expect that the development of a complementary client-side programming language will require few changes to WEBLOG. One final note on scope: WEBLOG makes no attempt to address noSQL-based web applications.

3. WEBLOG

Our main thesis is that many of today's web applications are conceptually simple but are written using programming language constructs that are unnecessarily difficult for the compiler to analyze. WEBLOG is a web development language that eliminates the hard-to-analyze programming language features while including domain-specific constructs that help the programmer overcome that lack of expressiveness. WEBLOG is an investigation into whether it is possible to design a domain-specific language that is expressive enough to build real-world web applications while simultaneously being *inexpressive* enough that the language itself can both soundly and completely eliminate a plethora of security vulnerabilities (possibly even those we have yet to identify).

WEBLOG is a server-centric language similar to PHP, Java servlets, and Ruby-on-Rails. By *server-centric*, we mean that a developer focuses on writing the code that runs on the server and treats the client as simply a mechanism that renders the server's output in human-readable form and solicit's additional input.

WEBLOG's attempt to balance expressiveness with inexpressiveness is based on two key ideas. Instead of giving programmers the ability to choose from a wide variety of data structures (*e.g.*, binary trees, arrays, lists), it supports a single data structure that is both necessary and sufficient for typical web applications. Second, it ensures that the language for manipulating that data structure is written using purely declarative constructs that can be analyzed by state-of-the-art automated reasoning tools.

Data-centric Programming Model WEBLOG supports a single data structure: the relational database. Conceptually, a programmer writes code that takes as input one relational database and outputs another relational database. This database-centric programming model is a natural fit for the web domain because all the main data structures manipulated by typical web application can be construed as relational databases. Obviously the backend relational database of the web application fits the paradigm. The form data a client submits to the server in an HTTP request is a collection of key-value pairs, which we can represent as a database table with two columns. Even the auxiliary data structures a web application commonly manipulates (the *cookies* for the client and the *session* for the server) are sets of key value pairs. The output of a web application is also often just a relational database, but one rendered in HTML.

Purely Declarative Because the only data structure in WEBLOG is the relational database, the obvious language for describing the input/output functionality of a web application is the most prevalent one for managing relational databases: SQL. Besides being a purely declarative, well-known language that is well-suited for the task, large fragments of SQL can be deeply analyzed using the theorem provers, model builders, and SMT solvers developed by the automated reasoning community over the last 50 years (see [5, 11] for the relationship between SQL and first-order logic).

3.1 Syntax

At the top-level, a WEBLOG application is a collection of *servlets*. Each servlet is a self-contained piece of web server functionality that takes an HTTP request as an input, modifies the server's session and RDBMS, and returns an HTML page to the client.

Definition 1 (Servlet). *A servlet has the following fields.*

- ***transducer**: a collection of SQL update statements that describe how data sent to the servlet changes the RDBMS, cookies, and session, and how to compute the output.*
- ***guard**: a collection of SQL integrity constraints dictating the conditions under which the servlet can be executed.*
- ***renderer**: a description for how the output data is displayed on the client.*

The input to a servlet is a relational database, some of whose tables represent all the usual sources of information for a servlet[2]. The user data contained within an HTTP request is stored in the two-column table `HttpInput`. The cookie data is stored as the two-column table `Cookies`. The session data is stored as the two-column table `Session`. The remaining tables in the servlet's input are the backend RDBMS tables.

A servlet's guards are written as SQL integrity constraints over the relational database provided as input to the servlet. If any of those guards fail, no changes are made to the cookies, session, or RDBMS, and WEBLOG automatically sends a response to the client describing what the failure was.

If all of the guards succeed, the servlet's transducer is executed on the input database. Any changes made to the RDBMS tables are sent to the RDBMS. Any changes to the `Cookies` table are reflected in the HTTP cookies sent back to the browser. Any changes to the `Session` table are carried over to the server's actual session object (and if there is any session data stored, a WEBLOG-managed session ID cookie is set automatically).

Once the transducer execution completes, the resulting database is given to the servlet's renderer, which creates the HTML page to send to the browser. Conceptually, any query results that the renderer needs has already been computed by the transducer and stored in a table agreed upon by the transducer and the renderer. The renderer is free to display any data present in the relational database however it likes, though the compiler checks to ensure the renderer never releases information it should not.

In our running example application, the web page for creating a new user sends an HTTP request to the server with the user's first and last name, an email address, a login ID, and a password, which causes the server to insert that data into the RDBMS and log the user into the application. To implement this functionality in WEBLOG, a developer creates a servlet whose transducer is the following two SQL update statements. The first inserts the user's data into the database, and the second sets the session's username to her login ID, thereby logging her into the application. This is shown in Listing 1.

To require that the user's selected login ID has not already been chosen by another user, a WEBLOG developer would include a guard with SQL integrity constraint shown in Listing 2 guaranteeing that the login ID in the HttpInput table does not already exist in the User table of the RDBMS.

While this example requires no real data be sent back to the client, consider a web page that returns all auctions whose titles include a query string chosen by the user. To implement the search servlet, a WEBLOG developer writes a SQL update command that inserts all the auctions from the RDBMS table `Auctions` whose titles match the user's search string (stored in the `HttpInput`

[2] We use the term *relational database* to mean a collection of named *tables*. A *table* is a collection of rows, all of which have the same number of columns of atomic data.

Listing 1.

```
INSERT INTO Users (login, first, last, email) SELECT login, first, last, email FROM HttpInput
INSERT INTO Session (user) SELECT login FROM HttpInput
```

Listing 2.

```
CHECK (NOT EXISTS
  (SELECT * FROM Users U, HttpInput H WHERE U.login = H.login))
```

table) into a temporary table, here called `SearchResults`, as shown in Listing 3. Those search results are then rendered to the client.

Because the same SQL statements can be used in many different servlets, WEBLOG enables a developer to organize SQL code into modules and to combine modules using a simple form of inheritance. Each SQL module is either an *update* module, meaning that it includes just SQL update statements (*i.e.*, INSERT, DELETE, or UPDATE), or it is a *guard* module, meaning that it includes just integrity constraints. SQL update modules are defined with the `defupdate` command; SQL guard modules are defined with `defguard`. A servlet's transducer is a *sequence* of SQL update modules. A servlet's guard is a *sequence* of guard modules. When a servlet is invoked, the guard modules are checked in the order they appear in the servlet definition; the first module in which an error appears (*i.e.*, a constraint is violated) halts the execution of the servlet, and WEBLOG returns all errors in that module to the user. If no errors occur, the update modules are executed in the order they appear, and the servlet's output is rendered and returned to the user. Listing 4 is the WEBLOG code for the user-registration servlet described above.

From the perspective of basic functionality, the renderer for a servlet can be any piece of code written in any language that takes a database as input and outputs HTML. But for the sake of security, WEBLOG requires that the compiler be able to perform three tasks. First, the compiler must be able to analyze the rendering code for each servlet to compute exactly that fragment of the database the renderer requires in order to produce the client. Said differently, what fragment of the database can WEBLOG hide from the renderer without altering its output? This requirement is not much of a restriction in practice because it is often a simple matter to require each renderer declare which tables it will read (and enforce that declaration by only providing the renderer with exactly those tables).

Second, the compiler must be able to analyze the rendering code to compute the HTML context (or the lineage of HTML tags) in which each piece of user data is to be embedded. For example, if the renderer takes a user's profile and displays it on the screen in an HTML table, then the context for each of the profile's data elements might be `<html><body><table><tr><td>`. This requirement is far more difficult to attain because all looping and recursion constructs must be analyzable, and dead code must always be identifiable.

Third, the compiler must be able to control the behavior of all the web forms that are produced. At the very least, the compiler must be able to supply code for each form's event handlers without modifying the client's overall behavior, and it must be able to reference and modify the form's values.

Currently, WEBLOG is outfitted with a simple rendering mechanism that satisfies the properties above. It transforms the results of a servlet's execution into one of several languages: XML, JSON, or HTML with cookies. Rendering data as XML and JSON is straightforward and can be carried out by WEBLOG autonomously, but rendering HTML requires additional developer involvement. In WEBLOG, we view an HTML page as a way of displaying data to the user or requesting data from the user. We call the specification for how data is to be displayed in HTML a *table*, and the specification for a request for data a *form*, reflecting common use cases for the HTML elements of the same name.

The renderer operates similar to HTML templates in traditional development frameworks. The developer writes an HTML page along with several table and form specifications. At runtime, WEBLOG inserts into that HTML page renderings of data and renderings of requests for data, as per the table and form specs.

Definition 2 (Renderer). *A renderer has the following fields.*

- ***HTML**: an HTML page*
- ***forms**: a set of substitutions of the form* htmlID/form
- ***tables**: a set of substitutions of the form* htmlID/table

The substitution htmlID/form *means that the HTML element with ID* htmlID *should be replaced by an HTML representation of* formname. *Similarly for tables.*

A form specification is a database schema (a collection of table names and column names) along with guards that dictate the permitted combinations of table values and the servlet to which data should be submitted. A table specification is just a database schema combined with the name of one of several algorithms built into WEBLOG for rendering a database table in HTML.

Definition 3 (Form, Table). *A form has the following fields.*

- ***schema**: a database schema*
- ***guard**: a list of guards*
- ***target**: the servlet to submit data to*

A table has a schema and the name of one of several algorithms built into WEBLOG *for rendering data.*

Forms are created with the `defform` command; tables are created with `deftable`; schemas are created with `defschema`; renderers are created with `defrender`. Listing 5 shows the renderer for the new-user registration page, which includes a form with a guard requiring that the two passwords the user provides are equal. The HTML page WEBLOG generates automatically ensures that the user's data satisfies any guards on the embedded forms before the user is allowed to submit that form to the server.

Notice that the user-registration renderer supplies the argument `:lang HTML` to `defrender`, which dictates that the renderer is one that outputs HTML. Writing a renderer that outputs XML or JSON requires simply changing the `:language` and ignoring the `:html`, `:forms`, and `:tables` arguments.

Admittedly, the renderer infrastructure for outputting HTML is not as expressive as we would like because it requires the developer to choose from one of several pre-built rendering options for each table and form, and clients are limited to static HTML pages. A more ambitious approach to rendering is studied in [20], where the basic rendering language mixes HTML with arbitrary code from a

Listing 3.

```
INSERT INTO SearchResults (id) SELECT A.ID FROM Auctions A, HttpInput H WHERE A.Title LIKE H.query
```

Listing 4.

```
defservlet new-registration ()
   :guard (unique-login)
   :transducer (save-registration
               login)
   :renderer reg-renderer

defupdate save-registration ()
   INSERT INTO Users (login, first, last, email) SELECT login, first, last, email FROM HttpInput

defupdate login ()
   INSERT INTO Session (user) SELECT login FROM HttpInput

defguard unique-login ()
   (NOT EXISTS (SELECT * FROM Users U, HttpInput H WHERE U.login = H.login))
```

Listing 5.

```
defrender user-registration (:lang HTML)
   :html "path/to/HTML-file.htm"
   :forms ("userdata"/new-user)
   :tables ()

defform new-user ()
   :schema userreg
   :guard (passwordsEq)
   :target new-registration

defschema userreg ()
   CREATE TABLE Userinfo (login, password, password2, firstname, lastname, email)

defguard passwordsEq ()
   NOT EXISTS (SELECT * FROM Userinfo WHERE password != password2)
```

traditional language like Ruby. This work is attractive because it builds on the common paradigm of HTML templates but achieves the analysis required by WEBLOG using a type system to detect HTML contexts. In the future, we plan to develop a richer client-side development language that complements the server-side programming support within WEBLOG. In the remainder of the paper, the only thing about the rendering language we assume are the three requirements described earlier in this section.

3.2 Semantics

The semantics of WEBLOG is basically the same as any traditional web development framework. The main difference is that WEBLOG provides primitives for the developer to write the entire application by simply manipulating a collection of database tables. That collection, which we denote with Δ, includes tables representing all of the traditional data sources in a web application: the client's cookies, the server's session, the backend RDBMS, the payload of the HTTP request, and any data output to the client. Algorithm 1 defines the functional semantics of WEBLOG in terms of how Δ is constructed from the traditional data sources, how a servlet changes Δ, and how changes to Δ are carried back to the original data sources.

Algorithm 1 SERVE(URL, HTTPdata, Cookies)

if the servlet S referenced by URL does not exist **then** throw a 404 error
Set Δ to be the RDBMS data
if Cookies includes a session token **then**
  if a session E for that token exists **then**
    $\Delta = \Delta \cup E$
  else
    throw a Lost-session error
$\Delta = \Delta \cup$ Cookies
$\Delta = \Delta \cup$ HTTPdata
/* Δ is now fully constructed ***/**
for all g in SERVLET-GUARDS(S) **do**
  if Δ violates g **then** throw a Guard-failure error
for all t in SERVLET-TRANSDUCER(S) **do**
  $\delta =$ COMPUTE-UPDATES(t, Δ)
  $\Delta =$ APPLY-UPDATES(δ, Δ)
/* Δ is now fully modified ***/**
Update session and RDBMS data to match Δ
Extract output data O and cookie data C from Δ
return APPLY(SERVLET-RENDERER(S), O) and C

The main semantic question about the WEBLOG implementation is how the servlet's transducer is applied. Recall that the servlet's transducer is a sequence of SQL update modules, each of which is a collection of SQL Insert, Delete, and Update commands. The update modules are applied in the order they appear. Applying a module means computing all those tuples that the module dictates should be inserted, deleted, and updated based on the current Δ (COMPUTE-UPDATES above) and once all the updates are computed, applying them to alter Δ (APPLY-UPDATES above). Said another way, if an update contains one insert and one delete command, WEBLOG first computes all those tuples that are to be inserted, all those tuples that are to be deleted, and then inserts and deletes those tuples from Δ. (Any tuple that a module both inserts and deletes is inserted into Δ by WEBLOG.)

4. WEBLOG Security Defenses

Every year the Open Web Application Security Project (OWASP) collects data on web vulnerabilities and ranks them by their prevalence, calling the resulting list the OWASP Top 10. In this section we detail the defenses we have designed for the WEBLOG compiler. Each of WEBLOG's defenses satisfy two main goals: *automation* and *transparency*.

The automation goal requires that, once the developer has written a functional description of the application, the compiler installs its cadre of defenses soundly and completely. Thus, were there formal definitions for each of the OWASP Top 10 vulnerabilities, we could have formally proved that the compiler guarantees that no WEBLOG application is vulnerable to any of the OWASP Top 10. We do allow for the possibility that the functional description does not contain enough information for the compiler to infer how the application ought to behave in response to an attack, in which case the developer provides that information as a security policy (*e.g.*, access control). But that policy is written independently of the application's functionality, and it is the compiler's job, not the developer's, to see that the policy is obeyed by automatically weaving together the application's functional description and its security policies.

The transparency goal requires that for non-malicious users, the functional description of the web application operates the same whether or not the compiler has automatically installed any defenses. Thus the web developer need not even be aware that the defenses are put in place or have any knowledge of how they operate. Transparency is convenient for developers and enables new security defenses to be installed in an existing WEBLOG application by simply re-compiling the application using an updated version of the WEBLOG compiler.

Defenses that have been implemented are marked with ✓. Those that have only been designed are marked with ✗.

4.1 SQL Injection Attacks (SQLIAs) ✓

Of the OWASP Top-10 web application vulnerabilities SQL injection (SQLi) consistently ranks as one of the most prevalent. A SQLi attack is one in which the attacker includes SQL commands inside a text string that the application typically treats as an atomic entity, *e.g.*, a last name or an email address. SQLi attacks cause the application to do things the developer did not intend if those embedded SQL commands are turned into actual commands when the application interacts with its backend RDBMS.

For example, consider the running example where the application retrieves the list of auctions that match the user provided auction title. There is a single input `query`, and we want to retrieve the titles of auctions that match the query. In PHP, we might write the following code to find all the appropriate books.

```
sql.execute("SELECT * FROM Auctions WHERE
    title LIKE " + $_POST['query'])
```

The problem, of course, is that the user can supply SQL commands in the string `query`, which, when concatenated with the SQL fragment above, results in a string that manipulates the database in a way the developer did not intend.

WEBLOG prevents SQLi attacks by requiring developers to write all of their code in a single programming language (SQL) instead of two separate languages (e.g., PHP and SQL). This important design choice allows us to deal with defending SQLi in a natural way: SQLi is only possible because code written in a language such as PHP generates SQL code at run-time by concatenating SQL commands together with user input. In contrast, WEBLOG developers write all the SQL commands directly, without trying to combine the query "code" with input. User input affects the results of the queries and updates in much the same way, but those commands are expressed in a safer syntax that ensures that user inputs are never treated as SQL keywords.

4.2 Cross-site Scripting (XSS) ✓

A cross-site scripting attack (ranked by OWASP as the 2nd most prevalent) is one in which the attacker includes a command (*e.g.*, in JavaScript) that is meaningful for the web browser within a text string that the application does not expect to contain a command, *e.g.*, a text string representing an email address. When that string is sent back to another user's browser, commands can be executed and compromise that user's security or privacy. Just like for SQLi, commands supplied by the user are being executed as they were issued by the web application itself.

The standard defense from cross-site scripting is to sanitize every piece of user data before sending it to the browser (where the sanitization performed depends on the HTML context in which that data is to appear). Sanitization ensures commands embedded in user data are not interpreted as commands by the web browser. For example, the string

```
<img src = "javascript:alert()"></img>
```

is sanitized to

```
&lt;img src = &quot;javascript:alert()&quot;&gt;
```

thereby ensuring that the HTML command embedded within the string (the `<img>` tag) are not executed by the browser but are rather treated as data.

This defense, while thorough, is impractical for those web applications that actually want their users to submit HTML commands within their data, *e.g.*, so as to format blog posts or descriptions of items for sale. Thus for many applications, there are two kinds of data elements: those that are allowed to include HTML tags and those that are not. And even data elements permitted to include HTML are not typically allowed to include arbitrary HTML because of security vulnerabilities; rather, they are allowed to contain only certain HTML tags.

WEBLOG protects against XSS attacks by sanitizing all user-supplied data (depending on the HTML context in which that data is embedded) when that data is sent to the user, unless the developer marks the data element as not needing sanitization, and WEBLOG ensures that the values assigned to data elements not needing sanitization cannot produce XSS attacks. To mark an element as not needing sanitization, the developer declares a data element to be of type `HTML`, `integer`, or `boolean`. The `integer` and `boolean` types can only be assigned the obvious values; the `HTML` type can only be assigned strings from a fragment of HTML that is parsed consistently across all browsers and is (strongly believed to be) devoid of XSS attacks [22]. All undeclared data elements are of type `string` and are sanitized when output to the user.

These types are enforced in two ways. Whenever data is submitted to a WEBLOG application from a user, the types of that user data are checked, and an error is thrown if user data fails to be of the proper type. (Implementationally, the compiler adds a new guard to each servlet that checks types.) Furthermore, WEBLOG performs type inference and type checking at compile time to ensure that a developer does not, by omission or by commission, copy a data value of type `string` into a data element declared to be of type `integer`, `boolean`, or `HTML`, thereby circumventing the sanitization that ought to have been performed on the data. This requires ensuring that no implicit casting is performed and that there are no unsafe builtins that perform type casting. WEBLOG's type system ensures that a data element's type follows that data element around and hence when it is sent to the renderer can be properly sanitized according to its context as well as its content.

The reader might have observed that WEBLOG performs *output sanitization* (sanitization is performed only when data is sent to the renderer) as opposed to the more conservative *input sanitization* (sanitization occurs when the data is received by the application). Input sanitization fails to meet our design goal of transparency: the code that the developer writes is less likely to behave the same if the XSS defense were turned off. For example, assume the developer wishes to check the length of a stored string value. With input sanitization (which may convert "<" to "&lt") the length of a string value is different after sanitization, whereas output sanitization only changes values after the web application has finished processing them.

4.3 Parameter Tampering ✓

Similar to SQLi and XSS, parameter tampering attacks involve submitting data to a web server that the developer did not expect. A parameter tampering attack is one where the attacker circumvents the client's user interface to submit data to the web server that the client would have rejected. Parameter tampering attacks are often successful on web forms that include a drop-down list with a fixed set of choices for the user. If a malicious user chooses a value not in the list (*e.g.*, by manually sending an HTTP request to the web server), and the server neglects to check that the submitted value is one of the permitted choices, an attack can compromise the integrity of the application [6].

For example, WeBid asks a user to select one of her pre-registered financial accounts to pay for any new merchandise she wins at an auction. If instead of selecting one of her pre-registered accounts from the drop-down list WeBid provides, she submits someone else's account number, the server might charge the other person for her merchandise.

The cause of parameter tampering vulnerabilities is that application developers must write and maintain separate code bases for the client and server, which over time can become unsynchronized. If the client performs data validation that the server fails to perform, no amount of client testing will reveal the unintended behavior of the application under parameter tampering attacks because testers will always submit data that passes the client validation checks.

WEBLOG addresses parameter tampering attacks by automatically replicating any data validation checks performed by the client onto the server. This ensures that any data that the client would reject is also rejected by the server; hence, all parameter tampering attacks are eliminated. This replication process requires three steps. First the WEBLOG compiler reformulates the application so that each servlet processes exactly one form, *i.e.*, that every form is submitted to a distinct servlet. If k forms submit to the same servlet, the compiler makes k copies of that servlet and changes the targets of the k forms to point to different copies. Second, the WEBLOG compiler walks over all forms and adds each form's guards to the guards of the corresponding servlet. Finally, the compiler generates a new guard for each servlet that ensures the only form fields submitted is one of those that appears in the form. This last guard prevents negative tampering attacks, which are described in [7].

4.4 Access Control ✓

Access control is the problem of ensuring that only certain users can manipulate sensitive resources in permitted ways. It is not mentioned directly in the OWASP Top 10 but addresses two of those vulnerabilities nevertheless. One kind of Session Management vulnerability (OWASP 3) is when the application places sensitive information in the user's Cookie instead of the Session or RDBMS. Access control protection ensures that all the data sent to the client, whether in the cookies or in the HTML page, obeys the access control policy. The other vulnerability addressed by access control is called Insecure Direct Object References (OWASP 4). These can arise when the user requests data by issuing a URL that the developer did not anticipate. Proper access control protection ensures that no user is sent data she is not authorized for, regardless of how or when it is requested.

Typically, access control is enforced implicitly by a web application's code. In WEBLOG, however, a developer writes an access control policy separately from the application's functional description and WEBLOG weaves the two together to implement the functionality of the application while simultaneously obeying the access control policy. WEBLOG allows a developer to express such a policy using SQL statements that describe the fragment of the database (the RDBMS, Session, Cookie) that the application is allowed to read and write, conditioned on the current database.

For example, in WeBid, to require that a user profile is only writable by the user herself, the developer would state that the tuples of the `User` table in the RDBMS that are writable are those where the `username` is the same as the `username` of the Session as shown in Listing 6. These statements are syntactically similar to SQL's GRANT/REVOKE statements.

Currently, WEBLOG only supports *write* policies, since they are easier to enforce than *read* policies. *read* policies are more difficult to enforce because the compiler must ensure that given the output of the servlet and the source code for the application, the user can only *infer* information that she is allowed to *read*.

To enforce a `write` policy on a servlet, WEBLOG analyzes the servlet code that inserts tuples and the servlet code that deletes tuples. Because of SQL's syntax and WEBLOG's support for only a fragment of SQL, it is straightforward to extract all the conditions (written in SQL) on the HTTP inputs, session, cookies, and RDBMS under which the servlet inserts data into a given table. It is convenient to think of these conditions as a (possibly complex) SQL integrity constraint. Likewise, it is easy to extract all the conditions (written in SQL) under which data is deleted from a given table, and it is easy to extract all the conditions under which the access control policy allows a given table to be written. We use ι_t to denote the conditions under which the servlet inserts tuples into table t, δ_t to denote the conditions under which the servlet deletes tuples from table t, and ζ to denote the conditions under which the access control policy allows table t to be written.

Conceptually, a servlet obeys an AC write policy if for every table t and for all possible HTTP inputs, sessions, cookies, and RDBMS databases, all the tuples inserted and deleted are allowed to be written, *i.e.*, that the following is always true: $\iota_t \vee \delta_t \Rightarrow \zeta$.

This analysis can be delegated to off-the-shelf, first-order automated reasoning systems because WEBLOG supports only that fragment of SQL that can be easily translated into first-order logic. Thus the formula above can be viewed as a formula in first-order logic, where if that formula is valid (*i.e.*, true for all HTTP inputs, sessions, cookies, and RDBMS databases), then the servlet obeys the access control policy. For lack of space, we give no details about

Listing 6.

```
ALLOW write ON SELECT User.* FROM User, Session WHERE User.username = Session.username
```

converting SQL to and from first-order logic but refer the reader to well-known results on the topic [5].

If the formula above fails to hold (which we discover because the automated reasoning system invoked by the compiler provides a counterexample or the system fails to find a proof in a reasonable amount of time), it is a simple matter to modify the servlet in question to enforce the access control policy. The compiler adds a new guard to the servlet that checks if the combination of the HTTP request data, cookies, session, and RDBMS data violates the formula above, and if so rejects the data. By adding such a guard, the compiler guarantees that the servlet will never be executed on inputs that will violate the access control policy. The guard that the compiler constructs is simply the formula above converted from first-order logic back into SQL. This is a rather direct implementation of the access control policy; the real difficulty lies in simplifying that guard and eliminating checks that the servlet's other guards perform. The check that the formula above is true for *all* databases can be seen as an extreme attempt at simplification: one in which the guard is eliminated altogether.

4.5 Cross Site Request Forgery (CSRF) ✗

CSRF attacks (ranked at OWASP 5) arise when one web application fools a user into executing functionality on a different web application. For example, a third-party application could produce a web page with a link labeled as "Home" that when clicked sends an HTTP request to WeBid that places a new bid on an existing auction. Such attacks are only possible because the WeBid server cannot tell whether the request originated from a legitimate WeBid client page or from another application.

The typical defense against CSRF attacks is to embed a unique token in every client web page that is sent to the server whenever sensitive operations are performed. The server only performs those sensitive operations when the right token is included in the HTTP request. Since a WEBLOG application declares what forms / links are present on each page, the compiler can automatically add the required tokens along with guards that ensure the proper token is received. Moreover, the compiler can also automatically detect which servlets cause side effects (by inspecting whether they make updates to the RDBMS/cookie/session), and hence can add tokens for only those forms / links whose targets will cause side effects. This alleviates the problem of *overprotection* (protecting requests that are do not change state at the server), as tokens will only be checked for requests that can make state changes to the server.

4.6 Session Management Vulnerabilities ✗

Session Mangement Vulnerabilities (OWASP 3) are of two sorts. The first arise because the developer made simple mistakes about the mechanics of creating a cookie representing the session ID for a given request. Similar to many modern web development frameworks, WEBLOG directly implements session management and hence addresses mechanical session management vulnerabilities. A WEBLOG developer need manipulate the session for each request, and WEBLOG automatically includes the necessary session ID cookie in the response (whenever the session is non-empty). Similarly, each incoming request with a session ID cookie causes WEBLOG to load the corresponding session data automatically. The second kind of vulnerability arises because the developer mistakenly sends sensitive information to the user through cookies. This type of session management vulnerability is addressed by WEBLOG's access control protection, described in Section 4.4.

4.7 Cryptographic storage ✗

Cryptographic storage vulnerabilities (OWASP 7) arise when sensitive data stored in the RDBMS (or in files) is not encrypted to protect against attackers who gain access to the database itself. We envision the developer writing a separate cryptographic security policy dictating which fragments of the database ought to be encrypted upon storage. Given such a policy, the compiler automatically (a) adds a final update to each servlet that encrypts data just before saving it to the backend RDBMS and (b) modifies each servlet so that the data is decrypted before any guard is checked or update performed on that data. The compiler could improve the performance of this basic approach by only decrypting that data that the servlet needs when it needs it. For example, if a servlet only checks the equality of two sensitive pieces of data and the encryption algorithm is deterministic, decryption is unnecessary and the compiler could avoid inserting the decryption code.

4.8 Transport layer ✗

Transport layer vulnerabilities (OWASP 9) arise when sensitive data is not encrypted in messages sent between client and server (*e.g.*, the application fails to use HTTPS when requesting credit card numbers). Similar to cryptographic storage vulnerabilities, WEBLOG could allow the developer to write a transport layer policy dictating which fragments of the database ought to be protected in transit, and then the compiler could choose HTTPS for any servlet sending or receiving information that is derived from or saved to a sensitive fragment of the database.

4.9 Forced browsing ✗

A forced browsing attack (OWASP 8 & 10) occurs when the attacker requests URLs in an order that the application did not anticipate. For example, an attacker could try to skip crucial pages in an e-commerce shopping cart application to manipulate the total price of her purchases. WEBLOG's underlying access control model ensures that no single servlet invocation will leak sensitive information, but does not ensure that multiple servlets will interact as they were intended (*e.g.*, redirects and forwards). We are currently working on adding a workflow policy language that enables developers to describe how servlets ought to interact so that the compiler can automatically enforce that policy.

5. Evaluation

To evaluate WEBLOG, we addressed the following questions. Which common web application features is WEBLOG expressive enough to implement? And, can WEBLOG be used to implement a real-world application in its entirety, and how does that implementation's security compare to an implementation in a traditional web development framework? When evaluating security, we concentrated on the four defenses our implementation currently supports (implementations for the remaining defenses are underway): SQLi, XSS, parameter tampering, and access control.

5.1 Web Application Features

To understand which features are important in today's web applications, we surveyed two existing ones: WeBid (an online auction website used as the running example in this paper) and B2Evolution (a blogging platform) [1]. We analyzed WeBid closely and found that the features it uses are limited to CRUD (creating, retrieving, updating, and deleting information from the database), sending emails, basic file IO (*e.g.*, uploading file from disk), processing credit cards/paypal payments, captcha support, basic computation (*e.g.*, image manipulation for creating thumbnails), AJAX support, and HTTP redirects. The following table summarizes the prevalence of these features in WeBid in terms of the number of PHP files concerned primarily with each feature. For B2Evolution, we made a cursory analysis looking for features not appearing in WeBid but found nothing noteworthy.

74%	CRUD + HTTP redirects
8%	Email support
7%	File IO
3%	Payment processing
3%	Captcha
3%	Computation
1%	AJAX

CRUD (Create, Retrieve, Update, Delete) CRUD operations are the actions necessary to manipulate the data contained in the backend relational data management system (RDBMS) of an application: create new elements, retrieve existing elements, update existing elements, and delete unwanted elements. In both WeBid and B2Evolution, for example, user profiles must be created, the details of a profile auction must be retrieved from the database so as to be displayed to the user, profiles must be updated if the user wants to change her email address, and profiles must be deleted if the user decides to terminate her use of the application.

Both WeBid and B2Evolution are implemented in PHP, where all of the CRUD operations (which are implemented manually) follow the same basic outline. Check that the user-provided data is well-formed and either reject malformed data or sanitize it. Dynamically construct SQL statements by concatenating developer-written SQL fragments with user-provided data. Execute the SQL statement. Iterate over the results of the execution and output HTML tags to mark up each of the results. Typically, each CRUD operation is implemented by a separate piece of PHP code, at the end of which a different SQL command is executed. Listing 7 contains examples of SQL commands for CRUD operations.

When developing CRUD operations with WEBLOG, we can often combine the code for CUD into a single SQL update module. The servlets for creation, updating, and deletion can then all use this same module. The only reason the Retrieve functionality cannot be included is that instead of moving data from the user to the RDBMS, the R operation moves data from the RDBMS to temporary tables for output to the user. This is shown in Listing 8.

Search While analyzing WeBid, we discovered that half of the CRUD-only PHP files are limited to simply reading from the database, but not writing to it. These files can therefore be viewed as providing search functionality; here we focus on implementing an advanced search, a common feature of today's applications. The advanced search mechanism allows a user to search for information by specifying conditions on different attributes. For example, WeBid allows users to search for an auction by putting constraints on the auction title, description, and maximum bid price.

The PHP implementation of WeBid's advanced search dynamically constructs the appropriate SQL query by iteratively combining developer-written SQL fragments with user-data. The difficult part is ensuring that only those attributes that the user gave conditions for are used in the resulting query. For example, if the user selected a maximum bid price and included a query string for the title but imposed no restrictions on the description, the SQL query must include the bid price and the title in the WHERE clause but not the description. The following PHP snippet gives the flavor of how the PHP code constructs such a query.

```
$query = "SELECT * FROM auctions";
if ($title != "" || $desc} != "")
   $query .= " WHERE ";
if ($title != "")
   $query .= "title = ".$title;
if ($desc != "")
   $query .= "OR description = ".$desc;
```

Implementing this feature in WEBLOG requires care because SQL queries cannot be generated dynamically. Instead of dynamic generation, we can think of the construction of the search results as a sequence of database updates, each of which filters the auctions found so far by a different search attribute. In our example, the first update creates a temporary table with all of the available auctions. The second update eliminates all those auctions that fail to satisfy any `title` search criteria or is a noop if no search criteria are imposed. The third update eliminates all those auctions that fail to satisfy the `description` search criteria, and the fourth update handles the `bid` critera. See Listing 9.

Web Form Validation Today's web applications typically include web forms for soliciting user data that validate the user's data before sending it to the server. For example, both WeBid and B2Evolution check that when someone creates a new user, the email address has the right format. Because client-side validation cannot be trusted by the server (an attacker can disable JavaScript or manually send an arbitrary HTTP request), the same validation must be duplicated on the server. Writing and maintaining two different code bases (often in different languages) implementing the same functionality is a notoriously difficult problem.

While PHP includes some support for validation (`http://www.php.net/manual/en/book.filter.php`), the developer typically writes the JavaScript validation code, the PHP validation code, and the HTML for displaying the form. Ruby on Rails (ROR) has built-in support for server-side validation but still requires manually written JavaScript code for client-side validation. The Google Web Toolkit (GWT) is the forerunner in this category because it allows the developer to dictate which server-side code should be duplicated on the client.

In WEBLOG, a developer wanting to build a web form dictates what kind of data the form is supposed to solicit from the user and allows WEBLOG to do the rest. For a basic form without client-side validation, the developer gives just a database schema for the user to fill out, and WEBLOG generates HTML for building that form. To include client-side validation, the developer adds SQL guard modules, and WEBLOG then automatically generates the JavaScript for checking those constraints. WEBLOG also checks those constraints on the server when data is submitted. Thus, the developer only writes a single validation code base, and WEBLOG duplicates that validation code wherever it is needed.

Limitations One of known limitations of WEBLOG is lack of support for systems operations, such as sending emails, writing files, caching, Apache configuration. We will only add such support if doing so does not diminish the compiler's ability to eliminate security vulnerabilities. For example, file manipulation is likely to make deep analysis far more difficult and will likely not be supported. Another class of limitations is that of administrative control: when significant customization or sophisticated administrative interfaces are used. For example, a page that accepts an arbitrary SQL query and returns the results cannot be built in WEBLOG. A third class of limitations arises when significant computation is necessary, *e.g.*, image manipulation. Such algorithms can be written in traditional languages and then "called" by referencing special database tables

Listing 7.

```
sql.execute("INSERT INTO users VALUES ($username,$pwd,$email,$bio)");
sql.execute("SELECT * FROM users WHERE username = $username")
sql.execute("UPDATE users SET email = $email, biography = $bio WHERE username = $username");
sql.execute("DELETE FROM users WHERE username = $username");
```

Listing 8.

```
defupdate user-cud
   DELETE FROM Users WHERE EXISTS (SELECT * FROM HttpInput WHERE HttpInput.login = Users.login)
   INSERT INTO Users (login, first, last, email) SELECT login, first, last, email FROM HttpInput
```

Listing 9.

```
defservlet display-search-results
   :transducer (upd0 upd1 upd2 upd3)

defupdate upd0
  INSERT INTO Search * SELECT * FROM Auction

defupdate upd1
  DELETE FROM Search WHERE EXISTS (SELECT * FROM HttpInput H WHERE H.title != "" AND H.title LIKE Search
      .title)

defupdate upd2
  DELETE FROM Search WHERE EXISTS (SELECT * FROM HttpInput H WHERE H.desc != "" AND H.title LIKE Search.
      desc)

defupdate upd3
  DELETE FROM Search WHERE EXISTS (SELECT * FROM HttpInput H WHERE H.bid != "" AND H.bid >= Search.
      maxbid)
```

in WEBLOG, but we must investigate how the addition of such algorithms affects WEBLOG's security guarantees.

5.2 Expressiveness and Security

Next we evaluated whether or not WEBLOG is sufficiently expressive to build an entire web application and how the resulting application compares in terms of security to the same app written by someone of roughly the same skill in a more traditional web development framework. We experimented on the existing application WebSubRev [4], an open source application for submitting papers to a conference that has been used at several dozen venues, and asked one student to re-implement it in WEBLOG and another to re-implement it in Sinatra (a Ruby-based framework).

Implementations The most important result is that it is possible to implement WebSubRev in its entirety using WEBLOG. WebSubRev is mainly a collection of CRUD operations (saving submitted papers in a database), a task for which WEBLOG excels. The WEBLOG and Sinatra implementations also turned out to be quite similar syntactically and required roughly the same amount of time to write, about an hour. Their similarity can be attributed to the correspondences between language constructs in Sinatra and WEBLOG (see the below table for a summary).

RUBY/SINATRA	WEBLOG
`get '/submit'`	`defservlet new-submit`
`post '/submit'`	`defservlet submit`
`.erb files`	`defrenderer`
`DataMapper models`	`defschema`

Security The second interesting result was that despite their similar syntax and development times, the two versions differed in terms of security/usability. Both applications are free of SQL injection attacks. For Sinatra, this was a byproduct of using an object-relational mapper (ORM), which safely handles the common functions like writing an object to the database. However SQL injection attacks would be possible if extending the experiment to include functionality not covered by the ORM, such as advanced search. In contrast, the WEBLOG application developer could not introduce a SQL injection attack even if she tried.

For cross-site scripting (XSS), the Sinatra implementation of WebSubRev was vulnerable to attack. Any HTML code submitted via the form is blindly stored in the database and sent to the browser unsanitized. The developer relied too heavily on the ORM's built-in functionality and neglected to consider the problem of XSS. Had we used Ruby on Rails, an XSS defense is built-in, but that defense must be disabled to allow users to format their data using HTML, thereby making it vulnerable to XSS attack.

For parameter tampering, the Sinatra implementation was not vulnerable to attack because it included all the proper data validation on the server; however, it included no client-side validation since doing so required writing validators in JavaScript. The WEBLOG implementation was also immune from attack but included both client-side and server-side validation, despite the developer having only written client-side validation. The automatic security of WEBLOG enabled the developer to build a more user-friendly application that was just as secure as the Sinatra application.

Finally, for access control neither implementation had any access control policy violations, mainly because WebSubRev had so few features that there was little opportunity.

6. Related Work

There have been numerous approaches to web development based on the declarative paradigm and SQL, *e.g.*, Hilda [23], SAFE [18], FORWARD [14], Strudel [13], Spicey [15], and SVC [25]. Typically this work is concerned with providing a language where the compiler can automate the implementation of conceptually simple but technically tedious or delicate functionality. For example, FORWARD allows a web developer to build clients that display a fragment of the application's backend database where updates are automatically propagated via AJAX. To use FORWARD, the developer writes the SQL query describing the fragment of the database that should be displayed, and the compiler automatically generates the necessary AJAX and server code. In contrast to languages aimed at providing additional functionality, WEBLOG was designed to provide security guarantees—to completely eliminate those security vulnerabilities that are most prevalent in today's web applications.

Within the security community, the work most related to WEBLOG falls under the category of *by-construction security*, which [17] describes comprehensively. The most relevant work is is SELinks [12], SIF [10], Swift [9], Resin [24], UrFlow [8], [19], [20], and [16]. All these works are based on fully expressive, traditional programming languages (such as Java and Haskell) and are carefully designed to eliminate one or two known security vulnerabilities from web applications. But because their underlying languages are fully expressive, extending these approaches to eliminate additional vulnerabilities requires redesigning the language, if it is possible at all. In contrast, because WEBLOG is less expressive it is far more likely that additional security guarantees can be implemented by simply improving the compiler. When WEBLOG was designed, we only considered protections against SQLi, XSS, and parameter tampering. All of the other defenses (including access control) were added on after the design was complete. In short, this paper reports on the benefits and drawbacks of languages with reduced expressiveness for securing applications deployed on the World Wide Web.

7. Conclusion

WEBLOG is a declarative web development language designed to eliminate today's most prevalent security vulnerabilities. WEBLOG's compiler takes a description of an application's basic functionality together with independently authored security policies and generates code that simultaneously implements the desired functionality while respecting the developer's policies. We evaluated WEBLOG by implementing real-world applications, analyzing their security properties, and investigating the WEBLOG development process. Overall, we found that the reduced expressiveness of WEBLOG enables many strong security guarantees while enabling the development of web applications common in small businesses.

8. Acknowledgements

This work was supported in part by the National Science Foundation under awards CNS-1228697, CNS-1141863, CNS-1035914, CCF-0916438, DGE-1069311, CNS-1065537 and CNS-0845894.

References

[1] B2evolution app. http://b2evolution.net/.

[2] Common weaknesses enumeration. http://cwe.mitre.org/.

[3] Webid app. http://sourceforge.net/projects/simpleauction/,.

[4] Websubrev app. http://people.csail.mit.edu/shaih/websubrev/,.

[5] S. Abiteboul, R. Hull, and V. Vianu. *Foundations of Databases*. Addison-Wesley, 1995.

[6] P. Bisht, T. Hinrichs, N. Skrupsky, R. Bobrowicz, and V. Venkatakrishnan. NoTamper: Automatic Blackbox Detection of Parameter Tampering Opportunities in Web Applications. In *ACM Conference on Computer and Communications Security*, Chicago, IL, USA, 2010.

[7] P. Bisht, T. Hinrichs, N. Skrupsky, and V. Venkatakrishnan. WAPTEC: Whitebox Analysis of Web Applications for Parameter Tampering Exploit Construction. In *Proceedings of the 18th ACM Conference on Computer and Communications Security*, Chicago, IL, USA, 2011.

[8] A. Chlipala. Static checking of dynamically-varying security policies in database-backed applications. In *USENIX Symposium on Operating Systems Design and Implementation*, 2010.

[9] S. Chong, J. Liu, A. C. Myers, X. Qi, K. Vikram, L. Zheng, and X. Zheng. Secure web applications via automatic partitioning. In *Proceedings of the ACM Symposium on Operating Systems Principles*, pages 31–44, 2007.

[10] S. Chong, K. Vikram, and A. C. Myers. SIF: Enforcing confidentiality and integrity in web applications. In *Proceedings of the Usenix Security Symposium*, 2007.

[11] E. F. Codd. A relational model of data for large shared data banks. *Communications of the ACM*, 13(6):377–387, June 1970.

[12] B. J. Corcoran, N. Swamy, and M. Hicks. Cross-tier, label-based security enforcement for web applications. In *Proceedings of the ACM SIG for the Management of Data*, 2009.

[13] M. Fernandez, D. Florescu, A. Levy, and D. Suciu. Declarative specification of web sites with strudel. *The VLDB Journal*, 2000.

[14] Y. Fu, K. W. Ong, Y. Papakonstantinou, and M. Petropoulos. The SQL-based all-declarative FORWARD web application development framework. In *Proceedings of the Conference on Innovative Data Systems Research*, 2011.

[15] M. Hanus and S. Koschnicke. An ER-based framework for declarative web programming. In *the Symposium on Practical Aspects of Declarative Languages*, pages 201–216, 2010.

[16] A. Krishnamurthy, A. Mettler, and D. Wagner. Fine-grained privilege separation for web applications. In *Proceedings of the International World Wide Web Conference*, 2010.

[17] X. Li and Y. Xue. A survey on web application security. Technical report, Vanderbilt University, 2011. URL http://www.truststc.org/pubs/814.html.

[18] R. M. Reischuk, M. Backes, and J. Gehrke. SAFE extensibility for data-driven web applications. In *Proceedings of the World Wide Web*, 2012.

[19] W. Robertson and G. Vigna. Static enforcement of web application integrity through strong typing. In *Proceedings of the Usenix Security Symposium*, 2009.

[20] M. Samuel, P. Saxena, and D. Song. Context-sensitive auto-sanitization in web templating languages using type qualifiers. In *Proceedings of the ACM Conference on Computer and Communications Security*, pages 587–600, 2011.

[21] The Open Web Application Security Project. The Ten Most Critical Web Application Security Vulnerabilities. https://www.owasp.org/index.php/Category:OWASP_Top_Ten_Project.

[22] E. Z. Yang. HTML Purifier. http://htmlpurifier.org.

[23] F. Yang, J. Shanmugasundaram, M. Riedewald, and J. Gehrke. Hilda: A high-level language for data-driven web applications. In *the International Conference on Data Engineering*, 2006.

[24] A. Yip, X. Wang, N. Zeldovich, and M. F. Kaashoek. Improving application security with data flow assertion. In *the ACM Symposium on Operating Systems Principles*, 2009.

[25] W. P. Zeller and E. W. Felten. Svc: Selector-based view composition for web frameworks. In *Proceedings of the USENIX Conference on Web Application Development*, 2010.

GlassTube

A Lightweight Approach to Web Application Integrity

Per A. Hallgren
Keyflow AB &
Chalmers University of Technology
Gothenburg, Sweden
per.zut@gmail.com

Daniel T. Mauritzson
Ericsson AB &
Chalmers University of Technology
Gothenburg, Sweden
daniel.mauritzson@gmail.com

Andrei Sabelfeld
Chalmers University of Technology
Gothenburg, Sweden
andrei@chalmers.se

Abstract

The HTTP and HTTPS protocols are the corner stones of the modern web. From a security point of view, they offer an all-or-nothing choice to web applications: either no security guarantees with HTTP or both confidentiality and integrity with HTTPS. However, in many scenarios confidentiality is not necessary and even undesired, while integrity is essential to prevent attackers from compromising the data stream.

We propose GlassTube, a lightweight approach to web application integrity. GlassTube guarantees integrity at application level, without resorting to the heavyweight HTTPS protocol. GlassTube prevents man-in-the-middle attacks and provides a general method for integrity in web applications and smartphone apps. GlassTube is easily deployed in the form of a library on the server side, and offers flexible deployment options on the client side: from dynamic code distribution, which requires no modification of the browser, to browser plugin and smartphone app, which allow smooth key predistribution. The results of a case study with a web-based chat indicate a boost in the performance compared to HTTPS, achieved with no optimization efforts.

Categories and Subject Descriptors [*Security and privacy*]: Web application security

General Terms Security, integrity, man-in-the-middle-attacks

Keywords web application security, data integrity, lightweight enforcement, application-level security policies

1. Introduction

With the overwhelming expansion of the World Wide Web and increasing reliance on it by the society, the security of web applications is a crucial challenge to be addressed.

1.1 Integrity in Web Applications

Information integrity is a vital security property in a variety of applications. In general, integrity is a versatile property. Indeed, security textbooks [16, 30] agree that it is hard to pin down the essence of integrity, and surveys [26, 32, 33], tutorials [18], and papers [4, 24] identify a range of integrity flavors.

PLAS'13, June 20, 2013, Seattle, WA, USA.

In the setting of web applications, *data integrity* is particularly crucial. Data integrity, or simply integrity in the rest of this paper, requires that data sent over the network must be accurate and consistent with the intended message. This inherently means that information sent cannot be modified, and that the consignor is authentic. In contrast, *confidentiality* requires that sensitive information must not be leaked to an unauthorized party. *Passive attackers* are able to eavesdrop on the network and reuse any obtained sensitive information such as session tokens to impersonate the client for the server, and vice versa. *Active attackers* pose additional challenges for integrity as they are able to suppress and modify messages in transit and mount fully-fledged man-in-the-middle attacks.

The treatment of *sessions* is important for web application integrity. Sessions in web applications, intended to personalize user experience, are typically implemented by passing session identifiers via cookies between the server and the client. The cookies are sent with each request over the stateless HTTP protocol. A range of attacks such as *replay attacks* [35], *cross-site request forgery* [2], and *session fixation* [20] target stealing and abusing the session credentials in order to hijack sessions and impersonate users towards the server. The communication of session credentials in clear text has lead to the common misconception that *confidentiality* is needed in order to have a secure session towards a web server, in order to achieve *integrity*.

The only other standard alternative to HTTP for web applications is to use HTTPS, a web protocol that encrypts all communication using TLS/SSL. TLS/SSL provide encryption of all data traffic at the transport layer, relying on asymmetric cryptography for key exchange, symmetric encryption for confidentiality, and *message authentication codes* (MAC) for message integrity. Achieving both confidentiality and integrity comes at a price of performance on both the sending and receiving ends.

1.2 Importance of Integrity

Browsers indicate to users whenever they access a site over an unencrypted connection. However, many users associate encryption with security, and not with confidentiality. It is intuitive to most users that their connection to the bank should be encrypted. However, users are commonly far less aware about when the data they send and receive can be distorted by an unauthorized party. If integrity was maintained by default, we claim that the web would uphold the intuitive amount of security for a general web page.

Ubiquitous open wi-fi networks exacerbate the problem. Under an open configuration of a wi-fi network, as frequently used at hotels, airports, and restaurants, the traffic between the user's device and base station is unprotected. Open wi-fi networks are susceptible to both passive and active attackers. This creates an ideal scenario for session hijacking attacks, as popularized by tools such as

Firesheep [5], a Firefox extension to impersonate users logged on to social networks such as Facebook. This type of vulnerability that can be exploited by script kiddies must be viewed as severe.

While it is essential that an attacker does not impersonate a user, hijacking sessions is extremely simple with many web popular services such as Wikipedia. This can be done using such popular tools as Wireshark for network monitoring and, for example, Opera to open a session with a user specified cookie. A successful attack can be mounted by non-experts in a matter of minutes. A man-in-the-middle can then freely modify any information sent between the server to the client. A victim service provider might suffer a damaged brand, reduced sales and general sabotage. A victim user might be infected with malware or provided with incorrect information.

We argue that integrity is vital for any web application, regardless of whether the application utilizes sessions. Clearly, there is a cost to maintain integrity, and in many cases the chances of a breach may not be so high as to weigh heavier than that cost. However, to neglect integrity implies both disregarding what a user sees on a site and disregarding what the server perceives that a user posts. To put it boldly, why communicate if you do not care if the content transferred between the two parties is arbitrarily modified?

1.3 Scenarios

From a security point of view HTTP and HTTPS offer an all-or-nothing choice to web applications; either no security guarantees with HTTP or both confidentiality and integrity with HTTPS at the price of performance. However, in many scenarios confidentiality is not necessary and even undesired, while integrity is essential to prevent attackers from compromising the data stream. Example scenarios include:

Public web site browsing. Open web sites such as Wikipedia allow users to manipulate public data. Data confidentiality is not needed, while attempts of malicious modification of content and impersonating users need to be thwarted.

Open source projects. Large volumes of data are transferred for publishing and downloading open source software projects. Since the data is public from the outset, confidentiality is not necessary. Integrity is however a must to prevent malicious modification of the code.

Provider or authority disruption. Even though in many cases a full-fledged man-in-the-middle attack may seem unlikely, they do exist even outside the scope of an unprotected wi-fi. For example, a service provider has all the relevant tools and may have reason to interfere with their users traffic. Indeed, some ISPs are known to inject code into their user's web traffic on a regular basis [10].

1.4 Goals

Motivated by the above scenarios, our goal is to create an approach to integrity in web applications designed to authenticate both the client and the server towards each other. While we focus on the mutual authentication and integrity towards both the client and the server for each message within a session, we note that the authentication of *users* is an orthogonal issue [21], which we leave to the application. Both parties must be able to check that all packets originate from the other party in the conversation, and must also be able to verify the integrity of each message. Users and servers will thus be protected from session hijacking. A key goal is to protect against man-in-the-middle attacks, thwarting any attempts of modifying the data stream by the adversary.

We aim at specifying a general yet practical approach for integrity in web applications. It is thus important to support the approach with a proof-of-concept implementation, in order to evaluate programming overhead for the developer as well as indicative performance overhead.

The performance of an integrity approach for web applications is vital: if it does not relieve the server compared to HTTPS, there is no tangible reason to choose it over HTTPS. Hence, an important goal is performance boost compared to HTTPS, decreasing the cost per client. When bandwidth, database access, and/or other I/O form a bottleneck, the costs are still reduced in terms of computational resources on the server side. It is particularly interesting to study the overhead in an entire application, because optimizing the building blocks for cryptographic primitives does not necessarily mean overall performance improvement [31].

The final goal is a flexible framework that allows extensions where the degree of integrity can be tuned in an application-specific way. This is in contrast with application-agnostic HTTPS where the encryption method is set to null, as discussed in Section 6. GlassTube will function well for singular services, without requiring global support by browsers.

1.5 Contributions

With the goals above in mind, we propose GlassTube, a lightweight approach to web application integrity. GlassTube guarantees integrity at application level, without resorting to the heavyweight HTTPS protocol. The design will protect web applications against man-in-the-middle attacks where the attacker has complete control of the network. GlassTube guarantees protection against the following:

1. Modification of the data stream
2. Session hijacking
3. Reordering and replay attacks

GlassTube provides a general method for integrity in web applications and smartphone apps. GlassTube includes an initial setup phase, including a key exchange phase, where the server and client collaborate to establish a session key, to be later used for creating and verifying message authentication codes (MACs). The setup phase requires a connection which guarantees end-to-end integrity and the authenticity of the server; this can be accomplished with the help of HTTPS. Once set up, the following messages in the session are sent over HTTP, with integrity assured by GlassTube MACs on per-message level.

GlassTube is easily deployed in the form of a library on the server side, and, as mentioned above, it offers flexible deployment options on the client side: from dynamic code distribution, which requires no modification of the browser, to browser plugin and smartphone app, which allows smooth key predistribution.

To evaluate GlassTube in practice, we have implemented a simple web chat service that uses GlassTube as library for integrity. The chat service requires minimal efforts from the developer to enable secure GlassTube sessions. Further, our experiments indicate a boost in performance compared to HTTPS, achieved even when no optimization efforts were made.

GlassTube opens up new possibilities for web application security. Application-level support implies flexibility in customizing the level of cryptographic protection suitable for different applications. It also opens up new avenues for application-specific confidentiality, where only selected information is encrypted, useful when the bulk of communicated data is public.

2. The GlassTube Approach

GlassTube is designed to provide integrity over insecure connection, preventing manipulation of the data stream. This section specifies the GlassTube approach. The approach consists of two phases. The GlassTube Setup is the first phase. It maintains distribution of code and the key exchange. The second phase of the approach is the

GlassTube Data Transfer (GTDT), which ensures integrity between the web server and the client.

2.1 GlassTube Setup

GTDT requires that the code running on the client is not modified by an attacker, and that a session key is shared between the client and the application server, henceforth called the data site, which is secret except to the data site and the client. GlassTube can be initialized in any fashion that meets these requirements. This section describes some options to distribute code and how keys can be exchanged, independently from each other.

2.1.1 Client Code Distribution

Since web applications are not present on the client per default, the client-side code often needs to be sent at the beginning of the session. If an attacker can alter the client's code at this stage, following packets must be considered compromised as e.g. script injection at this stage can change how transfers are made in the future. It is therefore vital that the code's integrity can be guaranteed. Client code can be distributed either *statically* or *dynamically*. Statically distributed code is previously present at the client (e.g. a browser plugin). Dynamically distributed code is sent when the web application is accessed by the web browser. Examples of both are presented in the following paragraphs.

Static distribution of client code refers to the installation and use of browser plugins or applications for smartphones. In this case, for an end user to communicate with a web server running GlassTube, he or she needs to acquire and install additional software prior to making the first request.

Dynamic distribution is the most common type for web applications, as it is used by almost every page on the web. Typically dynamic code consists of JavaScript, Flash, Silverlight, or Java applets embedded within the page. Dynamic code distribution for GlassTube must be done by a host which guarantees end-to-end integrity, and for which the client is able to verify the server's identity. This host is henceforth called the secure site. The secure site only communicates with the client during the setup of a GlassTube session. If code is dynamically distributed, the goal is that the client is reinitialized as rarely as possible, to boost performance by limiting the reliance on HTTPS. Instead, all content can be fetched with AJAX from the data site, and only the bare bones of the application are sent from the secure site.

2.1.2 Key Exchange

GTDT relies on a session key to be shared between the client and the data site, in order for both of them to be able to create and verify MACs. A new session key is negotiated at the beginning of each session. It is not possible to reuse keys negotiated during TLS; JavaScript, and many server frameworks, does not provide access to transport layer information.

We propose the use of a known protocol, the Authenticated Diffie-Hellman protocol [12–14] (ADHE) to exchange keys, an authenticated version of the classical Diffie-Hellman key exchange [13]. The scheme requires that the client possess a public key belonging to the data site. The public key can be acquired either by distributing the key with the code or by fetching it from a secure site after code distribution.

The Diffie-Hellman protocol uses two domain parameters, a generator g and a prime number p. The domain parameters are not necessarily secret. The two parties within a Diffie- Hellman key exchange each generate a random number to be their private key, x and y respectively. They then create their public key as $X = g^x \bmod p$ and $Y = g^y \bmod p$, which they send to the other party. Both parties can now compute their shared key $Z = g^{(xy)} \bmod p = X^y \bmod p = Y^x \bmod p$. An eavesdropper knows both X and Y, but neither of x and y, and thus cannot find Z [13]. The shared key will be called Z and *session key* interleaving throughout the paper.

Under the Authenticated Diffie-Hellman key exchange, the server's public key is signed using a DSA or RSA certificate. The client's public key can also be signed in the same manner, if client certificates can be distributed in a feasible manner. The client is thus able to verify the server's public key's integrity, preventing man-in-the-middle attacks [12, 14].

Random numbers are needed in the above key exchange. It is possible that the client does not have enough entropy to provide secure random number generation. In that case, the client can be supplied with random numbers by the secure site. It is possible for the server to compute the entire key as well as to simply generate a random number. It is preferred to let the client compute the keys instead, to relieve the server from the extra work. Random numbers sent from the secure site requires both integrity and confidentiality, as well as authentication of the secure site. In dynamic code distribution, the random numbers can be sent to the client embedded in the code. In that case, the code will need to be encrypted, as the numbers must remain secret. However, since the only practical protocol to securely distribute code is HTTPS, this would typically be done without any performance loss or modifications of the secure site.

2.2 GlassTube Data Transfer

Data transfers done with GTDT guarantees data integrity. The authenticity of the sender of each message is be verified, and messages are prevented from being replayed. This section details how this is accomplished.

2.2.1 Message Identifier

In order to prevent replay attacks it must be possible to distinguish each request from other requests containing the same data. The receiver must be able to determine whether a message identifier is valid. GlassTube addresses this by appending a unique identifier to each message, called *message identifier* or *I* for the remainder of this paper. I can be any entity using which the following two properties can be guaranteed:

- An attacker must not be able to forge messages by replaying them
- An adversary must not be able to reorder messages within a session

There are several common ways to guarantee freshness properties, each with their respective strengths and weaknesses. Timestamps are very common, as they are easy to implement and very efficient. As no additional information needs to be stored to verify if a timestamp is fresh, it is also a very scalable design. Timestamps does not, however, uphold either of the above properties. Unique nonces are also a common design, as they do not allow for a window in which messages can be replayed, and thus protect completely against eavesdroppers. However, nonces can be reordered if the attacker has sufficient access to the network. Sequence numbers provide desired security and can be efficiently implemented, making them a particularly suitable message identifier for GlassTube. Each party must for the duration of the session remember their own current sequence number, and which number is expected from the other party with the next message. When either party sends a message, they increment their own number by one. When receiving a message, the message identifier is verified by comparing the stored number with the received number; the received number must be equal to the stored number in order for the message identifier to be valid.

2.2.2 MAC

The data which is authenticated by the MAC in GlassTube includes all application-level information that defines the request or response, in the sense that if it is changed it will modify the data stream. A message should not be substitutable by a message which is not equivalent to the original. GlassTube must guarantee that the receiving end can verify the following based on the MAC, on application level:

1. The message has been delivered to the correct handler
2. No data used by the application has been modified, including headers values
3. This is the first time the message has been received
4. Messages are not being reordered

For a request, the defining data includes the complete URL (1), the request method (1), request parameters (2), and the message identifier (3, 4). For a response, defining data includes the response code (2), the response data (2), finally the message identifier (3, 4), and also the MAC for the request being responded to (1).

By including the URL in the MAC, the server can trivially verify which handler was intended to receive the request. For the client, there is no data in ordinary HTTP information which specifies a handler, as they are not apparent in traditional web applications. As a browser may execute multiple AJAX requests simultaneously, mapping responses to the correct handler is only possible by looking at port numbers, which is how the web browser determines the fact. GlassTube enables this to be done by the application by including the request's MAC in the response's MAC.

All header fields can not be included in the MAC, as content in header fields is frequently modified by intermediate hosts. Instead, the application can specify which headers it makes use of. Application headers included in the MAC are specified per request by the application using the X-GlassTube-Extra-Headers header field.

Reordering request parameters or header fields will produce a different MAC. Thus, the order of these are explicitly defined by the GlassTube protocol, rather than by the order in which they are received by the application. Both header fields and request parameters in HTTP are constructed as key-value pairs, and both are henceforth called message variables. A response cannot contain request parameters, and message variables in a response will thus only consist of header fields. We denote a message variable as $V_i = (k_i, v_i)$, for it's key k_i and value v_i. The union of all message variables are sorted alphabetically, resulting in a list ω, in order to deterministically determine the order on an arbitrary platform. The list of alphabetically ordered message variables ω are concatenated as follows while preparing the MAC, resulting in the string τ:

$$\tau = cat(k_0, "=", v_0) \quad (1)$$

$$\tau = cat(\tau, cat(k_i, "=", v_i, "\&")) \qquad \forall i \in [0 .. |\omega|] \quad (2)$$

Where $cat()$ performs string concatenation of all input parameters, with respect to order, and returns the result, while not modifying the parameters. The algorithm will result in a string which looks very much like GET request parameters.

As HTTP is an asymmetric protocol, the MAC is constructed slightly differently by both parties. The server will compute the MAC using a keyed-hash function Θ, τ as computed above, the session key Z, the message identifier I, the response body $body$, and the response code rc as:

$$MAC = \Theta(Z, concat(rc, \tau, body, req\_mac, I)) \quad (3)$$

The client computes the MAC using τ, the message identifier I, the request method $method$, and the URL url as:

$$MAC = \Theta(Z, concat(method, url, \tau, I)) \quad (4)$$

Message variables, the response body, and the response code are sent by the web application as usual.The MAC and the message identifier are included in each request and each response using two header fields, for the message identifier the header field is called X-GlassTube-Message-Identifier and for the MAC it is called X-GlassTube-MAC.

The HMAC-SHA1 MAC algorithm is particularly suitable for use with GlassTube as it is efficient and secure [28]. Cipher suite negotiations are common in similar protocols, but are not feasible in GlassTube web application, or smartphone app. In both cases, the client and the server are parts of a specifically designed system. The smartphone app is designed to work with a specific web service as a back-end, and the web app is sent by the web service by the beginning of the session. Thus, the programmer will decide ciphers as they construct the service. The browser plugin is more complicated, as it can be used towards several, different web services. In order for it to conform to the GlassTube protocol, browser plugins are restricted to HMAC-SHA1. Servers must announce GlassTube support to browser plugins unless they support HMAC-SHA1. Currently, only HMAC-SHA1 is supported by the GlassTube libraries.

2.2.3 Verifying a Message

Upon receiving a message, the recipient first calculates the MAC for the message, as described in Section 2.2.2. In the case that the MAC does not match the received MAC, the message is discarded. Otherwise, the message identifier must be verified. If the message identifier is valid, the message is accepted and sent to the application, and if it is not, it is discarded The procedure is illustrated in Figure 1.

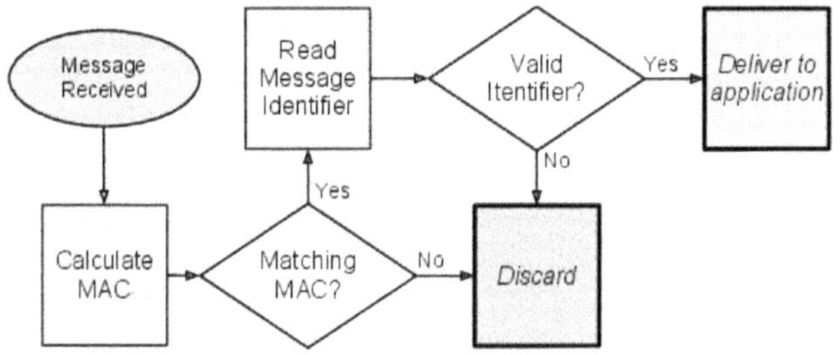

Figure 1. The verification process

Whenever the server discards a message, it must send an error message to the client, indicating what went wrong, so that a proper error message may be displayed to the end user. The error message is authenticated with GlassTube, as a normal message. Whenever the client discards a message, it must restart the session. The client is always able to address problems gracefully. If the client's message is faulty, it will receive an error message from the server, and resets the session. If the server's message is faulty (including if an error message is faulty, in the case that both the server's and the client's messages are being altered), the client resets the session.

3. GlassTube Instances

GlassTube offers a range of setup and deployment choices. This section outlines three different GlassTube instances to illustrate practical applications of the concepts presented in the previous section. Note that although all examples describe how a service may support GlassTube, the service may still choose to support HTTPS and HTTP for some pages at the site, in parallel with GlassTube.

However, it is important that the programmer is well aware that any HTTP transfers within a GlassTube session may void the integrity of messages later in the session, if used carelessly. For instance, many web applications depend on third parties to collect statistical data about how users traverse their sites. One such example is Google Analytics. Google Analytics is set up with a very short code snippet, which fetches another JavaScript file from Google's servers. It is vital that all transfers are all done using HTTPS, even when initiated by an included library or plugin. Otherwise, the site will be susceptible to man in the middle attacks. In the case of Google Analytics the request is done with SSL, and there is no need to worry.

3.1 Web Application

This section describes a setup for a web application which uses dynamic code distribution and server-side random number generation, illustrated in Figure 2.

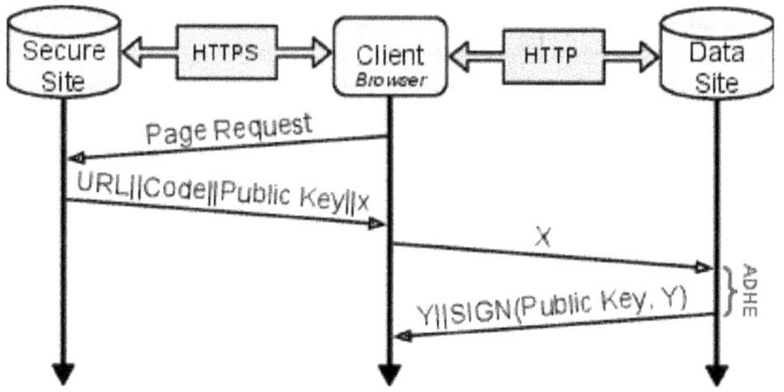

Figure 2. GlassTube for a generic web application

To start the session the client sends a `Page Request` to the secure site. The response from the secure site consists of four parts: a `URL` to the data site, `Code` that consist of GlassTube functionality and the web page's static elements and layout, the data site's `Public Key` and the client's private key x to be used in the ADHE key exchange. While sending the entire user interface from the data server might be somewhat cheaper, the user will experience some flicker and extra loading time, and thus sending a first view from the secure site will create a much smoother rendering of the page. When the client has interpreted the received code it will initiate a key exchange towards the data site using AJAX, after which it will have established a GlassTube session towards the server. Following requests should start to populate the rich web application, as the user navigates the already loaded UI, while never refreshing the web page, as that would incur another key exchange. The integrity of each message during GTDT will be guaranteed by GlassTube, and sensitive - though not secret - data can be sent confidently.

The developer sets up two sites, the secure site running HTTPS and the data site servicing HTTP. The secure site and data site may be hosted by the same machine, but may as well be distributed among different machines for load balancing. To add GlassTube functionality to the data site the developer may import a GlassTube library and mark individual pages to use GlassTube. As the secure site and the data site makes use of different protocols (HTTPS and HTTP, respectively), they are separate origins and separated by the same origin policy [3]. The data site must therefore explicitly allow the secure site to make Cross-Origin requests to it, making use of Cross-Origin Resource Sharing (CORS) [37]. A typical client code needs few modifications in order to work with GlassTube.

In a web application, it is common that data transfers are initiated when HTML is loaded on a page, making the browser fetch additional content. This happens when an ordinary image tag, such as `<img src="image.jpg" />` is rendered. The browser will fetch the image *image.jpg* from the server, without resorting to AJAX and JavaScript - indeed, JavaScript is completely oblivious regarding all data transfers which it does not initiate itself. The same is true for `<script>` and `<iframe>` tags, which means that if these tags are used by in the application to reference a resource at the server, they may break GlassTube. However, a programmer may make use the data URI scheme [25], which embeds the binary data of an element instead of referencing to its location, to achieve the same functionality that can be achieved with the traditional URL scheme.

GlassTube is fully transparent to the end user with this setup. Users access a GlassTube web page as any other web page, e.g. using a bookmark or following a link. A benefit of using this setup is that the application provider does not have to create, maintain and distribute a separate software for the client. The setup requires a secure site servicing HTTPS, and will thus have a slightly bigger impact on the server than a client with completely pre-distributed code and public key.

3.2 Generic Browser Plugin

Another way to set up a GlassTube session is by utilizing a generic browser plugin; generic in the sense that it is not bound to a certain web application or domain. This setup is outlined in Figure 3. Upon connecting to a web site, the plugin announces that it can handle GlassTube sessions, and the secure site will respond appropriately.

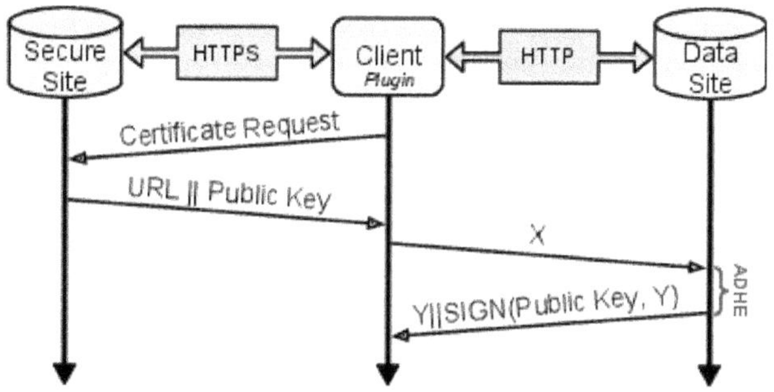

Figure 3. GlassTube as a browser plugin

A generic plugin removes the need for individual application providers to maintain and distribute plugins, and the end user only needs to take one action to be able to use any number of GlassTube sites. Benefits of using a plugin instead of dynamic code is potentially better client performance and the possibility to handle HTML-initiated requests. Note that due to the lack of a cipher suite exchange, the browser plugin will not be able to connect to services not supporting HMAC-SHA1.

An alternative approach is to store the public key along with the secure site's SSL certificate and the signature of the public key at the data site; the signature is created with the certificate. The browser plugin can then initiate the session directly towards the data site, and thus removing the reliance on HTTPS. The browser plugin verifies the data site's authenticity of the public key, and thus the data site, by verifying the signature using the certificate and the certificate towards the browsers installed root certificates.

3.3 Smartphone App

Many web applications might find it desirable to release an app that lets the users browse and edit the information, this setup is illustrated in Figure 4. It differs from the other two in the sense that no secure site is used, instead the data site's public key comes shipped with the app. This means that the overhead of first connecting to a secure site is gone, which gives a performance boost. As most apps, it is dedicated to one web site, thus an end user has to install one app per site.

For this setup the developer creates and releases an app. No secure site needs to be deployed, as the public key for the data site is shipped together with the app. Any functionality needed in the

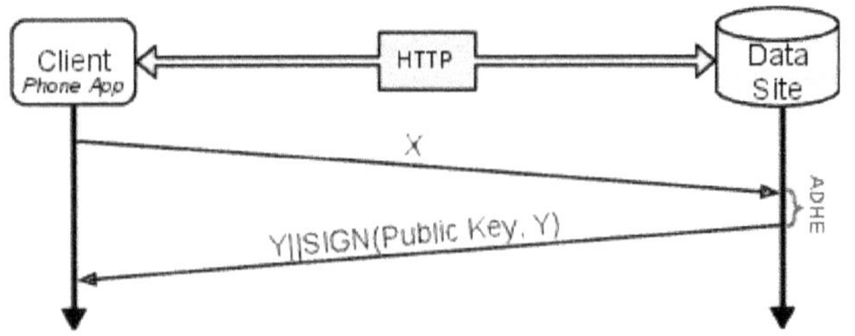

Figure 4. GlassTube as used by a smartphone app

app for key exchange and GTDT can be accessed from a library, thus very little extra work needs to be done. The data site is set up as in Section 3.1.

3.4 Notes on Scalability

The nature of GlassTube has some implications on large and complex systems, this section will briefly discuss how load balancers and cache servers integrate with GlassTube. As GlassTube enforces end-to-end integrity for the span of a session, the client will experience it as though a man-in-the-middle attach has occurred if a load balancer changes application server, and the application servers of the service does not somehow share GlassTube session keys.

Intermediate cache servers will not be able to cache any GlassTube requests, as each request is made unique by the message identifier. This fact should prevent caching completely, but misconfigured caches may erroneously cache GlassTube requests. If this occurs, the client will experience it as though an attacker is replaying old responses, and reset the session.

4. Security Considerations

This section discusses the security of GlassTube, and is divided into three parts. The first part details the different parts of the GlassTube approach, highlighting each part of a GlassTube session. The second part covers GlassTube's security guarantees. The third part pursues general security considerations.

4.1 The GlassTube Approach

This section covers the security within each stage of the GlassTube Setup, and the security of the GlassTube Data Transfer.

4.1.1 Client Code Distribution

To ensure that messages are handled correctly, it is important that the code running on the client is not modified by an attacker. Two options were presented in Section 2.1.1, one where the code is fetched from a dedicated code server, dynamically, and one where the code is available via a plugin or application on the client, statically. For both mechanisms, trusted third parties are used to securely distribute initial code.

For dynamic code distribution, the service is responsible for delivering the code to the client. As man in the middle attack can be attempted at any point during the transmission, end-to-end integrity must be guaranteed, and the client must be able to verify the server's identity. HTTP over SSL offers the required security and is a typical choice as it is broadly supported.

Static code distribution is an effective way to decrease the risk of a man in the middle attack against the client code, since the code is not sent over the network at the start of each session. It is still vital that the code is securely distributed to the client. The common distribution channels for smart-phone apps and browser plugins provide secure downloads and verifies the publisher. This means that most use cases of statically distributed code can be assumed to be secure.

4.1.2 Key Exchange

Authenticated Diffie-Hellman is a canonical way of exchanging keys in a secure manner, as it a part of TLS. Diffie-Hellman guarantees that only the communicating parties can compute the session key; eavesdropping is ineffective. Diffie-Hellman is, however, susceptible to man-in-the-middle attacks, where the attacker exchanges one key with the server and one with the client, as the identity of the server is not verified by the client. ADHE successfully thwarts man-in-the-middle attacks, as it uses a previously known server certificate, with which the client verifies the server's identity.

An attentive reader might notice that the server does not have any previous knowledge about the client, and thus a man-in-the-middle may seem possible by impersonating the client. However, this requires either that the impersonated client does not verify the server's signature in the key exchange, or that the adversary does not alter the server's Diffie-Hellman public key. In the latter case, the adversary can not interfere in the following session without being discover, and in the former the impersonated client is faulty.

4.1.3 GlassTube Data Transfer

The MAC of each message is the most vital part of GlassTube, as it ensures integrity of every message. By including the request parameters and the URL in the MAC, GlassTube asserts that the client will know if intended data is delivered to the intended service on the intended server. MACs are constructed in an asymmetric manner for requests and response, as responses and requests contain different information. Note that an adversary can not confuse the protocol by sending requests to the client or responses to the server, as such packages are discarded already by the browser or web server, and are not accepted by the application.

For a request, the attacker may try to forge the URL, the request parameters, or the message identifier. If the request parameters or the message identifiers are modified, the message will trivially be discarded by the GlassTube service. If an attacker modifies the URL, the request may be delivered to a different web application, in which case the client will reject the response. If the packet is delivered to the same application but using a different URL, the application will detect that the MAC is invalid, and will discard the packet.

With each response, the response code and data are included in the MAC along with the message identifier. The data and message identifiers are authenticated, and only handled by the client application, meaning that any modification will invalidate the MAC. Modifying the response code can have more complicated consequences, as the response code is interpreted by the web browser, but none of these cause anything else than truncation. By modifying the port numbers in a response, an adversary may cause a request to be delivered to the wrong response handler at the client. By embedding the request's MAC in the response's MAC, such attacks are prevented, as the client will be able to identify the request is handled by the intended request handler.

4.2 Security Guarantees

This section will describe how GlassTube protects against 1) Modification of the data stream, 2) Session Hijacking & 3) Reordering and replay attacks.

4.2.1 Modification of the Data Stream

A correctly set up GlassTube protects against most aspects of a man in the middle attack, except for when the attacker delays or completely removes packets from the stream, for which it is unfeasible to create a solution. GTDT will protect a correctly set up session during data transfer, as described above.

An active attacker may during a full man in the middle attack modify the entire packet, which includes TCP and IP headers. However, as both the client and the server verifies information on the application layer, nothing can be achieved except for truncation, if the attacker modifies the lower levels - assuming that no data from the lower layers are used by the application. By verifying each request using a secure MAC while keeping the session key secret, there can be no modification of the data stream during a GlassTube session.

4.2.2 Session Hijacking

An adversary cannot masquerade as the data site because each key exchange scheme uses public keys. The public keys are either distributed with the code, or fetched from the secure site, as detailed in Section 2.1.1. Both of these methods are considered secure, see Section 4.1.1. Once a session is set up an attacker can not impersonate the client, as the session is protected by each message being authenticated with MAC. If an attacker, Eve, would attempt to use the session cookie of another user, Bob, the server would at first glance think that Eve is actually Bob, thus using Bob's session key to verify the MAC. The verification would fail, as Eve does not know Bob's session key, and cannot create a correct MAC.

Note that both server and client may relay messages on to a third party, outside of the protocol. This does not violate any of the guarantees made by GlassTube, and there is no feasible way to prevent such behaviour. Once a session is set up, both parties have expressed explicit trust for the other.

4.2.3 Modifying HTTP headers

An active attacker can add, remove and modify HTTP headers. If the application uses HTTP headers, they must be included in the MAC. Any inherent behavior of the web server is considered to be the responsibility of the programmer; the configuration of the web server is part of the application. Thus, all malicious modifications of HTTP headers in a request is easily detected, and analysis of the server becomes simple. Any modified headers will either not be acted upon, or be included in the MAC. If headers are modified in responses, analysis becomes more complex, as we may not presume that the programmer is in control of the inherent behavior of the web browser.

It is possible for an attacker to modify HTTP headers in such a way that the message is interpreted differently by the browser. However, if an attacker forces the browser to modify a message, the MAC will be void. An attacker can use the Location header [15, p. 135] to force the browser to execute a new request towards another URL. Since the browser sends the *same* request to a different URL, this message will be treated in the same manner as a message with a modified URL, described in Section 4.1.3, and will lead to that the either the request is discarded by the server or by the client, depending on where the new URL points. Lastly, an attacker may attempt to change caching behaviour at the client. This, however, will not have any affect on the application, as each GlassTube request is unique and not cacheable.

When a benign intermediate host, such as firewalls and proxies, modifies header fields, a GlassTube session may be terminated or unable to commence. Thus, there may be false negatives over certain links, making GlassTube malfunction. These may completely prevent a client from reaching the service, but does not lead to a breach of integrity.

4.2.4 Replay and Reordering Attacks

GTDT uses message identifiers, as described in Section 2.2.1, to prevent both replay and reordering attacks. As the message identifier is unique for every message, the recipient will only accept a specific message identifier once. Thus, replay attacks are not possible during a GlassTube session. Reordering is made impossible by sequence numbers being sent in strictly increasing order.

4.3 General Security Considerations

The subsection will discuss general security issues, which are not confined within the limits of web applications integrity.

4.3.1 Entropy

JavaScript currently has no support for generating cryptographically secure random numbers. Unless a third party library is used, only `Math.random()` is available, which is not cryptographically secure. Although adding cryptographically strong random number generation to JavaScript API is only a matter of time [36], GlassTube does not depend on the ability of the client to generate random numbers. The client must not be used to generate random numbers if it cannot guarantee cryptographically secure random numbers. In this case, the secure site generates the random numbers and sends them securely to the client. This is the choice taken in our GlassTube instances.

4.3.2 User Authentication

Recall that user authentication is an orthogonal issue [21] left to the application. By design, GlassTube does not offer confidentiality, and it is therefore important that the application does not send authentication data in clear text. If the user gives the attacker enough information to authenticate as the user, there is often no need for integrity.

4.3.3 Denial of Service

GlassTube does not have a large performance impact on the secure site, as this site will always perform a fixed number of operations for every client; the extra workload caused by every separate GlassTube client will not increase with the number of clients.

Each session between a client and the data site requires that the data site stores information. The time to access this information will increase with each client, and thus each new session does not just add its own workload but does also affect the workload for all other sessions. This in turn means that the data site is more vulnerable to a resource exhaustion attack. However, it is very likely that the work done by the application itself will by far exceed that of any method for maintaining integrity.

5. Case Study

This section presents a working prototype of GlassTube, and investigates how it performs relatively to HTTP and HTTPS. The web application used in the study is a simple chat that allows the users to login, post messages, read messages, and logout.

5.1 GlassTube Implementation

This section covers a server implementation of GlassTube using Java and two separate clients implemented in Java and JavaScript. Java is chosen as the backbone for both the server and clients, using Google Web Toolkit [17] (GWT) to generate JavaScript as needed. Standard Java libraries are used whenever possible as they provide reasonable performance and are easy to use. The chosen implementation strategies are dynamic code distribution and server-side random number generation for the JavaScript client, with static code distribution for the Java client. A secure site and a data site are set up, but no actions have to be taken to prepare a web browser to use the JavaScript client.

The Java client is developed in order to benchmark the server, see Section 5.2. The JavaScript client is developed to assert that the user experience is not noticeably affected by GlassTube.

5.1.1 Server

Both servers are implemented with Java servlets using standard Java libraries for cryptographic functions as well as web application functionality. The implementation of the server-side part of GlassTube consists of 203 lines of Java, 66 at the secure site and 137 at the data site.

The secure site is capable of serving both the Java client and the web client respectively. The Java client uses static code distribution, while the JavaScript client makes use of dynamic code distribution. To the Java client, we thus only need to send the data site's public key, while for the web client there's also a need to serve JavaScript and the client's private key for the Diffie-Hellman key exchange. As the secure site only takes part in the setup phase no further data is handled by this server.

To make development at the data site easy, a GlassTubeServlet was created. It extends the HTTPServlet and adds GlassTube specific functions for the key exchange and for constructing and verifying MACs. The GlassTubeServlet demands that the first message from a client contains the client's public key for the Diffie-Hellman key exchange, from which the servlet computes the session key. The data site then signs its public key and sends the key as well as the signature to the client, concluding the key exchange. All servlets extending GlassTubeServlet on the data site are now ready to use GTDT. All information required for GTDT is stored in the server's session storage.

5.1.2 JavaScript Client

The JavaScript client uses GWT to convert all cryptographic functions from Java to JavaScript. The jQuery JavaScript library is used to provide smooth access to AJAX and different user interface functionality. Functions for exchanging keys and constructing and verifying MACs are thus coded in Java, while data transfers during GTDT are managed in native JavaScript using jQuery. The Java code is 75 lines long, and the JavaScript functionality needed is 14 lines long. This excludes the cryptographic functions (HMAC and SHA-1) that were needed to be imported because *javax.security* is unavailable to GWT.

Upon initialization, the JavaScript generated by GWT initiates the key exchange by computing the client's public key with the server-generated private key, embedded in the code. The client will also have the data site's DSA public key, which the client uses to verify the server's response. When the key exchange is complete, the web application is ready to be used by the end user.

5.1.3 Java Client

The Java Client is able to make use of Java's standard API to provide all needed cryptographic functions. It fetches the data site's public key and a server-generated private key from the secure site, to emulate a web client, after which the Java client commences the key exchange towards the data site. When keys have been exchanged, GTDT is ready to be used.

5.2 Benchmark

This section details the results of a series of tests conducted to verify how GlassTube performs in relation to HTTP and HTTPS. The first benchmark measures how well the server performs, and compares the average number of successful requests per second for the different techniques. The second benchmark compares the response time as experienced by the end user. As each GlassTube message must be uniquely identifiable, lest the protocol be vulnerable to replay attacks, intermediate caches will unfortunately not be able to help boost the performance of GlassTube. This is true also for HTTPS, while HTTP can obtain significant boosts by caching.

5.2.1 Server Benchmark

The benchmark is done against a very simple chat application called SimpleChat, using static fields to maintain the state of the web application. Each access to any of SimpleChat's functions is counted as a successful request by a client. A benchmark using each of the three different techniques, HTTP, HTTPS and GlassTube is performed. During the HTTP benchmark only the data site will receive traffic, during the HTTPS benchmark only the secure site will receive traffic, and during the GlassTube benchmark both will receive traffic. Therefore, the same machine is hosting both the secure site and the data site in order for the same computational resources to be available during all of the benchmarks.

The benchmarks were carried out towards a server running Tomcat 6, using standard configuration. The server machine used in the server benchmark is a Packard Bell Dot M/A-NCD/711, with a 1.2 GHz 64 bit processor with a single core, and 2GB of RAM. The SSL connection towards the server was for both clients using 256 bit AES in CBC mode, with SHA1 for message authentication and ECDHE_RSA as the key exchange mechanism.

Figure 5 plots the result of a benchmark conducted towards HTTP, HTTPS and GlassTube. The graph plots successful messages per second on the Y-axis, and the tests are carried out with an increasing number of clients for each test. The clients are configured to messages of 4096 bytes at an interval of between 10 and 300 milliseconds. The Max label in Figure 5 shows the maximal throughput for a server with unlimited processing power and a network without latency using the given client configuration.

The chosen configuration gives measurements with very little focus on how setting up new connections within the different protocols perform. However, it is very common that a user sends a multitude of requests to a server. Loading www.facebook.com, the authors observe 144 requests within the first 3 seconds at the time of writing. At the very least, a site will contain a script file, a style sheet and a couple of images besides the markup. Given that the user will navigate to a couple of pages within the site, the number of requests used during data transfer quickly grows to make the setup less prominent, when comparing the performance of the different protocols.

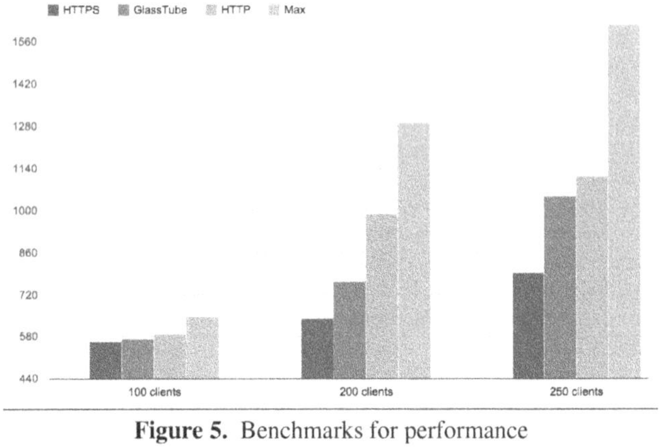

Figure 5. Benchmarks for performance

Figure 5 shows what the throughput limit for each setup is. HTTP will follow closely to the maximal limit until just about 1000 packets per second is reached, and reaches it's limit at around 1150 packets per second, while HTTPS can handle about 800 packets per second and GlassTube can process around 950 packets per second. The number of requests that can be served by GlassTube in this setting is at 250 clients 32% higher than that of HTTPS and 6% lower than HTTP, while HTTP can serve 41% more clients than HTTPS.

It is clearly visible that there is a performance gain in the above scenario when using GlassTube instead of HTTPS. GlassTube is also very close to the performance of HTTP at 250 clients, which is notable. While this does not mean that GlassTube will provide a performance boost as compared to HTTPS for an arbitrary service, it proves that it is possible to find cases where it is profitable to use application-level integrity enforcement, instead of resorting to lower-level techniques. Be it GlassTube, a derivate or later version of GlassTube, or a completely different protocol.

5.2.2 Client Benchmark

The client was benchmarked using Google Chrome, comparing the time for an AJAX call to be prepared, sent, received, and interpreted. The application used was SimpleChat, and each chat message posted was timestamped. Any timestamps in JavaScript inherently includes any time spent preparing and verifying HTTPS details. All GlassTube computations are included in the timestamps. The machine used in the client benchmark was a 13" MacBook Pro, running Intel i5 2.4 GHz CPU, and 4GB of RAM.

The average of 100 samples was 7.42 ms for HTTP, 9.9 ms for GlassTube, and 11.61 ms for HTTPS. These numbers are tiny, and the delay is not noticeable by a user. The results are consistent with the results on the server side, and shows that GlassTube can be implemented efficiently in JavaScript, as well as in Java.

6. Related Work

We share much of the motivation with work on application-level integrity described below. However, our work offers substantial added values: protection against active attackers and fine-grained application level integrity support.

SSL supports both null encryption and null authentication, both in which the respective security property is neglected. When null encryption is used, SSL functions as an integrity-only protocol. However, neither null encryption or authentication is allowed by any major browsers[22]. IPsec supports end-to-end integrity, using Authentication Header (AH) in Transport Mode. However, when AH is used in transport mode, the origin IP address is included in the signature[29]. This means that AH cannot be used in combination with NAT, and thus is not useful for most practical practical applications. We emphasize that in contrast to GlassTube, both SSL with null encryption and IPsec AH transport are protocol-level, lacking flexibility for expressing application-specific policies.

Adida presents SessionLock [1], a mechanism to protect a web session from eavesdropping. SessionLock uses HMAC to prevent eavesdroppers from simply reusing the session cookie to authenticate themselves. SessionLock does not prevent against active attacks, but prevents session hijacking and thus incapacitates tools such as Firesheep. However, an active attacker can easily alter the client's behavior by modifying a response to contain different JavaScript, which can then be used to either leak the session key or make use of the compromised client to construct signed messages.

BetterAuth [21] by Johns et al. describes a non-regressive approach to authentication, secure by default. BetterAuth is focused upon authentication, which does not handle integrity in its abstract sense. Orthogonal to GlassTube, the focus is on user authentication rather than application integrity. A common case with open services is to use authenticators specific for every application that uses the service, through e.g. OAuth [19], and to not only authenticate the user.

Dacosta et al. suggest One-Time Cookies [11] (OTC) as an alternative to using session cookies for authentication. OTC protects the session by sending a session key, encrypted, which is also used to sign the message together with each request. The stateless protocol is inspired by Kerberos, leading to a scalable design. However, the server responses are not signed, and thus the protocol is vulnerable to man in the middle attacks, in the same manner as SessionLock.

Singh et al. propose HTTPi [34], as an alternative to HTTPS that guarantees end-to-end integrity. They achieve convincing performance results by focusing on utilizing web caching. HTTPi shares much of the motivation with our approach when arguing that integrity without confidentiality is often desired. However, HTTPi occupies a somewhat different point in the design space. HTTPi is a direct alternative to HTTP and HTTPS, with possibilities for access control across HTTPS, HTTPi, and HTTP content. Similarly to HTTP and HTTPS, HTTPi relies on the support of the browser. In contrast, GlassTube is a lightweight approach that focuses on application-level support for integrity. GlassTube does not require browser modification. Being a customizable library, GlassTube features flexibility for supporting application-specific policies.

Choi and Gouda describe an integrity protocol for web applications, named similarly to the above protocol, HTTPI [7]. HTTPI is designed to allow intermediate cache servers to function, while still maintaining integrity. However, the protocol lacks protection from replay attacks, and it requires a plugin to function. Cache servers can be a great performance boost for web applications, which is most desirable. However, the choice of MD5 for hashing makes collision attacks feasible, leading to inferring the hash of the content, and hence opening for man in the middle attacks.

Chen et al. present App Isolation [6] against cross-site attacks that occur while accessing multiple websites simultaneously in the same browser, such as cross-site request forgery. They isolate browser sessions from each other. GlassTube provides the same level of protection when using JavaScript or a smartphone app without any additional efforts, as each browser window has a local and protected session key, which cannot be accessed by other windows. When utilizing a browser plugin it is up to the implementation of the plugin to provide this separation. Efforts such as App Isolation thus becomes redundant if GlassTube is employed.

The tools like SIF [8] and SWIFT [9] allow the programmer to enforce powerful policies for confidentiality and integrity in web applications. The programmer labels data resources in the source program with fine-grained policies using Jif [27], an extension of Java with security types. The source program is compiled against these policies into a web application where the policies are tracked by a combination of compile-time and run-time enforcement. The ability to enforce fine-grained policies is an attractive feature. At the same time, the enforcement is rather heavyweight: the programmer is required to use Jif as the programming language.

7. Conclusion and Future Work

We now summarize the results and give an outlook onto future work.

7.1 Summary

We have proposed GlassTube, a lightweight approach to web application integrity. Such an approach is vital when confidentiality is not needed or even undesired and when application-specific integrity policies are in place. GlassTube is compatible with several secure setup options with and without modified client. Upon successful setup, GlassTube guarantees per-message integrity, preventing a man in the middle attack from inferring changes to data between the client and the server, without being detected. GlassTube assures mutual authentication between client and server for each message within a session. As is common, the authentication of the user to the application is left to the application [21].

The deployment of GlassTube is lightweight, both in the web application setting and in the scenario of smartphone apps. Little effort is required of the developer to use the GlassTube library. GlassTube is fully transparent for the end user. The benchmarks from the case study show that GlassTube reduces the load compared to HTTPS. The performance results are encouraging, given that no optimization efforts were made. GlassTube provides a solid foundation for future implementations both refining security policies and optimizing performance, so that it can be efficiently implemented and easily deployed in existing applications.

7.2 Future Work

An important direction for future work is focused on detecting truncation attacks. When a user performs a number of actions in sequence, the adversary might cause unexpected results by dropping the last packets. A promising way to combat this is to implement application-level transactions.

GlassTube could further enhance flexibility over HTTPS-based applications if encryption could be supported by GlassTube. This will enable the programmer to specify application-specific confidentiality and integrity policies. We conjecture that sending a few packets encrypted with GlassTube while already having a GlassTube session negotiated is more efficient than setting up a new HTTPS connection for these transfers.

Another improvement that GlassTube can benefit from is freeing the programmer from using the binary data of each image, instead of its path. A similar improvement can be also made for dynamically loaded frames and scripts. This can be accomplished by having GlassTube deployed as a proxy or a module in the web server, similarly to the technique by Lekies et al. [23]. Future work includes studying the performance implications.

Acknowledgments

Thanks are due to Cedric Fournet, Martin John, and Frank Piessens for the fruitful feedback. This work was funded by the European Community under the ProSecuToR and WebSand projects and the Swedish research agencies SSF and VR.

References

[1] Ben Adida. SessionLock: securing web sessions against eavesdropping. In *Proc. International Conference on World Wide Web (WWW)*, pages 517–524, 2008.

[2] Aung Khant. A Most-Neglected Fact about Cross Site Request Forgery. `http://yehg.net/lab/pr0js/articles/A_Most-Neglected_Fact_About_CSRF.pdf?1334750354`, August 2010.

[3] A. Barth. The Web Origin Concept. RFC 6454 (Proposed Standard), December 2011.

[4] A. Birgisson, A. Russo, and A. Sabelfeld. Unifying facets of information integrity. In *Proc. International Conference on Information Systems Security*, LNCS, December 2010.

[5] Eric Butler. Firesheep. `http://codebutler.com/firesheep`.

[6] Eric Yawei Chen, Jason Bau, Charles Reis, Adam Barth, and Collin Jackson. App isolation: get the security of multiple browsers with just one. In *Proceedings of the 18th ACM conference on Computer and communications security*, CCS '11, pages 227–238, New York, NY, USA, 2011. ACM.

[7] Taehwan Choi and M.G. Gouda. HTTPI: An HTTP with Integrity. In *Proc. Computer Communications and Networks (ICCCN)*, pages 1–6, August 2011.

[8] S. Chong, K. Vikram, and A. C. Myers. Sif: Enforcing confidentiality and integrity in web applications. In *Proc. USENIX Security Symposium*, pages 1–16, August 2007.

[9] Stephen Chong, Jed Liu, Andrew C. Myers, Xin Qi, K. Vikram, Lantian Zheng, and Xin Zheng. Building secure web applications with automatic partitioning. *Commun. ACM*, 52(2):79–87, February 2009.

[10] C. Chung, A. Kasyanov, J. Livingood, N. Mody, and B. Van Lieu. Comcast's Web Notification System Design. RFC 6108 (Informational), February 2011.

[11] Italo Dacosta, Saurabh Chakradeo, Mustaque Ahamad, and Patrick Traynor. One-time cookies: Preventing session hijacking attacks with stateless authentication tokens. `http://smartech.gatech.edu/handle/1853/42609`.

[12] T. Dierks and E. Rescorla. The Transport Layer Security (TLS) Protocol Version 1.2. RFC 5246 (Proposed Standard), August 2008. Updated by RFCs 5746, 5878, 6176.

[13] W. Diffie and M. E. Hellman. New directions in cryptography. *IEEE Trans. on Information Theory*, 22(6):644–654, November 1976.

[14] W. Diffie, P. C. Van Oorschot, and M. J. Wiener. Authentication and authenticated key exchanges. *Designs, Codes and Cryptography*, 2(2):107–125, June 1992.

[15] R. Fielding, J. Gettys, J. Mogul, H. Frystyk, L. Masinter, P. Leach, and T. Berners-Lee. Hypertext Transfer Protocol – HTTP/1.1. RFC 2616 (Draft Standard), June 1999. Updated by RFCs 2817, 5785, 6266.

[16] D. Gollmann. *Computer Security (2nd Edition)*. Wiley, 2006.

[17] Google. Google Web Toolkit. `https://developers.google.com/web-toolkit/`.

[18] J. Guttman. Invited tutorial: Integrity. Presentation at the Dagstuhl Seminar on Mobility, Ubiquity and Security, February 2007. `http://www.dagstuhl.de/07091/`. Slides at `http://web.cs.wpi.edu/~guttman/`.

[19] E. Hammer-Lahav. The OAuth 1.0 Protocol. RFC 5849 (Informational), April 2010.

[20] Martin Johns, Bastian Braun, Michael Schrank, and Joachim Posegga. Reliable protection against session fixation attacks. In *Proceedings of the 2011 ACM Symposium on Applied Computing*, SAC '11, pages 1531–1537, New York, NY, USA, 2011. ACM.

[21] Martin Johns, Sebastian Lekies, and Walter Tighzert. Betterauth: Web authentication revisited. In *28th Annual Computer Security Applications Conference (ACSAC 2012)*, 2012.

[22] Kenji Urushima. SSL/TLS Supported Cipher Suites. `http://www9.atwiki.jp/kurushima/pub/pkimisc/SSLTLS_CipherSuite_Support_Table_.html`, March 2010.

[23] Sebastian Lekies, Walter Tighzert, and Martin Johns. Towards stateless, client-side driven cross-site request forgery protection for web applications. In *5th conference on "Sicherheit, Schutz und Zuverlässigkeit" (GI Sicherheit 2012)*, 2012.

[24] P. Li, Y. Mao, and S. Zdancewic. Information integrity policies. In *Workshop on Formal Aspects in Security and Trust (FAST'03)*, 2003.

[25] L. Masinter. The "data" URL scheme. RFC 2397 (Proposed Standard), August 1998.

[26] T. Mayfield, J. E. Roskos, S. R. Welke, J. M. Boone, and C. W. McDonald. Integrity in automated information systems. Technical Report P-2316, Institute for Defense Analyses, 1991.

[27] A. C. Myers, L. Zheng, S. Zdancewic, S. Chong, and N. Nystrom. Jif: Java information flow. Software release. Located at `http://www.cs.cornell.edu/jif`, July 2001.

[28] National Institute of Standards and Technology. Cryptographic Algorithm Object Registration. `http://csrc.nist.gov/groups/ST/crypto_apps_infra/csor/algorithms.html`, February 2011.

[29] B. Noble, G. Nguyen, M. Satyanarayanan, and R. Katz. Mobile Network Tracing. RFC 2041 (Informational), October 1996.

[30] Charles P. Pfleeger and Shari Lawrence Pfleeger. *Security in Computing (4th Edition)*. Prentice Hall, 2006.

[31] M. Roe. Performance of protocols. In *Security Protocols*, volume 1796 of *LNCS*, pages 147–152, 2000.

[32] A. Sabelfeld and A. C. Myers. Language-based information-flow security. *IEEE J. Selected Areas in Communications*, 21(1):5–19, January 2003.

[33] Ravi S. Sandhu. On five definitions of data integrity. In *Proceedings of the IFIP WG11.3 Working Conference on Database Security VII*, pages 257–267, 1994.

[34] K. Singh, H.J. Wang, A. Moshchuk, C. Jackson, and W. Lee. Practical end-to-end web content integrity. In *Proceedings of the 21st international conference on World Wide Web*, pages 659–668. ACM, 2012.

[35] William Stallings. *Cryptography and Network Security*. Pearson Education, fifth edition, 2011.

[36] W3C Web Cryptography Working Group. Group charter. `http://www.w3.org/2011/11/webcryptography-charter.html`.

[37] World Wide Web Consortium. Cross-Origin Resource Sharing. `http://www.w3.org/TR/2012/WD-cors-20120403/`, April 2012.

A. HTTP Header Fields

A.1 Volatile Headers

Headers listed in this section are frequently changed by intermediate hosts. Thus, including them in the MAC will often cripple an application. Potential attack vectors are considered for each header field.

An adversary can modify headers with the intent to make either browsers or server-side caches to present a cached version instead of a fresh response. This, however, will not be possible since each GlassTube message includes a message identifier which makes all requests unique and not cacheable. These include the fields Cache-Control [15, p. 108], Date[15, p. 124], Age[15, p. 106], If-Modified-Since[15, p. 130], If-Unmodified-Since[15, p. 134], If-Range[15, p. 133], Vary[15, p. 145], Expires[15, p. 127] and Last-Modified[15, p. 134].

A number of header fields are used mainly to keep track of different properties of intermediate hosts. Modification of such may lead to truncation of the data stream, but none modifies the application data in any way. They include the Via [15, p. 116], Warning [15, p. 145] and Connection [15, p. 146] header fields. Other header fields used in relation to proxies and intermediate hosts are Max-Forwards [15, p. 136], Proxy-Authenticate [15, p. 137] and Proxy-Authorization [15, p. 137]. The Max-Forwards header field can never have any other effect on a stream than truncation, as it only specifies how many times a packet can be forwarded by intermediate hosts. The Proxy-Authenticate response header is used by proxies to require the requester to supply a Proxy-Authorization request header. The first is sent out by proxies, and the latter is used to authenticate the end user towards a proxy. If a request or response causes caches or proxies to modify the message, the MAC will become invalid, and the session will be reset.

A.2 Application Headers

Headers mentioned in this section should be safe to include in the MAC, while leaving them out of the MAC will not allow an adversary to modify the data stream if they are not used by the application. Many of these headers are not modifiable form JavaScript, but they are still consider mutable as the adversary will have full access to modify messages sent over the network. If any header is used by the application, it must be included in the MAC.

The Retry-After response-header field [15, p. 140] is used to inform the client of how long a resource is expected to be unavailable, or for how long the client should stall before following a redirect. The data stream can not be modified in any way through the use of this parameter, it may however cause truncation of the stream.

The Content-MD5 header field [15, p. 121] is the MD5-signature of the entity body. If the Content-MD5 header field is modified, without the entity body being modified, the receiving party must decline the request. If both the Content-MD5 header field and the entity body is modified, in such a way that the header field is the MD5 hash of the entity body, the GlassTube MAC will be incorrect for the received entity body, and the request will be declined. This header field is completely redundant in a GlassTube session and should not be used.

The Range request header field [15, p. 138] is used to specify what parts of (which range of bytes) an entity is wanted by the application. This can be useful when retrieving a large entity. The server may decide to disregard a range request. Whenever a certain range of bytes is sent in a response, the exact range returned is specified in the Content-Range entity header field. If the Range request header field is modified, the client will need to send additional requests in order to retrieve the entire entity. If the Content-Range response header field is modified, the received bytes will be interpreted as a different byte range than the original, which will cause the MAC to be invalid, as the response body will be interpreted differently by the client than by the server.

The Accept-Ranges response-header [15, p. 105] is used to advertised to the client what, if any, byte ranges the client can request. Byte ranges may still be requested regardless of whether Accept-Ranges have been received by the client or not. Modifications of this field will lead to performance losses at worst, by introducing extra round trips. The same effect can be accomplished by the adversary by simply dropping packets.

The WWW-Authenticate response header field [15, p. 150] includes a challenge to enable the user to authenticate him- or herself. If this header field is modified, the user will not be able to be authenticated, and the result is the same as stream truncation. If a response contains a WWW-Authenticate header field, the client should respond with a request containing the Authorization header field [15, p. 107]. The Authorization header field is used to authenticate the user. However, since the Authorization field would be sent in cleartext using GlassTube, WWW-Authenticate and Authorization must never be used during a GlassTube session as it could allow an adversary to impersonate the user. Note however, that this does not violate any of GlassTube's guarantees, as the user's session is still has valid integrity.

The Allow header field [15, p. 106] is used to specify which request methods are supported for the requested resource. An attacker can set not allowed methods to be advertised as being allowed, however, they will not be served by the origin server. If the adversary changes allowed request methods to be disallowed, the data stream will be truncated the. However, nothing except for truncation can be accomplished.

The Host header field [15, p. 128] identifies the resource being requested, on a host running web services for multiple domains it controls which site is served. Modifications to the Host header field was discussed in section 4.1.3. Any modifications to this field can only lead to truncation of the data stream.

The From header field [15, p. 128] is used to identify the person responsible for a request, but only for logging purposes and never for authorization. The From header can thus never affect a current session in any way.

The Location response-header [15, p. 135] is used to redirect the client to another resource together with a response code in the range 300-399. If a GlassTube request is responded by a redirect, it will have the same effect as if the original request is modified so that it is delivered to a different service, as the browser will resend the exact same request to another host and/or URL. Signatures will not match on the target machine, and a GlassTube service will thus discard the packet. A service not running GlassTube will respond, but without adding a MAC to the response, which means that the client will discard the message. Redirects must not be used within a GlassTube session, as the client can not successfully follow them. Attacks that modify this header are void, as even benign usage leads to declined messages.

The Pragma header field [15, p. 135] is used solely to supply implementation-specific directives, to any machine along the message path. As only the active client and intended service can construct a correct MAC for a modified packet, modifications by any other party are not interesting. The only standardized value of the Pragma header field is $no - cache$, which will not cause any issues with GlassTube (removing the header may cause truncation of the data stream).

The header fields Accept [15, p. 100], Accept-Charset [15, p. 102], Accept-Encoding [15, p. 102], Accept-Language [15, p. 104]), Expected [15, p. 126] and the TE [15, p. 142], controls in what formats a response is accepted. An adversary can thus try to change the response by changing these headers, if the application reacts to them.

The two conditional request-header fields If-Match [15, p. 129] and If-None-Match [15, p. 132] are used to control whether a request is served, i.e. if a PUT is applied or if a GET is returned. If-Match and If-None-Match match against entity tags according to known entities. Entities are introduced by the ETag [15, p. 126] response-header field.

The Referer field (misspelled in the standard [15, p. 139]) may be used by the application to keep track of from which resource the request-URI was obtained.

The User-Agent [15, p. 145] field is often used to tailor user experience, as different browsers use different rendering engines and in some cases the size of the users screen can be guessed from the user agent, as is the case with smartphones. The Server response header [15, p. 141] informs the client what server software is serving the request.

The header fields Content-Language [15, p. 118], Content-Length [15, p. 119], Content-Location [15, p. 120], Content-Encoding [15, p. 118] and Content-Type [15, p. 124] are used to inform the receiving party about how the entity body is formatted. If these headers are modified by an attacker, a web browser may transform the data, e.g. by only reading the number of bytes specified in the Content-Length header field from the entity. If this occurs the MAC will not match - if the application can interpret the result at all.

The Transfer-Encoding header field [15, p. 143] describes what codings have been applied to the message during transfer. This coding applies to the message, and not to the entity - as is the case with Content-Encoding, and it is thus applied by the web server or web browser, before it reaches the application. If an attacker modifies the Transfer-Encoding header field, MAC will not match on enclosed data, and it will be decoded incorrectly.

The Trailer header field [15, p. 143] describes what header fields are present in the trailer of a chunked message. If this header field is modified by an attacker, it may change how the data reassembled. If it is, the MAC within the data will either not match the data, or will be indistinguishable.

The Upgrade header [15, p. 143] is used to change the application-layer protocol, to e.g. change from HTTP/1.0 to HTTP/1.1, or from HTTP/1.1 to FTP/1.0. A GlassTube service must decline any upgrade requests.

Position Paper: The Science of Boxing

Analysing Eval using Staged Metaprogramming

Martin Lester
Department of Computer Science, University of Oxford
martin.lester@cs.ox.ac.uk

Abstract

The ubiquity of Web 2.0 applications handling sensitive information means that *static analysis* of applications written in *JavaScript* has become an important security problem. The highly dynamic nature of the language makes this difficult. The **eval** construct, which allows execution of a string as program code, is particularly notorious in this regard. **eval** is a form of *metaprogramming* construct: it allows generation and manipulation of program code at run-time. Other metaprogramming formalisms are more principled in their behaviour and easier to reason about; consider, for example, Lisp-style code quotations, which we call *staged metaprogramming*. We argue that, instead of trying to reason directly about uses of **eval**, we should first transform them to staged metaprogramming, then analyse the transformed program. To demonstrate the feasibility of this approach, we describe an algorithm for transforming uses of **eval** on strings encoding program text into uses of staged metaprogramming with quoted program terms. We present our algorithm in the context of a JavaScript-like language augmented with staged metaprogramming.

Categories and Subject Descriptors D.3.3 [*Language Constructs and Features*]: Metaprogramming

General Terms Languages, Verification, Security

Keywords JavaScript, eval, staged metaprogramming, static analysis, program transformation

1. Introduction

The **eval** construct of JavaScript takes a string and parses and executes it as program code. For several years, authors of static analyses for JavaScript argued that they could ignore it because it was rarely used or used only in trivial ways [9]. Their real reason was probably that analysis of such a powerful construct seemed utterly hopeless, particularly when considering the language's lack of protection mechanisms, as it allows arbitrary behaviours to result from an unstructured data value.

However, a recent survey [18] showed that a majority of the most popular websites use **eval** and that they use it in many varied (and often misguided) ways. Correspondingly there has been a surge of interest in techniques for dealing with **eval**. Some authors argue that static analysis of **eval** really is hopeless and instead develop dynamic analyses that monitor execution of **eval**ed code [11, 20], enforcing security policies by terminating the program immediately before a violation. Indeed, this is probably the most reliable and mature technology currently available [6], but given the benefits of catching violations early in development or deployment, the attitude seems somewhat fatalistic.

Furthermore, there are fundamental limits to dynamic monitors: they can only enforce safety properties. For example, *noninterference* [8], which is one of the best known information flow security properties, is not a safety property [22]. Consequently, it can never be *precisely* enforced by a monitor [19], although it is possible to enforce more restrictive properties such as isolation of untrusted code [16].

Some recent work [13, 17] considers how to determine what arguments may be passed to uses of **eval** and hence how to replace occurrences of **eval** with code that does not use it. However, these approaches seem limited to handling certain fixed patterns of usage. We argue that reasoning about **eval** could better be viewed as two distinct problems: the first is determining what code may be executed; the second is reasoning about the behaviour of that code. As each is difficult in its own right, we are more likely to be successful if we focus on one problem at a time. In previous work [15] we addressed the second problem by showing how to analyse information flow in a JavaScript-like language augmented with Lisp-style code quotations or *staged metaprogramming*. We now tackle the first problem by showing how to translate uses of **eval** in this language into staged metaprogramming.

We begin in Section 2 by explaining what staged metaprogramming is and why it is a suitable formalism for most uses of **eval**. We describe our algorithm for translating **eval** into staged metaprogramming in Section 3 and discuss future directions in Section 4. We briefly review related work in Section 5, before concluding in Section 6.

2. Metaprogramming

2.1 Staged Metaprogramming

The language Lisp allows programs to construct code templates as data values, splice them together and run the resulting code. We refer to these features collectively as *staged metaprogramming*. Following the language λ_S of Choi and others [3], we can add these features to a programming language with three constructs:

- **box** e turns the expression e into a code value; it does not evaluate e.
- **run** e evaluates the code value e.
- **unbox** e may only occur inside a **box** expression. It forces evaluation of e; the resulting code value is spliced into the surrounding code template.

PLAS'13, June 20, 2013, Seattle, WA, USA.

Booleans	b	::=	**true** | **false**
Strings	s	$\in$	*String*
Numbers	n	$\in$	*Number*
Names	x	$\in$	*Name*
Constants	k	::=	**undef** | **null** | b | s | n
Expressions	e	::=	k | x | **box** e | **unbox** e | **run** e
			| **fun**$(x)\{e\}$ | $e(e)$ | **if**$(e)\{e\}$ **else**$\{e\}$ | $\delta(\overline{e})$
			| $\{\overline{s:e}\}$ | $e[e]$ | $e[e] = e$ | **del** $e[e]$

let $x = e_1$ **in** e_2 is an abbreviation for **fun**$(x)\{e_2\}(e_1)$

Figure 1. Abbreviated syntax of *SLamJS*

In previous work [15], we took a subset of λ_{JS}, the core calculus for JavaScript developed by Guha and others [10], and added staged metaprogramming with **box**, **unbox** and **run**. We called the resulting language *SLamJS*. An abbreviated syntax is in Figure 1.

For example, in *SLamJS*, **box** $(x * 2)$ evaluates to a code value, which can be stored in a variable or passed to a function like any other value: **let** $y =$ **box** $(x * 2)$. When that code value is run, for example with **run** y, it evaluates to double the value of x in the current scope, which may be different from the scope in which the code value was defined. If we **let** $z =$ **box** 2, we can create the same code value with **let** $y =$ **box** $(x * ($**unbox** $z))$.

2.2 Expressivity of Metaprogramming

Although JavaScript's **eval** is only a single language construct, metaprogramming can increase the expressivity of a programming language in several distinct ways. In most cases, we find the expressivity is matched by staged metaprogramming:

Composing Code Templates In JavaScript, code templates can be encoded as strings and spliced together using string concatenation. For example:

```
var f = function(z) { return 3 * z };
var y = "2";
var x = "f(" + y + ")";
eval(x);
```

Adding **box**, **unbox** and **run** to JavaScript, we could express this as:

```
var f = function(z) { return 3 * z };
var y = box(2);
var x = box(f(unbox(y)));
run(x);
```

We show how to automate this transformation in Section 3.

Changing Scoping When code is run with **eval**, it is evaluated in the scope of the **eval**, not the scope in which the code was defined (as is the case for functions). This example (left) returns 2, not 1; again, it can be modelled in staged metaprogramming (right):

```
(function(x){
 return (function(y) {
  return (function(x) {
   return eval(y)
  })(2)
 })("x")
})(1)
```

```
(function(x){
 return (function(y) {
  return (function(x) {
   return run(y)
  })(2)
 })(box(x))
})(1)
```

The precise choice of scoping rules may vary between languages. For example, λ_S has less permissive variable capture rules than *SLamJS*; the latter's are closer to those of JavaScript. However, JavaScript's **eval** has the peculiarity that, if it is called via an alias, it evaluates in the global scope, rather than the local one.

Changing Evaluation Order It is folklore that metaprogramming facilities allow a programmer to mix uses of call-by-name and call-by-value evaluation in a single program. This intuition is made more concrete by Inoue and Taha [12]. While this is expressible in both JavaScript **eval** and staged metaprogramming, the analyses we consider are not sensitive to the change, so we do not discuss it further here.

Serialisation In metaprogramming terminology, turning a data value into its corresponding code value is called *lifting* [23]. This is not generally possible in JavaScript: there is no facility to turn a function into its source code. It is possible for primitive data values as these can be converted into strings. In fact, JavaScript string concatenation does this implicitly.

To model this behaviour in staged metaprogramming, we need an operation **lift** e that evaluates e and, if it evaluates to a primitive value, turns it into the corresponding code value. (Note that this is in contrast to **box** e, which does not evaluate e.) Using **lift**, this example:

```
var y = 2;
var x = "f(" + y + ")";
```

would become:

```
var y = 2;
var x = box(f(unbox(lift(y))));
```

We did not consider **lift** in our original work on *SLamJS*. Fortunately, for primitive datatypes, it can be added to our language and analysed in the same way as basic arithmetic operations, by defining a new primitive operation.

Deserialisation If code can be treated as a data value, it can be read from files or the network and dynamically loaded using metaprogramming facilities during program execution. Some JavaScript libraries support incremental loading in this way. This is also possible using staged metaprogramming, although it requires support from the language runtime environment to turn data from the network into code values, in much the same way that it already provides support for turning strings passed to **eval** into code.

Static analysis of code using incrementally loaded libraries is difficult because not all of the code will necessarily be available at once. However, this is not a problem peculiar to **eval** or even JavaScript, although the haphazard infrastructure of Web applications does complicate it. We discuss this and related concerns further in Section 4.3.

Aside: Reading the popular JSON format is one simple example of deserialisation; JSON encodes data as the JavaScript source code string that evaluates to that data. However, because of security concerns, current "best practice" is not to **eval** JSON code, but instead to use a library function $JSON.parse()$. Perhaps a new best practice should be not to manipulate code templates with string concatenation, but to use (as yet unwritten) library functions $Stage.box()$ and $Stage.unbox()$? This would provide a path for developers using **eval** to migrate to staged metaprogramming, making it less likely that they would unwittingly introduce security holes through sloppy use of **eval**.

Intensional Uses Some metaprogramming formalisms, such as the SF calculus of Given-Wilson and Jay [7], allow code values to be examined internally and broken into their component parts. This is not possible in our staged metaprogramming formalism. It is possible in JavaScript but is rare, presumably because it is difficult to achieve using unstructured strings. A JSON parser *written in JavaScript* using regexes and substring operations would be an example of an intensional use.

3. The Boxing Algorithm

3.1 Overview

We now describe our algorithm for transforming uses of **eval** into staged metaprogramming. We illustrate our algorithm with examples in $SLamJS$, although we believe that the idea is sufficiently general that it could be applied to many other languages with an **eval** construct, such as Perl and PHP.

The basic idea is that we transform:

- code constants into **box** expressions;
- concatenation of code strings into splicing using **unbox**;
- **eval** into **run**.

For example:	becomes:
let $x =$ "y" **in**	**let** $x =$ **box** y **in**
eval x	**run** x
while:	becomes:
let $f =$ **fun**$(z)\{3 * z\}$ **in**	**let** $f =$ **fun**$(z)\{3 * z\}$ **in**
let $y =$ "2" **in**	**let** $y =$ **box** 2 **in**
let $x =$ "f(" $+ y +$ ")" **in**	**let** $x =$ **box**$(f($**unbox** $y))$ **in**
eval x	**run** x

In order to use our algorithm, certain conditions must hold:

- We need a sound dataflow analysis for the target language, including metaprogramming constructs.
- We need a string analysis for the target language that will give a sound over-approximation of the string values that may occur at different program points or be bound to different variables.
- The language must be parseable using `lex` and `yacc` or similar.

In previous work, we showed how to apply 0CFA [21] to $SLamJS$, so we reuse that analysis here. As 0CFA over-approximates the flow control of a program with a regular graph, it is easy to extract a grammar-based string analysis from the results. This is what we do in our implementation, although there are many techniques that could improve upon this [2].

3.2 Parsing

Our algorithm relies on using the existing parser for a language for part of the transformation; this makes our technique easily applicable to other languages. Typically, languages are parsed in two phases. The first phase, lexicographic analysis, transforms the program text into a sequence of tokens; the tool `lex` generates a *lexer* that does this using a deterministic finite state automaton. In the second phase, the actual parser turns the sequence of tokens into an abstract syntax tree; `yacc` generates a LALR *parser* to do this with a restricted form of pushdown automaton.

Normally, the lexer processes the characters in the program text in order from beginning to end. Similarly, the parser processes the token sequence in order from left to right (hence the second L in LALR). Our algorithm abuses these tools to process **eval**ed text out of order in fragments. Effectively, this gives us a finite way of parsing a string abstraction, which may encode infinitely many concrete strings of unbounded length. However, there is a price: we risk changing the meaning of the **eval**ed code. To avoid this (and hence keep our transformation sound), we must check that the lexing and parsing phases are unaffected by the change of order; we describe these checks in Section 3.4.

3.3 Algorithm Description

We must first modify the grammar of the language slightly: we add a new token `HOLE(x)` and a rule that this token constitutes an expression with corresponding abstract syntax tree **hole** x. An outline of a cycle of the algorithm is as follows; examples of some steps are shown in Figure 3:

let $foo =$ "o" **in**
let $x =$ "foo" **in**
if $(b)\{String.substr(x, 0, 1)\}$ **else** $\{$**eval** $x\}$

Figure 2. An example of an intensional use, which could not be transformed by our algorithm; b is a Boolean variable.

1. Use the dataflow analysis to determine which string constants S and results of string concatenations C flow into uses of **eval**.
2. Use the same analysis to determine which strings I flow directly to other string operations, such as object property lookup ($e[e]$) or substring operations. Check that $I \cap (S \cup C) = \emptyset$; otherwise fail. (Failure here usually corresponds to an attempted intensional use of **eval**; see Figure 2 for an example.)
3. Use the string analysis to approximate the values of strings used at different points in the program.
4. If a string value eventually flows to an **eval**, and the string analysis tells us it is a constant, then, if possible, statically parse the constant string to an expression e and replace the string value with **box** e.
5. To handle the remaining cases, where **eval**ed string values are not constant:
   (a) At a string concatenation c that flows to an **eval**, build a list of subexpressions that are concatenated together.
   (b) Use the string analysis to determine whether each subexpression refers to a constant string; if it does, replace it in the list with that string.
   (c) Merge adjacent constant strings in the list.
   (d) Run the lexer on each constant string in the list; replace it with the resulting sequence of tokens (removing EOF if necessary). Give up if the lexer fails.
   (e) Replace each non-constant subexpression e in the list with a unique `HOLE(x)`; record the mapping as $H(x) := e$; perform the lexing check described in Section 3.4 with e and the items immediately preceding and following it in the list; give up if it fails.
   (f) Concatenate all sequences of tokens in the list and parse the result with the modified parser. Give up if it fails.
   (g) In the resulting parse tree e, replace each subexpression **hole** x with **unbox** $H(x)$. (Recall $H(x)$ is the expression that generated the non-constant string corresponding to the hole.)
   (h) Taking the modified parse tree e', replace the whole concatenation c with **box** e'.
6. Check that all string expressions flowing to an **eval** have been transformed. If so, transform all instances of **eval** to our staged equivalent **run**.

The algorithm also needs to transform any primitive operations that operate on code values. For example, if we wish to model JavaScript's conversion of concatenated values to strings, we will need to replace uses of string conversion with **lift**.

A single cycle may be insufficient. The **eval**ed code may manipulate values that are used as code in an **eval**. So we must analyse the transformed program again and check that any transformations already performed are still valid in the presence of any new behaviours introduced by **eval**ed code. If they are not valid, the algorithm fails. If they are, we also need to check if any new **eval**s have been introduced; if so, we cycle through the algorithm again until no new uses are introduced.

1 let y = if(b){ "1" } else{ "2" } in
let x = "f(" + y + ")" in
eval x

2 $I = \emptyset$

3 $x \mapsto$ f(y) $y \mapsto$ (1 | 2)

4 let y = if(b){ box 1 } else{ box 2 } in
let x = "f("+y+")" in
eval x

5
(a)–(c) ["f(", y, ")"]
(d) [VAR(f) LP, y, RP]
(e) [VAR(f) LP, HOLE(w), RP] $H(w) := y$
(f) VAR(f) LP HOLE(w) RP $\mapsto f(\langle w \rangle)$
(g) f(unbox y)
(h) box(f(unbox y))

6 let y = if(b){box 1} else{box 2} in
let x = box(f(unbox y)) in
run x

Figure 3. Some steps in a run of the boxing algorithm.

3.4 Correctness

We now address some concerns as to whether the algorithm is sound; that is, whether it is possible that it alters the behaviour of a program. We do not formally prove soundness.

Side Effects If it is possible that we transform an expression e with side effects to a code value e' without side effects, we must be careful to preserve them. We can do this by executing e and discarding the result; that is, transforming e not to e' but to **let** $x = e$ **in** e', where x is fresh.

Lexing Suppose we have a language where (unlike in $SLamJS$) function application can be written as concatenation (without brackets) and consider the following:

let x = if(y){"(g(3))"} else{"g(3)"} in
let z = "f" + x in
eval z

Depending on the value of y, the values of z and its tokenisations might be:

```
"f(g(3))" ↦ VAR(f) LP VAR(g) LP INT(3) RP RP
"fg(3)"   ↦ VAR(fg) LP INT(3) RP
```

Suppose we try to transform the concatenation that is assigned to z. As x is not constant, we tokenise it as `HOLE(x)`; the concatenation then tokenises as `VAR(f) HOLE(x)`. Treating `HOLE(x)` as a wildcard, this matches the first case, but not the second. The problem is that the use of the hole has changed the tokenisation of the string.

Conceptually, we can view the lexer as a deterministic finite state transducer T. When strings x and y encoding program text are concatenated, we want to check that $T(x \cdot y) = T(x) \cdot T(y)$.

This hides some details of the problem, as in practice tokens that are identical in the automaton model often carry some data that distinguishes them (as with `VAR(f)` and `VAR(fg)` in the above example). What we really need to check is that concatenation does not change the positions of token boundaries in the program text. We can enforce this by checking (using the obvious algorithm) that, if X and Y are regular abstractions of strings that may be concatenated, whatever state the lexer's DFA may be in at the end of a string in X, it will emit a token and restart upon seeing any character that may occur at the start of a string in Y.

Parsing Consider arithmetic expressions in the program:

let x = "2" in
let y = "3 - 1" in
let z = x + " * " + y in
eval z

The result will be $2 * 3 - 1$, which is 5. We might be tempted to transform this to:

let x = box 2 in
let y = box $(3 - 1)$ in
let z = box ((unbox x) $*$ (unbox y)) in
run z

However, the **eval**ed expression then becomes $2 * (3 - 1)$, which is 4. (Arguably this may have been the intent of the author of the program.) The problem arises because the grammar of expressions in the language is ambiguous. The proposed transformation corresponds to one possible parsing of `2 * 3 - 1`, but not the one chosen by the language's `yacc` parser.

We can avoid this problem by requiring that the language has an unambiguous grammar. This is not an onerous requirement as, when `yacc` accepts ambiguous grammar specifications, it resolves the grammar ambiguity (perhaps arbitrarily) and produces a parser for a more restricted, unambiguous grammar, which would itself be valid as a grammar specification.

Disambiguation is often achieved by adding extra syntactic classes of expression. The example above might not be transformable in this case, as while x and y should clearly encode valid expressions, it might no longer be permissible to multiply arbitrary expressions. Replacing the final concatenation with "(" + x + ") * (" + y + ")" would allow the transformation.

Termination Unless the program has an infinite sequence of **eval**s that generate new **eval**s, the algorithm is guaranteed to terminate. Even then, if using a dataflow analysis such as 0CFA, each cycle will add new edges to the dataflow graph, so it seems likely it will eventually be saturated and a fixed point will be reached. This is not obviously certain, as replacing strings with code can introduce new program points, increasing the number of nodes in the graph. If possible nontermination is an issue, the algorithm can simply arbitrarily terminate after a fixed number of cycles; it seems unlikely that a useful, realistic program will feature a pathological infinite sequence of nested **eval**s.

4. Evaluation and Future Work

4.1 Precision and Scalability

We have implemented our algorithm, but have so far only tested it on a few examples. Consequently, we do not yet know how good it is in practice. This work was motivated by a desire to check information flow properties in JavaScript; we intend to chain the boxing algorithm with our information flow analysis for $SLamJS$ to evaluate its effectiveness. We are confident we can handle most situations where a use of **eval** receives only a constant string, but we are more interested in situations where there may be many strings encoding expressions of different shapes.

Our current implementation is based on 0CFA, which is fast, but also relatively imprecise. If this turns out to be a problem, we can apply the same approach to CFA2 or some other, more precise analysis.

Some aspects of our algorithm are not fully specified. For example, we do not prescribe in what order to transform code string-manipulating expressions in the source program, and this may affect whether the algorithm succeeds. In general, we would like to transform the smallest possible code-manipulating subexpression, as this results in a transformed program that most closely resembles the original program; our current implementation uses this greedy heuristic. However, there are situations where this causes the algorithm to fail (for example, because it results in the lexing check being violated), but other choices would succeed. Tuning such aspects of our algorithm is another area for future investigation.

4.2 Soundness and Applicability

Although we have argued for the soundness of the algorithm, we have not yet proved formally that it is correct or that it always terminates. This is an important next step, particularly if the transformation is to be used in security-related analyses.

As with many more theoretical works on programming languages, we handle an idealised version of the language that interests us (JavaScript). It would take further effort to apply our work to the entirety of a real-world programming language. There is a compositional, semantics-preserving translation from JavaScript to λ_{JS}, on which $SLamJS$ is based, so we think we can reasonably claim applicability. INRIA's Prosecco has produced an unambiguous Menhir (`yacc` for Ocaml) grammar for JavaScript, so it meets the criteria for our algorithm to be applied.

One area that would require particular attention in handling full JavaScript is the range of different possible scoping behaviours for **eval**. In $SLamJS$, we currently model how **eval** executes code with dynamic variable scoping, but do not consider quirks such as running code in the global scope when **eval** is called indirectly via an alias. The latest version of JavaScript complicates matters by introducing a new "strict" mode of **eval** (which generally behaves better) but retaining the old behaviours for backwards-compatibility. The latest version of λ_{JS}, called S5 [14], goes to some lengths to model the different variations in scoping rules. To take account of the different scoping rules, the boxing transformation would need to include a static analysis to determine in which modes each instance of **eval** can be run.

4.3 Infrastructural Issues

In considering applications of the algorithm, one should also consider when it will be run and by whom. So let us now discuss more generally the infrastructural requirements for static analysis of Web applications. In the context of information flow analysis of JavaScript, the precision of dynamic analysis is good enough for many practical situations, even though there are inherent limitations. By definition, dynamic analysis occurs when code is run. For client-side JavaScript, that means being run by a user, in a browser; this usually requires a modified browser, although monitoring within JavaScript is possible [16].

The primary advantage of static analysis of code is its ability to identify possible errors or security problems before code is run, ideally during development. So while one could imagine a static analysis being part of a browser, it would make more sense for it to be used on the webserver or by the developer.

This scenario introduces further challenges, as a complete Web application is unlikely to be a single, monolithic piece of code. For example, it may use libraries, which may be loaded incrementally during execution. This is not especially problematic, as the developer presumably knows which libraries could be loaded, has access to their code and may have control over the server from which they are loaded. So in principle, the application could be treated as a single piece of code (including all libraries), although this might not scale well to large libraries.

In the event that the developer does not control which version of the libraries is served, the application would need a mechanism for identifying which library has been loaded and a policy to follow if an unknown library is loaded. For example, the application code could include hashes of libraries against which it has been analysed. The browser would be responsible for checking hashes of libraries as they are loaded. In the event that an unknown library is loaded, either the application could fail or it could fall back to some dynamic analysis.

The situation becomes more difficult when third-party content (such as adverts or user-supplied plugins) is involved. In this case, some of the code might not even be written until after development of the core application. If all code, including adverts and plugins, is served from the same webserver, then it is still the case that in principle the application could be treated as a single piece of code. However, authors of adverts and plugins might need to take some responsibility for ensuring their code was amenable to static analysis.

Once again, if the code is not centrally distributed, the application needs a mechanism for identifying well-behaved code, but it is no longer possible to use a whitelist. Instead, the application would have to include some form of software contract specifying acceptable behaviours of third-party content and the browser would need to stage static analysis of code as it was loaded to check this contract. In order for this to be practical, either the contract would need to be easily verifiable syntactically [4], or the content would need to include an easily verifiable certificate witnessing that it satisfies the contract.

5. Related Work

Dynamic Analyses of Eval There are various dynamic or monitoring analyses for enforcing information flow policies in JavaScript that tackle **eval**. Chugh and others [4] propose initially using a static analysis of a program, but then running it in a monitor that performs a simpler static analysis of code when it is **eval**ed. Hedin and Sabelfeld [11] develop a dynamic type system that enforces termination insensitive noninterference. However, note that a monitor that immediately stops any program will also enforce this.

Fundamentally, we think it is preferable (although harder) to verify properties of programs before running them rather than to terminate them when an error occurs at run-time.

Tools for Removing Eval Jensen and others [13] produce a tool called *Unevalizer*, which uses the JavaScript analysis framework TAJS to identify and automatically remove uses of **eval**, so that other static analyses may be used. They have few problems with constant strings, but only seem able to handle non-constant strings if they match one of a fixed number of built-in usage patterns.

The tool *Evalorizer* [17] is also aimed at removing uses of **eval**, but the use case is different: the aim is to assist a developer in removing **eval** from code. The developer runs and tests JavaScript code in a browser configured to use a proxy provided by the tool. The tool collects uses of **eval** and categorises them to suggest how they might be rewritten.

Staged Metaprogramming There is a wide body of literature discussing metaprogramming, although it is still relatively poorly understood from a semantic perspective. There is not so much work on automated verification and analysis of metaprogramming. Choi and others [3] propose a translation for removing staged metaprogramming, so that existing automated tools can be used. However, their limited variable capture semantics may make it hard to apply their work to $SLamJS$ or JavaScript. Berger and Tratt develop a Hoare-style program logic for a version of ML with metaprogramming [1], but there do not seem to be any automated tools based on this work.

String Analysis of Code A common source of security vulnerabilities in Web applications is accidental execution of untrusted code resulting from careless splicing of user-supplied data into code templates. String analyses are a popular method for detecting such vulnerabilities, and are used effectively to analyse the shape of parse trees [24], but the behaviour of the resulting code is not usually analysed. Like us, Doh and others [5] use string abstraction and a modification to the language's parser to analyse dynamically generated code. Their string analysis is more advanced than ours, but the end result is a grammar, rather than a translation to staged metaprogramming. As Choi and others [3] point out, it is difficult to analyse the behaviour of code generated by such a grammar, as it is not clear how to concretise it in a precise way.

6. Conclusion

It is both necessary and possible to analyse statically the behaviour of JavaScript's metaprogramming construct **eval**, but the complexity of the task means it is best split into two problems: a transformation to a more principled form of metaprogramming and an analysis of this more principled form. Taking into account our previous work on analysis of staged metaprogramming, we have now developed the theory to handle both problems. In particular, this demonstrates how to analyse information flow statically in languages like JavaScript in the presence of **eval**.

Acknowledgments

We thank our anonymous reviewers for their comments, particularly with regard to future work.

References

[1] M. Berger and L. Tratt. Program logics for homogeneous metaprogramming. In *LPAR (Dakar)*, pages 64–81, 2010.

[2] T.-H. Choi, O. Lee, H. Kim, and K.-G. Doh. A practical string analyzer by the widening approach. In *APLAS*, pages 374–388, 2006.

[3] W. Choi, B. Aktemur, K. Yi, and M. Tatsuta. Static analysis of multi-staged programs via unstaging translation. In *POPL*, pages 81–92, 2011.

[4] R. Chugh, J. A. Meister, R. Jhala, and S. Lerner. Staged information flow for javascript. In *PLDI*, pages 50–62, 2009.

[5] K.-G. Doh, H. Kim, and D. A. Schmidt. Abstract lr-parsing. In *Formal Modeling: Actors, Open Systems, Biological Systems*, pages 90–109, 2011.

[6] J. S. Fenton. Memoryless subsystems. *Comput. J.*, 17(2):143–147, 1974.

[7] T. Given-Wilson and B. Jay. A combinatory account of internal structure. *J. Symb. Log.*, 76(3):807–826, 2011.

[8] J. A. Goguen and J. Meseguer. Security policies and security models. In *IEEE Symposium on Security and Privacy*, pages 11–20, 1982.

[9] S. Guarnieri and V. B. Livshits. Gatekeeper: Mostly static enforcement of security and reliability policies for javascript code. In *USENIX Security Symposium*, pages 151–168, 2009.

[10] A. Guha, C. Saftoiu, and S. Krishnamurthi. The essence of javascript. In *ECOOP*, pages 126–150, 2010.

[11] D. Hedin and A. Sabelfeld. Information-flow security for a core of javascript. In *CSF*, pages 3–18, 2012.

[12] J. Inoue and W. Taha. Reasoning about multi-stage programs. In *ESOP*, pages 357–376, 2012.

[13] S. H. Jensen, P. A. Jonsson, and A. Møller. Remedying the eval that men do. In *ISSTA*, pages 34–44, 2012.

[14] S. Krishnamurthi. Semantics and analyses for javascript and the web. In *SAS*, page 4, 2012.

[15] M. Lester, L. Ong, and M. Schaefer. Information flow analysis for a dynamically typed functional language with staged metaprogramming. In *CSF*, 2013. To appear.

[16] S. Maffeis and A. Taly. Language-based isolation of untrusted javascript. In *CSF*, pages 77–91, 2009.

[17] F. Meawad, G. Richards, F. Morandat, and J. Vitek. Eval begone!: semi-automated removal of eval from javascript programs. In *OOPSLA*, pages 607–620, 2012.

[18] G. Richards, C. Hammer, B. Burg, and J. Vitek. The eval that men do - a large-scale study of the use of eval in javascript applications. In *ECOOP*, pages 52–78, 2011.

[19] A. Russo and A. Sabelfeld. Dynamic vs. static flow-sensitive security analysis. In *CSF*, pages 186–199, 2010.

[20] A. Sabelfeld and A. Russo. From dynamic to static and back: Riding the roller coaster of information-flow control research. In *Ershov Memorial Conference*, pages 352–365, 2009.

[21] O. Shivers. Control-flow analysis in scheme. In *PLDI*, pages 164–174, 1988.

[22] T. Terauchi and A. Aiken. Secure information flow as a safety problem. In *SAS*, pages 352–367, 2005.

[23] L. Tratt. Compile-time meta-programming in a dynamically typed oo language. In *DLS*, pages 49–63, 2005.

[24] G. Wassermann and Z. Su. Sound and precise analysis of web applications for injection vulnerabilities. In *PLDI*, pages 32–41, 2007.

Author Index

www.ingramcontent.com/pod-product-compliance
Lightning Source LLC
Chambersburg PA
CBHW081552220326
41598CB00036B/6651
* 9 7 8 1 4 5 0 3 2 4 4 0 3 *